IVAN & ME

Jennifer Faus

This Special Edition of *Ivan & Me* includes
The Life Stories of the Bloody Sunday Victims
by Jennifer Faus © 2003-2015
Excerpt from *Rathlin*
by Jennifer Faus © 2015
Ivan & Me Copyright 2012 © by Jennifer Faus
Special Edition Copyright 2015 © by Jennifer Faus

All rights reserved. No part of this book may be reproduced or transmitted in any form or by any means without prior written permission of the publisher except in the case of brief quotations embodied in critical articles and reviews.

Published by Koser Howe Publishing
233 S. Lochinvar Street Wichita Kansas 67207

koserhowebooks.com

Printed and bound in the United States of America
ISBN: 978-0985471002

Cover design: Chris Parks
chrisparks.me

IVAN'S HEART

I've lost count of how many times I walked by his side, sat with him in a pub, or lingered over dinner as he talked. I listened from the passenger seat of his Mercedes on our many travels together and then at home his recorded voice spoke to me on the bus, soaking in a warm bath, or sitting at my desk, a large black dog nudging my elbow. How many times Ivan Cooper told me his story, I cannot recall. Over our five years together I learned his telling this story is a plea for forgiveness. Ivan wants forgiveness for putting people on the street on a crisp January day. He wants forgiveness for the fourteen murdered that day. Forgiveness for the fourteen again who sustained life-changing injuries, and for an entire city that was scarred for decades. For these perceived transgressions Ivan has not been able to forgive himself and for that he carries this burden. And so, I listen:

With the exception of internment without trial all of the other civil rights demands had been met. In other words, one man one vote had been conceded. An end to electoral gerrymandering had been achieved. The Derry City Corporation, the old corporation, had been shelved and replaced by a commission. There was legislation invoked in relation to discrimination in employment and legislation was invoked with regard to the fair allocation of houses. But one civil rights demand was still outstanding which perhaps was the Achilles heel of the whole civil rights movement and that was internment without trial.

Despite all of the warnings of anti-unionist politicians like myself and John Hume, the then prime minister of Northern Ireland, in order to appease his unionist backbenchers, had decided once again to embark on internment without trial. In nineteen and seventy-one, internment without trial had been used exclusively against the Catholic community. The nationalist community. The problem was that a large number of people who had been interned were people who were elderly in some cases, and in other cases, people who had had no connection with the IRA for many years.

It should be remembered that many people had been interned who had no connection with armed uprising. There were people perhaps who had an interest in Irish music and Irish culture who decided because of their interest to write their names in Irish, to be addressed in Irish, to speak the Irish language. Many of those people in the 1930s, 40s, 50s, and 60s, had been interned because of their interest in Irish music and their interest in Irish language. So at the very root at all of the feelings of alienation from the unionist system at Stormont lay the whole subject of internment without trial.

A few days after I had met the IRA and I believe that others had met them as well and sought similar assurances to what I had sought I was advised that no IRA personnel would carry guns in the vicinity of the march. I was told that no IRA personnel would fire any shots at the British Army. I was given a firm assurance. I was told the personnel would be withdrawn to the Creggan Estates and that all guns would be removed from the Bogside area. In retrospect, I accept that that undertaking given by the IRA was honored.

And so on the last Sunday in January nineteen and seventy-two, twenty thousand men women and children assembled in the Creggan Estates, not far from Creggan Chapel. It was a bright, pleasant January day. The weather was crisp, marginally cold. It was a carnival atmosphere. At the start of the march the lorry was followed by the twenty thousand men, women and children some of whom were singing the civil rights song 'We Shall Overcome.' This was the anthem which had been used by the civil rights movement from nineteen and sixty-eight. The entire civil rights movement from nineteen and sixty-eight in Northern Ireland had been demanding the same rights as the people of London, Cardiff, Glasgow, and Birmingham. If we were part of the United Kingdom, we had told the British Government, then we wanted precisely the same rights.

Prior to the march starting off I had become aware that there was a very heavy body of troops situated in William Street which has now become known as Barrier 14. There was no question of them permitting the march to proceed to the Guildhall Square. They would not. And so it was decided, in consultation with others, that once the march reached the apex of William Street and Rossville Street that the lorry would turn to the right. It would drive over along Rossville Street to Free Derry Corner stop there and the meeting would be held there. It was our view that while some young people might well try to break off, to engage in confrontation with the Army, the bulk of the marchers would follow the lorry to hear the speeches.

Now it must be said that a fairly large group of young men who were intent at throwing stones at the Army expressed anger at the fact that the march was not proceeding directly to the Guildhall Square and they made their way down to Barrier 14. The bulk of the civil rights marchers followed the lorry along Rossville Street to Free Derry Corner. I had gone to Barrier 14 in an attempt to get some of these young people who had broken off from the main march to return to the main march to hear the speeches at Free Derry Corner. Some of these young people proceeded to collect missiles to throw them at the Army. I saw General Ford in command strutting around like a peacock —arrogant, intolerant, *obviously there that day to do business. For a period I remonstrated with these young people and then I decided it was important to get the meeting underway so I made my way to Free Derry Corner.*

I wasn't on the platform very long when in the distance, in the vicinity of Barrier 14, I could hear the thud of rubber bullets being fired. I remember listening to the thuds on the platform and I said to Bernadette Devlin, 'Rubber bullets.' Her reply to me was, 'It's lead, Coops.'"

MARSEILLE

My first real trip out of the US was in 2000. I say first 'real' because if you are from the United States, Canada and Mexico don't count. It is embarrassing to admit I was thirty-one years of age my first trip to Europe. To a certain population of my family you hadn't really been anywhere until you'd been to Europe. And so, at thirty-one years of age, I was finally going.

Marseille was wonderful. I traveled with a group of teachers on an exchange. We had hosted teachers from France in Chicago for ten days and this was the return. On our first day we visited a school where children shared with us French civics lessons. We were served lunch in the school cafeteria during which wine poured freely and I was thus converted to the French way of living. For the following ten days we were steeped in educational initiatives, culture, food, and wine. We visited public and private schools, lunched on bouillabaisse at a housing project, and took photos by the locker of a famous soccer/football star. We learned a young child could be sent to the corner store for a bottle of wine for the family dinner and no one thought a thing about it.

We climbed a steep set of stairs on a warm starry night to a restaurant on the alley with a very long table and a very old woman who cooked for us and at the end of our six-hour meal sang 'Autumn Leaves' (in French). The moment could only have been improved had she danced with me and then proposed.

Hungover and on very little sleep, I chastised the French football league for violence at games as my colleagues and friends hung their heads, slunk down in their chairs, and silently renounced our association.

We dined regally in Aix au Provence, where I decided Chanel Allure would become my fragrance as power and grace flowed easily from the beautiful woman seated to my left. When I asked what fragrance she was wearing, her response, "Alluuura," took me to great rooms, ball gowns, secrets with rare men, and gilded chairs. I later purchased the largest bottle I could find. I didn't bother to ask the price. This perfume, after all, could change my life!

We lunched with the Mayor, drank cocktails at the home of the US Ambassador, walked along the Mediterranean under clear-blue skies. At the end, I couldn't bear to leave and stayed on two days extra, wandering the cobbled streets of Aix, dreaming of writing in a small, sparsely furnished flat. On fair days I would open the eight-pane pocket doors that overlooked the square. Evenings I would dine al fresco with a carafe of red wine. You would see me shopping in the market, carrying a basket with cheese, bread, meats, wine, and fresh flowers. On a rainy day, you might see me in a cafe reading a newspaper, an espresso for company, a large lazy dog at my feet.

Alas, I could not even afford a hotel room and begged a spot on the floor at a teacher's home and on that fated second day, boarded a jet that took me to Paris and home, the flight attendants' French slowly transforming to English as we flew the arc back to Chicago.

My city. Once vibrant and continental. The city that made my heart beat wildly and passion race through my veins. Post Marseille, post Europe, Chicago was now plain, ordinary, uninteresting. I was smitten. So when it came—two years later—the chance to return. To fly the arc of the Atlantic. I grabbed on with both hands.

DUBLIN

In 2002, I began working toward a Master of Theology degree. As part of the program one must complete a cross-cultural experience. Advertised as one of the options was a trip to Ireland. You may wonder why I was working on a theology degree. I wonder that myself. It is not something I've analyzed. I know I was trying to please my mother. I am also fairly certain it had something to do with my father's recent death. Not because of God or any mystical reason. Ministry was my father's field. Perhaps it kept me connected to him.

The year before my father died I left my job to help my mother care for him. I felt it was important. I thought, "this is what family does. We take care of each other." And so for more than a year I traveled once, sometimes twice, sometimes three times a week from Chicago to Richmond, Indiana to help.

As the time grew short, my father met with many people. They all described these meetings in glowing terms. That Bob had touched them with his words with and to them. I hoped that my dad would have something to say to me too and as we sat alone in the house one afternoon, I asked him. His response was, "I don't think I have anything to say to you."

I was sitting with him by the window. Hospice had been called in. The doctors said a week maybe two. I sat with him and told him I was sorry. I said, I thought maybe as he was dying, maybe he had something he wanted to say to me? I thought he would have some wisdom he wanted to share. I thought he might tell me he loved me or was proud of me or give me some advice. He said, "I don't think I have anything to say to you." I didn't follow up. I wanted to follow up. To ask what he meant by that. Why didn't he have anything to say? I didn't follow up and now I couldn't and I can't. And so I clung to his memory in a most unsuitable way. I attended to seminary. And through seminary, I traveled to Ireland.

I've heard stories of people going to Ireland on vacation only to send a note back to the States instructing the recipient to send their things. "Jane went to Ireland on vacation and she never came back. Just sent for her things." Now here I was landing in Dublin and I felt a strange sensation of home. I'd never felt at home anywhere in my life and here, as the wheels touched ground, I felt home.

An awareness looms that I may become one of those people who returns from Ireland describing it as haunting, spiritual, intoxicatingly romantic. I am not this person. I am a thinking introvert not a feeling introvert and I don't wax poetic about St. Brigid, sheep, or green rolling hills where the wind has 'a sound like a soft sweet song' and so I hope it is a falsity. Like Target.

Every time I enter Target I am overcome by a deep uncontrollable compulsion to spend. To part with hard-earned cash on cheap goods for which I have neither the need nor truly the desire. No one would seriously romanticize the Target-effect. But tourists do it every day in Ireland. They go to Ireland, are enchanted by the beauty and develop a mystical connection. I don't have a mystical connection with small kitchen appliances just as no one has a mystical connection with Ireland. But if you are going to fuck-all and abscond to another country, Ireland is not a bad place to do it.

We students were provided an itinerary detailing our sixteen days in Ireland. I had glanced over it as I shoved it in my bag on the way to the airport. We had a professor/guide who had worked it all out, so I really didn't see any reason to concern myself with the details. Leaving Newark I was not worried I didn't see anyone on the plane from the group because I knew no one in the group. I thought sometime in the next six hours an elderly man with glasses and protruding nose-hairs would stop by my seat and enquire if I were indeed Jennifer Faus.

After the in-flight supper the sinking feeling began. I was the only one of the group on this flight. I dug out the itinerary and found the address to Fatima House the first B&B of our trip. Problem was, I hadn't even looked at a map of Ireland, let alone Dublin and so had not a clue as to where it might be. Truthfully, neither Ireland nor Dublin. I knew of course that Ireland was over the Atlantic somewhere but as I skipped geography in my stellar public school education that was it. The extent of my knowledge about Ireland and its place on the map was it is somewhere beyond Lake Michigan. A rather uncomfortable exchange with a member of some Irish football team behind me ensued:

ME: Do you know where this B&B is located?

HIM: "Fatima House?"

ME: Yes. My group is supposed to be on this plane but I don't think they made it.

He consults with his cohort.

HIM: "What would you be doing staying at Fatima House? It's pretty low-scale. Not a very nice place."

ME: Well it's a cross-cultural experience. We are supposed to be experiencing the culture.

HIM: "Well, you wouldn't need to stay in a crap place to experience the culture. You wouldn't think much of Irish culture if you stayed in a shit place, would you?"

OOPS.

ME: (trying to recover) Well, what I mean is we aren't supposed to be hanging out in our hotel rooms but be out doing things, you know? (it's not working) Anyway, can you tell me how to get there from the airport? Should I take a taxi?

HIM: (quite finished with me) "No. There will be a bus. Just ask at information when you arrive."

He hands me back the itinerary. I turn around and keep face-forward the rest of the flight. I don't even get up to use the restroom for fear of the leers I will get from the football stars. Which, as it turns out, were just a bunch of firefighters back from a soccer match with a bunch of other firefighters in the states. Football stars. Ha!

He was absolutely correct. Information directed me to the bus and told me the stop I'd need and in an hour I was checking into Fatima House. Our room had six single cots. Cots. Not beds. Good old fashioned wartime cots. I dumped my luggage on a cot, grabbed my itinerary, and headed out to the streets of Dublin. Our forward-thinking professor laid out the entire day's activities so I just followed the list: Christ Church, Book of Kells, Marsh's Library, Grafton Street, the Ha'penny Bridge.

I bought a map and boarded a tour bus to acclimate myself to the city. I complained their map was upside down —if we were driving north toward 'X' why, did you have to turn the map upside down to follow along? Didn't they follow map-making convention? North goes on the top. The bus driver said she didn't look at maps. They didn't make any sense to her. This was not to be my only cartography challenge over the course of my relationship with Ireland.

At about 6:00 p.m., which I soon learned was 18:00, I decided to immerse myself in the culture. I dismissed the trifling fact I was not a drinker. (I was always at a loss as to what to order in American bars, so I was truly out of my league in Dublin.) The only phrase I knew in Irish drinking vernacular was, "Pint of Guinness." So I walked in, plunked myself down and said, "Pint of Guinness." Everyone stopped talking and looked at me. It was a local, meaning locals only. I was the sole foreigner and sole female. I was wearing a bright-red Northface jacket. Not only was it red, but far too big. I needed a rain jacket for Ireland, and being frugal by nature bought the men's XL off the clearance rack, knowing my son would use it post trip. I couldn't have been more American had I been waving a Confederate flag and saying, "Hey, Ya'll!"   "First time in Ireland?"

Yes!

The bartender tosses his friend sitting to my left a look and pulls me a pint. After the third pint I know the men in the Sinn Fein pub all have Disciple's names – Tommy, Paul, Jimmy, and Phil….Johnny, the barkeep, has a photo of Michael Collins taken by a relative pasted onto a cigar box. He shows it to Paul, "Some American offered me 120 for this."

"Wow."

"Yea, he asked me what I waaaanted for it. I told him I'd not seeeeeellit."

"Never."

"Yea, you don't sell this for nothing."

"Americans. They'll pay for anything."

"Do you know who this is?" He shows me the box.

Michael Collins. (and in an effort to show my vast knowledge) He negotiated the deal that divided the Republic and Northern Ireland. (I'd learned that from the only research I completed before the trip watching the movie, conveniently titled, Michael Collins).

"Michael farking Collins."

"Yea." To Paul, "She knows."

"So, missssss-eh, what else ya know 'booooout Ir'land?"

And so it went. We drank and they talked politics until Paul asked would I like some fish and chips. I must have fish and chips he pressed, as I was in Dublin and he knew where the best fish and chips could be found. Turns out, the chip shop was a cart near his apartment. As you know, I'd never been to a third-world country. (Chicago's west side is as close as I'd come.) But I imagine it would look something like Paul's neighborhood.

Behind a half-built and obviously abandoned stadium, half-burned cars smoking, laundry hanging everywhere, we picked through the rubble, climbed through a hole cut in a chain-link fence and ducked into a dirty white building. I cursed myself for forgetting my camera. His apartment was tiny. He had tiny fridge and a hot plate. Later I learned the tiny fridge is not a peculiarity in Ireland. But at that time, I thought it told me something about him. I ate my fish and chips and he put his in the icebox for later.

I sat on his couch and began to doze off as I had been awake for over 24 hours. He jostled me and asked, "Do you want to go to bed with me?"

What?

"Do you want to go to bed with me? I've got a bed in the other room. Will you go to bed with me?"

I thought it best to be moving on while he was still asking. I had no idea where I was. With the realization crashing around me that no one in the world knew where I was—except that they could confirm I'd boarded a flight to Dublin and checked into a dump—I suggested we head back to the pub. To my great relief he just shrugged and said, "OK."

With dawn approaching, and after witnessing several tussles and one outright brawl involving a woman and, eventually, the Garda, I decided to head back to the B&B. I agreed to meet Paul back at the bar the next afternoon so he could take me to get some photos of the city. It occurred to me he might just be saving the kill for the next day, but the opportunity to photograph where he lived was too enticing to pass up.

Back at Fatima House, I crawled over sleeping women to my cot in the corner. The next day I would not be able to find the pub. Eight years on, and more than a dozen trips to Dublin and I still have no idea where that pub sits.

And so went the next twelve days. In Waterford I met the harbormaster and went drinking with him til dawn. In Clonakilty I shared the best first-kiss of my life with a young man from South Carolina. In Clonmacnoise I worked as the kitchen helper to John and Kate who weren't expecting us for dinner. There I set the table and performed kitchen-tasks as directed while drinking glass after glass of 'the good wine' reserved for those who worked in the kitchen. After dinner there was Poitín all around and the group went en-masse for a midnight walk to Clonmacnoise. Someday I will meet someone who will marry me in the nun's church there. Then, there was Derry.

It must be said that in the sixteen days we traveled in Ireland, we stayed in two places with hot water. John and Kate's and a place owned by Australians in Ballintoy. Long nights of drinking followed by long days of walking interspersed with long hours on a tour bus wore on each of us differently.

Each person met their end in their own way, then picked up and kept going. There was the day our leader—not an old man with glasses and nose-hair but a robust young man with a big smile and a shaved head—simply said, "You have your itinerary for the day, see you tonight," turned, and walked off. The afternoon the curly-haired woman broke down and sobbed when there was no ice to be found for her water. And my favorite—a comforting thought still today when life is challenging—was my roommate's lament that she longed for Ecuador where she bathed in a polluted river and was devoured by bugs in 120 degree heat.

For me, I awoke in Derry planning to take walk around the walls as the sun came up. It seemed romantic to me to walk these historic walls at sunrise. I hoped to take a quick shower, and, by being the first in would have the best chance at some warmth in the water. There was no lightbulb in the bathroom. The icy water ran on and on, the floor was covered in hair, the towels, dirty. I abandoned my mission. I got back into my clothes, laid back on the cot and refused to get up.

My roommate who longed for Ecuador coaxed me with the promise of hot coffee and buttered toast. This of course was not to be found in the breakfast room of the hostel and so we all shuffled outside to wait for the bus to take us to the Carrick-a-Rede Bridge. Our ever-patient driver promised a petrol-station stop for coffee and buns and we were cheered. Slightly. Sincere moments of bonding occurred that day among the younger of us on the squishy island across the bridge. With each of us exhausted and on fragile footing, we knew to survive the next four days, we would have to stick together.

Our second day in Derry Produced a tour of the Walls. Martin McCrossan led us around the walls with lively anecdotes about Derry. At the end of the tour we were met by Ivan Cooper. An older-looking man in a navy three-breasted suit, he wore a lavender checked shirt, bright purple tie, and a colorful breast-pocket hankie. He spoke about his role in the civil rights movement but I was still thinking about coffee and buttered toast. Later that day I saw Ivan in the street and asked him if we could go for coffee.

It may seem a strange thing that I approached a relative stranger in the street and asked him to coffee. It is legitimate to say I needed information. A paper was required for the class. We were to chose a subject we found interesting on the trip and write about it. This is the excuse I used with Ivan. In some ways it would get me into more trouble than I bargained for. I told Ivan I was interested in Bloody Sunday. It was, in fact, his reference to Bloody Sunday was the only thing I could recall from his speech.

In response to this, Ivan directed me to the Bloody Sunday Family Centre to meet John Kelly and Mickey McKinney. This I did. These two things, telling Ivan I was interested in Bloody Sunday and meeting John and Mickey set-off a chain of events that culminated in a book called 'Any Mother's Son.' This I will explain later. The most important thing to know now is that on a sunny June day in 2002 I met Ivan Cooper.

Ivan and me. To say Ivan is one of the loves of my life is true. To say Ivan and I were having a love affair and I am the only one who didn't know it is also true. It is true that in our time together, I learned many things about Ivan. It is also true he kept much from me.

I don't know if Ivan ever thinks about our first meeting. I think about it often. I don't remember what we said. I remember sitting across from him drinking coffee like we'd been doing it all our lives. I was initially a bit nervous. After all I'd just lied to him to get him to go to coffee with me. But as we cleared the queue with our coffee and biscuits, Ivan and I were old friends and by the time our cups were empty, we'd solidified plans for dinner.

After coffee, Ivan had a meeting. I went to the Bloody Sunday Family Centre to meet John and Mickey and then, I bought a dress. Ivan and I went to dinner at the Tower Hotel. Two steaks, two bottles of wine, two coffees, and a shared chocolate later, Ivan elicits information about my father and I start to cry. I never cry. I think it must be the wine. Thankfully Ivan announces, *Let's go annoy the Provos!* I don't know what that means but I am relieved he has changed the subject.

I expect outdoors to be damp and chilly but it is a beautiful night. At midnight there is still light in the sky. The Tower Hotel is just round the corner from Peadar O'Donnell's but I don't know that yet. It's all cobblestone streets, walls, and arched walkways to me now. So I toddle along next to Ivan under the arch and down the steep street to the pub. We are late.

The evening is winding down. The band is playing its last. I sit smiling like an idiot as Ivan chats with everyone around. Then the ginger-headed mayor's son invites us to a party. Hand-in-hand Ivan and I walk along with the crowd to an old brick building which stands along the outside of the walls. In the living room of someone's flat Sinatra is playing and the mayor's son takes me in his arms and we dance. I catch glimpses of Ivan sitting on the couch surrounded by people. He is telling stories.

Seems like it's about four a.m. when Ivan and I are ushered into a dark blue Mercedes. I am driven around the corner and dropped off. I've forgotten the hostel locks its doors at 2:45 and there is absolutely no way in. Basically, I am really drunk, in a strange town, haven't a clue where anything is in relation to the hostel, and already can't remember that I've only been brought round the corner from the party.

There is much I am sure I don't remember about my time in Ireland. Walking back around the corner is one of them. I do recall standing on the street looking up at a red-brick building calling, Hello? Is anyone up there?

Someone in my group relayed the story that in Ireland, you can knock on a stranger's door and they will let you spend the night. Does this story have roots in Ireland's pub culture? I don't know. This is what I suppose it is about and so I call out again, Hello?

I am calling up because I can hear bottles clinking above me as if someone is cleaning up from a party. I make absolutely no connection that it is actually someone's home nor that it is the home I just spent several hours drinking, dancing, and most unfortunately, singing at. After the third "Hello?" a face appears at the window.

"You alright down there?"

The hostel is closed.

In my inebriated state, this is the entirety of my answer.

"You need a place to kip?"

Kip? What the hell is kip? Did I hear her right? I don't know. I stand blinking in the street light.

"You need a place to kip?"

Oh hell, I guess I better just say, Yes!

"Come on up then."

I think maybe this is where the party was but I don't remember the party being three flights up. I am tucked in on what I think is the sofa on which Ivan perched in the early morning hours as he chatted up the party guests and I danced to Sinatra with the mayor's son. After the two bottles of wine at dinner, I can't recall what or even if I was drinking. I sleep fitfully keeping one eye on the window, watching for the sun. The cleaning crew continues around me, and then, suddenly, all is quiet. I wonder if they wondered what they would do with me if I was still there when they awoke. I wonder if they still laugh about the drunk American blinking in the street light.

My bus leaves at 8:30. My hangover is severe enough I can't feel anything—yet. As the sun lifts over the Derry hills, I creep out of the flat, down the stairs, up the cobblestone street, through the gate, into the hostel, and pack my things. I skip the cold shower in the bathroom with no light. Fourteen days of cold showers across 1100 miles of Ireland. I am thinking I will get a hot shower in Belfast.

On the bus to Belfast I didn't know it was too late for me and Ivan. We had forged a bond. Part of our relationship includes that book. Ivan "facilitated" the creation of that book. He facilitates in a way that is akin to why no one likes blind dates. And if you don't know why no one likes blind dates then you have lived an enchanted life. Ask a friend who didn't marry their high-school sweetheart and they will tell you. I just don't have the energy today to explain it. I did once, but then I mistakenly threw those pages away so you are just on your own here. But 'Before Bloody Sunday' is a book about something. It is a book that matters. Ivan facilitates my writing a meaningful, touching book that empties my children's college funds, my savings, and as a final blow puts me on the verge of bankruptcy. But I pull through and it is the next book that finally drains the rest of my finances. Being an unsuccessful writer is a tough gig.

'Before Bloody Sunday' does not make me Bukowski or Sedaris or Royko or that <u>Running with Scissors</u> guy. It will not be one immortal novel vis a vis <u>Catcher in the Rye</u> or <u>To Kill a Mockingbird</u>. It will not be optioned for a movie but a Derry theatre will base a play on it and I will hear about it from a third party. I will not win a Pulitzer or an Angus. I will not have my fifteen minutes. But it will be a book that matters. In this world of <u>Harry Potter</u>, Oprah's Book Club, and <u>Twilight</u> there is a book that means something. A book that matters. And it exists because of Ivan Cooper.

This is what I say to make myself feel better when I think of the dismal sales of the book. When I think about how I threw years of my life away and then repeated the show all over again on another go-nowhere project. Ahhhh, the bells of altruism. Do you hear them ringing?

We arrived in Belfast to learn Helga House has cold showers. Yes, I know you are supposed to flip the switch or pull the cord. But the water does not heat. It's a diversionary tactic that cord. The stained carpet and grey sheets prompt me to drop my tourist façade. After accomplishing the obligatory: strolling the Botanic Gardens, visiting Queen's College, perusing the Seamen's Church, shopping along Donegal Place, taking in the political murals, and visiting C.S. Lewis' childhood home, my colleagues and I see three movies and stay out drinking for two straight nights to avoid touching anything at Helga's.

Every time I pass through over the next five years I will stay at the Belfast Hilton. At first I will feel badly about it. I should after all support some local B&B. Then the day will come. Sitting in business class—American Airlines has seen fit to bump me up God Bless them—traveling from London to Chicago. I am seated next to an English expat and I come to terms with it.

She tells me she was home in England for a visit. She's been living in the States for eight years. She had a lovely time at home, "But," she leans in and whispers, "I'm American now."

Really? Why do you say that?

"Well, I complained a bit. I wanted ice. I wished there were more channels on the telly. I complained about having to pay for TV. I missed a good steak. And quite frankly, I really enjoy a hot shower." She freed me. I was finally able to book accommodation without guilt. I am American. I require hot water.

INTERLUDE

Ever have a feeling that you shouldn't be doing something but you do it anyway? My entire life is that feeling. I don't think I can explain to you what it is like to go through life without a thought in your head except what you are doing right now. But with me that is how it is. Goldfish. The attention span of goldfish.

A conversation with me might go something like this, "I am so sorry to hear about the tragic unexpected death of your mother. You must be terribly broken up over it. Oh my, aren't those cute shoes?" Goldfish. Twenty years of single parenting will do that to a person. Everyone gets exactly 1.75 seconds of your time and only if you can spare it.

Single parents have to make every single decision for their families, accomplish every single task, and bear every single responsibility. Especially the single parents of my species which are the ones with no family around to take up any slack. There's no calling my mother or aunt or cousin when I need a hand. I am the only one on speed dial.

I am also a "lifer." This means I didn't get divorced for a minute-and-a-half then then marry a rich banker who tells everyone how proud he is of me for all those difficult minutes I spent as a single parent. I left my husband with no higher education, three kids under age 4, and $12.00. Twelve dollars. I never looked back. After that marriage I never even considered crossing that threshold again. My kids are now in college and that makes me a "lifer."

Getting back to my point, as a single parent your days are filled with stop-gap measures, because your days are filled with crisis management. There is no one to pass-off to. No one to discuss a problem. No one to help make a decision. And when it is just you and your kids the problems come at you rapid-fire. There is some level of crisis everyday. And you learn to deal with each one as efficiently as the next. So the "I forgot my lunch" crisis and the "Your child needs emergency surgery and your insurance is expired" crises are met with equal calm calculation. Mastering this efficient disposal of crises is important because when your days are filled with them you need to be fresh to deal with the next, which is due to arrive in about 1.75 seconds.

NEW YORK

Having never been to New York I chose a flight to arrive in the morning. I am eager to see Ivan and I want to see the sights but this morning I am not visiting Ground Zero or Ellis Island or the Museum of Modern Art or Times Square. I am swinging on the swings in Central Park across from the Essex Hotel. I am waiting for Ivan on the swing set. Not shopping on Fifth Avenue or lunching at Tavern on the Green. Swinging on the swing set in Central Park. My eyes are fixed on the Essex sign. I swing in my favorite black dress and four-inch heels because I don't want to be off sightseeing when Ivan arrives. I have never been so excited. Ivan and I are meeting in New York!

It is a perfect day. Fresh air, bold blue sky, billowy white clouds, and hope. Ivan is late but I am confident he will eventually arrive and I am anxious for our reunion. We are meeting to attend the Bloody Sunday premiere. Ivan is telling the media that *Paul Greengrass has delivered the single most important film on Bloody Sunday. It is a stunning piece.* Ivan is the central character in the movie so I may be just a bit leery of his assessment. No matter. I am in New York! To attend a movie premiere! Wow!

I imagine Ivan and me on the red carpet. Lights shimmering, cameras popping. Hand-in-hand. Smiling. Ivan would stop to chat with reporters as I stood quietly by. Adoring. Confident. Fabulous.

I was worried I might be too shy. Concerned my general aversion to meeting new people and paralyzing fear of crowds would get the best of me and I would sit frozen in our room unable to cross the threshold and go out into the glamorous life of Manhattan. I decided not to focus on reality and instead mentally rehearsed walking into the theatre blinded by the flashbulbs of the paparazzi. I never actually pictured us inside the theatre just gliding up to the doors.

Ivan and I would drink champagne. He would be charming. I would be witty. My beauty and grace would surely catch the eye of a George Clooney or Matthew McConaughey who would be bewitched by me and whisk me away to his Italian villa or Texas RV. One could rationally argue I was perhaps just a tad too focused on me. A wee bit too focused on the dress I would wear, the shoes, the make-up. Turns out, Paul and Ivan were not in New York so I could attend a movie premiere. They were there to promote the movie.

Thankfully Ivan rings and pulls me out of my fantasy. I shoot across the street to the Essex and we pile into a limo with John Kelly and Mickey McKinney of the Bloody Sunday Family Centre and are whisked off to lunch with a bony black-haired woman. Upon seeing Ivan she exclaims, "Darling!" and kisses both his cheeks. She greets John and Mickey with handshakes and looks down her narrow nose to me. "I was told there would be three of you. I reserved a table for four."

She apologizes profusely to the waiter for my presence, fusses about new table arrangements, and then spends the entire lunch complaining that she wanted Spring Greens and Prosciutto and nothing else. Could they not get that right? She sends it back saying and gesticulating "Nothing, Nothing, Nothing!" I order a hamburger which I interpret from her sniff is something a New York woman would never

ever do. I imagine she thinks my 5'7" one hundred thirty pound frame is slightly south of hippo.

She looks to John, Mickey, Ivan, and me for support in her Spring Greens and Prosciutto crisis. None of us can manage to stop staring at her as if she were an alien. Her gaze turns on us and we are shocked back to reality. Better she take it out on the waiter than us. I keep my head down the rest of the meal. I am not involved in the conversation. I am also not wearing my microphone which means this is my last memory of this lunch.

In retrospect I could kick myself for not being properly suited up with my mini digital recorder tucked in my bra under my arm, the microphone clipped between my breasts. But it occurs to me that Ivan and I may not have reached the recording every word part of our relationship yet. The experience with the bony woman was so bizarre, so out-of-body, so uncomfortable other than what I have just written my only other memories of this lunch are about white tablecloths, flowers, the large window at the front. I don't recall the conversation. I feel that I was so put off by her I looked down for the majority of the meal and that I why I have only these peripheral sensory memories.

I wish I had asked Ivan about that lunch later. I would love to know his impression but we never talked about it. I never asked. I was so focused on getting Ivan's memoirs down I often forgot to engage in a present relationship with him. I was oblivious to the fact that everyone around us was certain we were in a relationship. I think they thought we were in a romantic relationship. People asked me about it from time to time but I just shrugged them off. If was not until one of our last times together that it struck me. We were visiting Kevin McKinney and his wife (two of my favorite people in the world, I just admire them and their love for each other and commitment to their family, but I am getting off track). So Ivan and I stopped in because I wanted to confirm where Kevin's father was buried. Gerry McKinney is not on the roles of the City Cemetery. During the conversation Kevin and his wife invited Ivan and me to dinner when next I was in town. This was the moment I realized everyone thought Ivan and I were a couple. It was the way they asked us. They asked US. As if it was a forgone conclusion we would be together. OK, so yes, we were always together but, not in that way. I remember feeling dumbstruck as I turned and looked at him. Then it seems I suddenly ended the conversation and left.

Meanwhile, back in New York….

After lunch we are delivered back to the hotel where Ivan is late for a photo shoot. We are marched across the street where Paul is walking up a path from the park while a photographer snaps away. Then he walks back down. Then up again for more snaps. Then back down. The glamorous life of a film maker. They are looking for Jimmy who was due but is now missing. It is Ivan's turn to walk up and down the pat and I can't figure out where to stand. First I block the light, then I am in the background. After I trip over the camera bag I retreat to the top of the hill to loiter by the street.

A tall thin man in tight pants and shirt is there pulling out a cigarette. I ask the guy if I can bum one. He doles out two. We stand together smoking. Two onlookers. It's taking a long time. The photographer can't seem to get the perfect angle. We stub out our smokes and the guy doles out two more.

He has an Irish accent so I point to Ivan and say, You know who that guy is? I am eager to share my vast knowledge of the Irish civil rights movement and my connectedness to the famous and infamous Ivan Cooper.

"Who? Ivan? Yeah." Paul is now walking up toward us. I straighten to say hello. After all, it is important this guy know I am acquainted with the director of Bloody Sunday. Paul nods hello to me and says, "Hey Jimmy."

"Hey Paul."

I thought he looked familiar. Jimmy Nesbitt. He will later win best actor for his role as Ivan Cooper in Bloody Sunday, but now he's just hanging out on Central Park South with his new friend Jennifer Faus. Ivan heads toward us and in a flash Jimmy switches off 'guy smoking on the street' and becomes 'famous actor.' He is ready for his session.

Hello Jimmy. I see you've met Jennifer.

"Aye." Jimmy turns to me and formally shakes my hand. "Hello Jennifer. How are ya Ivan?"

Very well. Best get on they're waiting for you.

The energy emanating from Jimmy as he saunters down to the photographer is nuclear and I am jealous. I want that inner-light, endless energy, magnetism. Maybe I could be like Jimmy. I stand on the sidewalk staring, trying to channel Jimmy Nesbitt: 'I am confident. I am sexy. People want to be near me. I am fabulous.' Ivan takes my hand. *Come on Jennifer, you look knackered. Let's get you a drink.* Maybe not.

The crowd at the bar look like they are going to church. Suit coats with button down shirts and khakis on the men, long casual skirts on the women. Perhaps I am a bit over dressed in my short black dress made from scuba-suit material. My make-up has been done by an over zealous Yves Saint Laurent counter girl also eager to be this close to a movie premiere. I do look fabulous. The approving looks of the bell-hops and elevator attendants confirm my feeling.

The group is piled like puppies around a table in the bar. Drinking and laughing, they are painfully welcoming as Ivan and I approach. They welcome me like the relative who smokes cigars in the house, drinks too much, cusses in front of the kids, and—lovely—has just arrived for an extended holiday. They will tolerate me best they can, knowing it will soon be over.

Into the limo once more. Paul, two twenty-something assistants, Producers Pippa Cross and Steve Morrison, John, Jimmy, Mickey, Ivan, and me. While waiting for the limo Jimmy gives me an approving nod and a cigarette. He has a power. He makes me a bit weak in the knees. Later Jimmy will get in a bit of a bother for making too many women weak in the knees.

The limo pulls up to a cement auditorium. There are no lights, cameras, no carpet. I've stepped in gum and my mascara is running from one eye and clumping on the other making me look like a winking raccoon. I am thus appropriately relieved there are no photographers. A publicist appears and picks out the important few: Ivan, Jimmy, Paul, Pippa, and the two young, giggly, good-looking assistants. I wander down a hill and over to the side of the building and take a picture of the Julliard School sign with my disposable camera.

Walking back up to the entrance, I face my reality. This morning I stood on the street smoking with the venerable

Jimmy Nesbitt. Tonight, my companion is a foot shorter than me and balding. He has a gap between his two front teeth, which accentuates his hissing laugh. Dark slits of eyes pierce me from behind wire-rimmed glasses. "Shall we sit together for the movie?"

Steve Morrison. CEO of Granada Films, the maker of 'My Left Foot.' I am supposed to be impressed. Quite frankly he creeps me out. We sit together. He confirms my feeling. Early in the film he grabs my hand and squeezes it with such ferocity throughout the movie I think I feel my bones snapping.

The film receives a standing ovation. Ivan is correct. It is a truly stunning work. After winning dozens of awards awards around the planet, Bloody Sunday will be banned from the Oscars because it was shown on television in Ireland prior to its release in the states. Never mind the television showing was required by the film boards that partially funded the film. I suppose the Academy worried a film might win on its merits rather than via the clout of the studio behind it.

No matter, Paul will go on to direct 'The Bourne Supremacy.' It will gross more than $50 million during its opening weekend and earn more than $175 million in the US alone. This is followed by an Oscar nomination for 'United 93,' and the multi-million dollar career he so deserved. As I grind away typing memories from years ago, I ardently admire Paul for his genius and his ability to move on.

After the premier we retire again to the hotel bar and drink until the early hours of the morning. Ivan and I set out at sunrise to find a genuine New York diner. Ivan's travels have taken him to every continent but he professes love for

American dining. *It's not American food, per se, it is the wide variety of choices and high quality of food offered in America.* His confession may not be colorful but it comes from the heart and the genuine delight on his face as we peruse the menu satisfies me more than warm blueberry muffins and hot coffee.

A few blocks from the Essex, we find what could be the backdrop for any 1950s American movie. The restaurant has a large "DINER" sign on its stainless steel exterior. Booths line the windows. A u-shaped counter with barstools—the kind with the seats that swivel— stands in the middle. We spend three bliss-filled hours talking over hot coffee, creamy oatmeal, buttery eggs, and the biggest muffins I've ever eaten.

We laugh about the dinner we attended with potential film distributors and the speech Ivan gave. He tells me he had no idea they would ask him to speak. I told him he was wonderful. As I work though a second muffin, Ivan reminisces:

I think the first inclination I had that I might be capable of public speaking was when I joined the Young Farmers Club. I think I was fourteen.

What's the formal name for that? Is it like 4-H?

That was it. The Young Farmer's Club - YFC. It was almost entirely Protestant. If not all. I think it was all Prod. I remember they had these social gatherings and debating competitions. I remember they had an under eighteen debating competition. I think I was fourteen and I had entered it. I was the youngest and I won it. I won a gilt - a young pedigree female pig. I won the pig. I kept the pig and the piglets and I managed to get more and I looked after the pig myself and I managed to expand to I think to eight to ten mother pigs - sows. Then my mother said, 'You are not going to be a farmer so those pigs are going to have to go.'

Why did she say you are not going to be a farmer?

I liked the pig very much. We developed a very close bond. I didn't like the idea of killing them and one day I came home and all the pigs were gone and my mother said, 'You need to devote your attention to your books and you can't devote attention to books if you are running after pigs!'

At the age of sixteen and a half I joined the local Young Unionists Association because that was the local structure of politics. I stayed in the Young unionist movement until I was eighteen and a half or nineteen. Then I was expelled.

And you're going to tell me why?

I don't remember the actual reason they gave but it had to do with causing a ruckus at meetings and cross-examining politicians. That was the real reason. I don't remember the reason they gave at the time but I was kicked out. I don't remember the reason they gave—it was some minor thing....

You were a pest!

Perhaps. Perhaps a bit of a pest.

We never see Ground Zero or Ellis Island, the Museum of Modern Art, or Times Square. But we are warmed in each other's presence as the red and yellow leaves of a New York autumn blow past the diner window.

THE GLENS OF ANTRIM

It is dark when we reach Ballycastle. We've whiled away the afternoon at the Adair Arms, 25 miles northwest of Belfast. Ivan had to stop for a meeting. We ended up holding court in the bar all afternoon. I am developing a great affection for dark mahogany, whiskey, and the company of men. I've not seen any women in the places Ivan and I haunt.

I've met only one. I went to her home in Belfast and spent the afternoon learning about her experiences as the wife of the man who blew up Palace Barracks and the mother of a daughter permanently disabled by a rubber bullet. I wrote to her after but she never responded.

It is late. I've probably been dozing. Ivan pulls off to the side of the road. *Alright Jennifer. That's it. We will go again in the morning.* I struggle in behind Ivan, pulling my wrap tight against the brisk November air. We are directed to the bar. It and the patrons are well-lit and bustling. It's not noisy but the crowd is lively. They seem to all be having a good time. My mind is foggy. I am not sure what night it is but the bar is packed as Ivan and I look for a seat. We always seem to find something facing the crowd. We sit next to each other and look out over the bar.

I try to shake off my exhaustion. I try to ignore the afternoon of alcohol in my veins. I sit up, smile, and receive Ivan's red wine and my whiskey cheerfully. People know Ivan. Everywhere we go people know Ivan. The evening falls away as we chat with people in the bar.

I am aware of laughing and joking but have no idea what is being said. I am on auto-pilot. After I've moved on to Bailey's a key is delivered and Ivan tells me to go on up and get some sleep. The hallways are simple and clean. The room is pale yellow simple and clean. I lie on the bed and the world is silent and black.

White caps crash on the beach. Wave after wave racing each other seeing who can hit the sand the hardest, the fastest. It would seem a joyful game, but there is no rest. The crashing surf's rhythm is constant, which, combined with the unrelenting wind, blocks out everything.

When I wake, my mind is quiet. The pale yellow room is soft and warm. My restless soul is calm. I pull on slacks and sweater and walk the stretch of Ballycastle Beach in solitude. The men at golf above me stay engrossed in their games. The pair of dogs chase imaginary prey. Their companion lends a silent nod.

I don't believe I've ever known what I presently feel in my soul. Peace. Stillness. I know I could stay here. I could find a small simple cottage and stay. Forever. Here my soul is content. The throbbing, racing, wildly passionate soul I have chased all my life is home. Quiet, content, at peace.

A short way down the beach is an old pier-like structure. It is not meant for boats, I don't believe, but fishing, perhaps. I walk a way out and watch the swirling rushing water. I am aware of the power of the ocean. I've been to the beaches on East and West coasts of the US but have never experienced water with this power. The waves don't come in and recede, but constantly pound the shore.

Ivan will be waiting. Sitting at the table with coffee and paper. Dressed in a suit. A purple, pink, or blue shirt, a flashy tie, and always, always, a silk hankie in his pocket.

I assumed there was only the bar of last evening but Ivan is past reception. I walk down the hall, turn right and find him in a small room with low tables. He encourages me to order breakfast but the coffee warms and fills me.

I told you a joke last night and you just looked at me smiling. Nothing registered. You were not a mighty pilot. I gave you a key and sent you to bed.

I'm better. I'll just drink this and get my things.

We have time.

We sit together for a few quiet moments. Ivan with his paper and me with my coffee. The small room is quiet and still. Our harmony together liquid and even.

The car is just up the road. Pausing at the empty terminal I wish for the ferry. It would take me across to Rathlin Island. Here the seagulls guard the path to the lighthouse. The seals aren't bothered by human bathing companions. They will gaze at you with such longing that before you know it you are stripping your clothes and entering the sea.

The island's lake is still, deep, and frigid. The sheer brutal cliffs protect puffins. I envision a small house with a fireplace and a desk. The dust jackets of my books reading, 'The author lives with her dog on Rathlin Island.' I want to stay. I ache to board the ferry but Ivan has a meeting. My musing interrupted, I return to the moment. We load our bags into the Mercedes, take our places, and continue our journey to the Glens.

Ivan is disappointed. *It's a miserable day. Just miserable.*

It's beautiful, Ivan, don't fuss.

It's just plain miserable.

And then, complaining finished for the moment, Ivan's phone rings and I begin my pre-meeting routine of taking off my seat belt and removing my coat. And we slip into another familiar dialogue, Ivan telling me, *You'll freeze without that.*

I need to take off my wire.

No one will know it's there.

I'll know it's there.

Ivan goes about reading text messages, holding his phone away, peering over his glasses, while I awkwardly remove the microphone clipped to the center of my bra inside my shirt, pulling out the wire, and eventually the small digital recorder I tuck into the side of my bra under my arm. It is now I realize Ivan and I are dressed like twins in matching dark suits. At least he is wearing a grey trench coat to my black long wool.

I decide not to mention it. Ivan is fussing because he wants me to see the valley but the day is foggy. The Glens of Antrim is one of the most beautiful places in the world. He's been telling me this for some time and now he thinks I am missing it. In his mind he's promised me beauty and given me a rainy mess. Standing on the ridge looking down from the sheep farm the valley is a soft even blanket of fog. Like the day, it is settled, enveloped, serene. Ivan huffs at my insistence that the fog is beautiful too. I push on saying I am just as pleased with a foggy valley as a clear one. Our petty disappointments will soon depart. Two weathered men approach us.

Brothers. One short. One tall. Both broad and muscled. Their caps do not conceal their lined faces. Calloused hands are exposed at the cuffs. They are otherwise covered. Three layers at least on top. Mud splattered boots at bottom. *This is Jennifer. She's a lawyer. You don't have to worry about her.* Ivan introduces me as a lawyer or writer or journalist, depending on the situation.

He then always follows up with how I am American and because I am American I am either frozen or hungry or tired or carrying some malady that will certainly kill me in the next few minutes if we don't move things along. Today, appropriately, Ivan chooses frozen. *Jennifer is from America. She's frozen. She's not used to our weather!* The men nod to me and lead us across the mud yard to the house saying, "Come along then. We'll get you inside."

We all squeeze into the small entry and close the exterior door before opening the next into the sitting room. Coats on against the cold. No one removes a coat though the room holds some warmth.

This is a feature of Northern Ireland. Every place you go people are wearing their coats. At coffee at lunch at dinner at meetings the coats stay on. The exception might be a fancy dress party. The taller brother exits the plain papered room through a door at the back. The shorter brother and I occupy the sofa against the long wall. Ivan perches near the entry door and the taller brother returns with a lad not much older than my son.

The young man sits in the middle, flanked by Ivan and the taller brother. He is slender and frail, a contrast to his father and uncle. He is just out of hospital for depression. Though the embarrassment of the brothers is obvious it is tempered by their concern for the young man. The taller brother, I gather is the uncle. The one who has called Ivan for help. The lad is in financial trouble. His narrow shoulders slump as he tells Ivan his story

"Well I opened the shop and we were doing well but not as well as we would have liked so we contacted Spar and became a Spar."

That's very well. What happened next?

"Sales were good but our employee costs were too high. We just couldn't seem to pay our bills. We had too many employees. We tried cutting down the hours of the shop, but still our employee costs were high. We couldn't ask them to take a pay cut......"

As I listen to his story I wish he had called Ivan sooner. His store could have survived. He just needed some guidance. Now failure overwhelms him. It shrouds the young lad's fragile frame. He is not sure he can go on. Ivan and the brothers discuss the options. Ivan will take the case. The uncle writes a check to cover the costs.

As my heart breaks for the young man I see Ivan in a new light. He went from fighting on a grand scale to helping one person at a time. Ivan could have conducted this business by phone. Instead, Ivan went to the top of Ireland to see this young man. To let the lad tell his story. To be present with the family.

I can see Ivan visiting homes without heat and water, filled with multiple generations. Homes overcrowded due to inequities in the allocation of housing. I know he sat through the night with women whose husbands had been interned. He must have grieved at the injustice of unemployment due to religion. And by his commitment to this singular person I see why every adult gaining the right to vote in Northern Ireland had been dear to his heart.

Ivan sitting in this house letting the lad tell his story must be why Catholics voted this Protestant into Parliament. Ivan understands the power of face-to-face interaction. He and his colleagues took their cause to the streets and fought for the rights of all. When they were stifled by the aftermath of Bloody Sunday, Ivan stepped out of the limelight, away from Parliament, away from large-scale public demonstrations and took up the causes of individuals.

The meeting winds down. Per usual, I have not seen a single woman. Per usual, no one acted as if it were unusual that I was there. Ivan deflects these questions I suppose when he introduces me as a journalist, a writer, a lawyer. He is kind. And if I am none of those things at least I am good at being invisible. We shake hands with the men. I resist the urge to hug the young man. Ivan and I take our leave.

I wish they had called me earlier. I really think I could have helped them save the business. That young man doesn't need to suffer so. I really think his business could have survived. It's been terrible for that family. He tried to take his life and nearly succeeded. I can help them now, but he won't be able to keep his business. It's too bad. Ivan pauses for a minute with his thoughts. I can see the weight of it on his shoulders. He takes a breath and says,

As I think about my childhood, incidents of no importance seem to shed light on my inclination to stand for justice and fairness. I remember, for example, our neighbor Mrs. McKenna. She did not like tap water and she drew her water from a spring. When a neighboring farmer let his cattle in to drink from her spring I went over and put her fence right again. She was so distraught about the encroachment on her water, and she being an elderly woman—at least to my young eyes!—I convinced my father to threaten the farmer with the law should he allow his cattle to breech her fence again.

I resented the farmers who treated their workers like slaves and I felt intensely sorry for the family down the road who lived in two rooms. I believe there were twenty family members under that one small roof. The mother used to dye flour sacks and use that fabric for dresses for her girls. I didn't think that people should have to live in such poverty. We didn't have central heat but we had fires in several rooms food for the coal-fired cooker and room enough. We had the resources to grow apples and plums, rhubarb, gooseberries, potatoes, and other vegetables. I remember thinking even as a small child that everyone ought to have the basics for sustenance, warmth, and clothes.

He takes a breath and looks at me. His head cocked slightly toward me. Eyes squinting. Taking me in as if his shadow has come to life and he can't figure what to do with it. *Well then, Jennifer, we're off.*

We've taken the coastal road from Ballycastle to the Glens. I am keen to take the scenic road to Torr Head. Ivan after all promised to show me the Green Green Glens of Antrim. *There's nothing green today, Jennifer. It's just, what is it you say? Yuck! Yuck, yuck, yuck. It's all grey. Nothing here to see today.* Ivan's dug in his heels. He looks at me and snorts. And, shaking his head, directs his car down the steep incline into Loughan Bay. Scattered about are the remains of small cottages. In the 1800's this part of the world was nearly inaccessible but the small community managed to work and raise families in the wild and woolly landscape. Sheep are so common here they regard the human inhabitants as a necessary evil and don't bother to acknowledge visitors at all, frequently blocking roads. Sleeping inches from the edge. Usually just at the pitch of a dangerous curve. The beauty lulls me and I hear Ivan's favorite refrain: *You're sleeping. You and John Hume. You sit in that seat and you sleep.*

John Hume's a popular guy. I'm in good company. But I don't snore and I'm much cuter. I've met him so I know for sure I am cuter than John.

You know Jennifer, John was once being monitored at Belfast City Hospital for sleeping habits. Some consultant in the United States had told him that his root problem was that his sleep habit was bad, so they were monitoring his sleeping. And I said to him, 'I never saw any problems with your sleeping patterns because as soon as you get in my car you put the seat back and you sleep.' Just like you my dear. And Jennifer, you're not that cute.

LA SOSTA

Ivan insists on feeding me before retiring to the Beech Hill. Ivan is always insisting I eat. Walking down Carlisle Road we duck into an alley, pass through wrought iron gates, and enter next to the restaurant's kitchen door. One false step and you are taking out trash or scrubbing pots and pans. It is a lovely cozy little restaurant and just as I am about to give over to its warm romance Ivan starts in, *Your phone is tucked in your pants.*

I don't have a pocket.

You know there are studies that show mobile phones cause cancer.

Are you concerned about my ovaries?

It is there. Tucked in your pants. There are studies...

It is here. Tucked on the fat of my ass. To my knowledge nobody has ever died of cancer on the fat of their ass.

Even with Ivan's sniping it is a lovely dinner. We drink a beautiful bottle of red wine. We eat delicious Italian food. No one rushes us. I shed my outer coat for the first time in days as the warmth of the restaurant, the wine, and the company envelop me. Ivan, usually prodding me about my upbringing, continues to open up about his.

Where I was brought up is very important. You've got to get that down. It was a very Protestant upbringing. Many of the feelings I have about civil rights are as important today as they were then. You know, my mother came across from Donegal to marry her Prod husband. I want you to try and grasp the nostalgic part. The humor that kept us going.

I used to go to the unionist meeting and our MP was Robin Chichester Clark. He used to come to one meeting a year and we never saw him again. He didn't have any advice for anyone. He didn't know anything about people's problems. You had to write to him in London! At the House of Commons in London!

I met other MPs like Edward Jones. Edward Jones had nothing in common with Derry. He didn't come from Derry. He only came here once in a blue moon. He had a cultured accent. I didn't have a cultured accent. He'd gone to public school in England. He had an Anglified accent. A posh accent. I had a Derry accent. The accent of an ordinary Derry boy. He had nothing in common with Derry people but he was their local MP.

The next to be elevated to the MP position was Aldrick Anderson. A man who was detested. An arrogant totally inadequate stupid fucker. Surely people are entitled to better representation than that. So I became very concerned.

My father had no respect for the 'big house.' My parents had no respect for the monarchy. As far as they were concerned you see, the poorest man in the land should be capable of getting to the highest office in the land. The ideology of it is important. Why should people be imposed of the monarch in Northern Ireland? My parents wouldn't fly the Union Jack either. As a young man I didn't like the idea of it and it was part and parcel to my upbringing. Why should these people, this privileged family, live from generation to generation in Buckingham Palace with all their wealth, their cars, their servants. They walk along and wave like this here. Why?! Why do we have to pay homage to them? I believed a lot of Protestant people felt as I did. But most important of all, I believed that someone should represent people from the

Protestant working class community who spoke with an authentic voice instead of coming from a big house.

So, from the time I was very young I felt very strongly. I didn't see why these people of privileged, formal education, aristocratic privileged people should automatically be selected as members of Parliament to represent working class people. Why should people who come from a more privileged background represent themselves as spokespersons for authentic working class? Working class people should be able to speak for themselves.

As a boy I used to drive around these Catholic areas with my dad. These women used to invite us into their homes. They were Catholic. They used to give me money and sweets and there were others like my mother who served as the local counselor and I don't mean that in a nominated position I mean hearing all the problems of the area.

I wanted someone to stand up and say, 'These people are living in terrible housing! People don't have water in their homes!' When I was a young man tens of thousands of people had no plumbing in their homes. I had, because my parents made certain that we had, which cost a lot of money. A lot of people didn't have any electricity in their homes. When I became MP in nineteen and sixty-eight there were still a lot of people who had no electricity and no water. No plumbing in their home. One of my first objectives was to ensure that those people in rural areas managed to get electrification and managed to get plumbing in their homes. A lot of those things that I felt strongly about are what I would call bread and butter issues: water, proper housing, electricity, jobs.

When I was eighteen I contested the county seat against a unionist called Mrs. Milligan. Mrs. Milligan's husband was a very prominent unionist and Mrs. Milligan was a very prominent unionist. Her husband had been editor of the Londonderry

Sentinel; a large Prod newspaper. Mrs. Milligan was an old establishment figure. She never had to fight for her seat. She was automatically selected. So I was about eighteen and a half and I decided to fight for her seat. I had no money for election addresses.

Why did you decide to fight her for her seat specifically?

Because I felt it was undemocratic for people to return year after year. To return without having any competition. Secondly, she didn't give a damn about the people she represented. The area was crying out for proper representation. So I threw my hat into the ring. I was eighteen with no money, so I put together a little program—an election manifesto—and I put out my program.

I didn't do terribly well. I was whopped. I think I might have got 40 percent and she got 60. But I got a lot of experience. I acquired a lot of experience canvassing. I knocked on doors and spoke with people and that led me to becoming involved in the housing situation in Derry. So before civil rights I was very much involved in housing protests in Derry.

The election canvasing heightened my awareness of the housing shortage and it focused my mind on power—how it can be acquired, how it can be utilized. I think my participation in the election campaigned sharpened me. I was whopped but I wasn't disgraced. I was only eighteen. So I suddenly realized that with a little more work I could become part of the political structures but I also realized what power was capable of delivering.

After dinner, Ivan and I take a long walk. Up Carlisle Road through the gate onto Ferryquay Street. Past our morning coffee place, Java. Past Ivan's office to where Austin's (Hasson's to the old timers) the world's oldest independent department store stands its Edwardian shadow cast over the Diamond.

Once the town square, the Diamond was the site of Saturday hiring fairs until 1953. Hiring fairs meant children were sold for periods of time to wealthy families. These children would be sent to work for the hiring family and not see their own family for days, weeks, or years. Some of these children were even sold and shipped to Australia.

The Diamond is now the home of the memorial statue which according to local legend was designed for Sheffield, England. However, when the people of Sheffield saw it they said, "There is no way we want that. It is far too aggressive looking!" Well, it wasn't too aggressive looking for Derry and they bought it on the cheap.

We walk down steep Shipquay Street past the Guildhall and round the corner toward Sandino's Bar. It is from Augusto Nicolas Calderon Sandino, that the Nicaraguan revolutionary group, the Sandinistas, and the bar in Derry derive their names. The bar welcomes everyone and everyone, it seems, comes.

As usual, the music is pouring out and the crowd spills into the street. Rather than fight our way through the hipsters for a drink Ivan and I continue up the road toward Craigavon Bridge pausing at the 'Hands Across the Divide' statue. Local sculptor Maurice Harron cast two bronze statues standing on separate columns with outstretched arms. The hands not quite touching.

I ask Ivan, Will the hands ever touch?

No.

Will the struggles ever end?

We're trying. Ivan sighs and tucks his arm in mine.

BELFAST

Ivan and I developed a routine. I took the overnight flight and transferred at Heathrow for Belfast City. At least until the British Government decided I was a terrorist and then I flew through Dublin. Flying to Dublin on American is painful because they fly Aer Lingus which is like traveling on a Guatemalan chicken bus. Although in saying that I really must apologize for the insult to Guatemalan chicken busses as they are likely more luxurious than Aer Lingus.

In Belfast Ivan sat reading the paper and drinking coffee while he waited for me. I showed up. Ivan complained about the weather made me eat breakfast. I tried always to appear awake and cheerful. We lugged my bags to his blue Mercedes. We drove into the hills of Northern Ireland.

Ivan talked about his life as we drove from appointment to appointment. His business and the nature of life in Northern Ireland required meeting people face-to-face. Taking notes was out of the question as was holding a recorder. To solve the problem I invested in a microphone. The digital recorder was tucked in the side of my bra under my arm and the microphone clipped to the center of my bra. We learned by trial and error that this placement meant the microphone picked up his voice pretty much anywhere and even if I wore a sweater. Ivan teased me a lot about wearing a microphone between my breasts. It gave him a lot of laughs over the years.

Ivan liked to go to a bar near the port in Belfast because they served great burgers. I don't remember the name. We often stopped in for lunch. For whatever reason, Ivan insisted I never wear the recorder in this particular bar. This didn't matter for on the few times I did the crowd was so loud picking up conversation was useless. Ivan insisted we always try to look very casual when we ate at this bar. However, the conversation we most often had at that bar went like this:

Would you like a burger? Cheese? A Stout? A Coke?

Sure. Then we have to talk about the book.

Do you have your microphone taped to your underclothing? I've never before in my life had an interviewer with a microphone taped to their bra. If I do write a book, I must put this in the book.

That's what we're doing. Writing a book. Right? That's why I've been flying over here?

That must go into the book - little American lady with a microphone stuck to her bra. Course you've got to flavor it and color it with what you say.

What exactly are we doing if we are not doing that?

You kept pushing your bust up so you could get the sound down!

So what are we doing? Are we writing a book together or what?

You haven't told me what to do. You told me you were writing a book on 1st PARA.

I am not doing that. I could never afford to do it.

You didn't tell me that.

We discussed it last time I was here. I said I couldn't do that book but I could write your memoirs or biography. You said you would answer the questions I brought last time. I left you with a list of questions, which you said you would return to me, which I have not seen the likes of.

You were attempting to write on the way to the airport. You are always attempting to write on the way to the airport.

I wanted to talk to you about the questions last time I was here and you said 'I'll answer them and I'll return them.' The question is - are we gonna do this together? Because you have other people pursuing you.

It doesn't matter. I like you. I liked your critique of Daly's book. I like when you said, 'I am bored with his perfect life. Yuck!' It was a very good critique. I like honest critiques. I hate people who grovel. I want to say the things I want to say. Things people won't necessarily like.

And that's what I see—if we are going to write a memoir or autobiography or….

But if you want to sell this book you've got to have that Daly stuff in it.

We can have the dancing through the fields….

You know one of the most important things in the book? Humor. Humor!

All I can say, after reading Daly's book, is it wouldn't be true to you and who you are to write a book that was only the good stuff. And no one wants to read about my bra and oh, how I kept leaning into you so you could speak into the bra. So Ivan tell me what are we doing? Are we writing a book together or what?

And with that, Ivan's phone rings, *Hello? Yes. She's sitting here right beside me. She's got a microphone taped to her bra. Yes. Right beside me. And whenever she asks me for a comment, I've got to lean in so I can speak into the bra. I'll ring you in the morning and we'll organize something. All the best.*

I bet he will be texting within the next half-hour. I want you to try and grasp part of the yucky nostalgic part. Middle age men like me read Bishop Daly's book and say - isn't that wonderful. Yea. Definitely we'll write a book. But you told me you were going to write a book on 1st PARA

We talked about that!

This is a very important point. Historically. And for the sake of academic study and for the sake of Ireland in my view it is important to write a book on 1st PARA. It won't sell very well. It'll bankrupt you. A book on Ivan Cooper will sell. It will sell if you do it with something about the individual himself. And the humor. Because it wasn't a great event that kept me going. It was the humor.

I often wonder about Ivan's frequent references to humor. He never told me any funny stories. It is only in retrospect that our jibes and petty arguments seem funny. Everything he told me was serious or sad.

'It was the humor that kept us going' is a common refrain in Derry. 'Oh how we laughed!' In the thirteen stories told in 'Before Bloody Sunday' there are humorous recollections. But Ivan is not telling me anything remotely laugh-worthy. It is certainly not laughable. Families struggling to feed and clothe their children is not funny. Soldiers in the street harassing women. I am having trouble finding the funny here. I can divide the information into that which is not funny but could be—shoeless children; cold water; outdoor plumbing; the same dinners week-in week-out; twenty people to a house; living in a Nisan hut. Then there are the things that are not funny and I cannot find the funny—having your home raided by the Army; checkpoints; discrimination; rubber bullets; murder. I am sure there are humorists who could turn this around but I am not one so I need Ivan to tell me the funny stories. But they are not forthcoming.

Listening to our tapes I find some of Ivan and my interludes fun. They make me laugh. I enjoy our unscripted moments together. But in my five years traveling to Derry I don't recall a moment doubled over with laughter. Listening to the tapes, I have the nervous laugh down. Pretty much after everything I say, I laugh. It is a good lesson in terms of improving my interviewing skills. But I still don't know if 'it was the humor that kept us going' or if that is just something people say to cope. I do, however, recall a joke I heard:

Mrs. Doyle was walking home from the market one day when she heard a tremendous boom. She set her groceries down and stopped two young men walking toward her:

"Boys! What was that noise? Was it a bomb or was it thunder?"

"Well Mrs. Doyle, we're sorry to tell you, that was a bomb."

Mrs. Doyle gathered her packages. "Thank God! I'm terrible afraid of thunder."

The A-6: DERRY TO BELFAST

I had diphtheria when I was three. I remember being at hospital. They had to fly a serum in from London and two brothers from Claudy—Catholic—went to the airport to collect it. Today I think nothing of driving but then the roads were dangerous. With frost on the roads it was quite a difficult drive and these two guys sped to the airport to collect the serum.

I remember when I was six. There was a concert at our school. Primary school. We all had to do something for this concert. So I dressed up as a cowboy and my mother made up a rhyme for me:

'Here comes I: Cowboy Joe. I come from the land called Mexico. I ride the range but I shoot too low. So send me to the cookhouse to make their dough. And watch that the pans don't overflow. And that was the end of Cowboy Joe.'

I remember she made that up in an evening. She was very resourceful. Colorful. There were seven in our family all together. I had a brother who was killed at the age of seven. A sister who died of diphtheria. They both died before my brother and I were born.

My brother was killed in an accident. My mother would never talk about it. Would never tell me about it. I remember one day I was wandering about the house and I opened a drawer and saw this registered envelope. I opened it and there was a lock of hair in it. My mother came in and saw me with this lock of hair and became very upset. She said that is your dead bother's hair. Give it to me and never touch it again. But but she never offered any explanation as to the circumstances of his death. Then about four years ago I gave a lecture in Claudy and an old lady who used to do house work at our home and take me to school came up to me. She told me the story.

My brother had been killed by a bread van. He used to be in the habit of going with the bread van vendor when he did his run and he saw the bread van and thought it was slowing down to stop. In those days the van had a little runner board to step up onto and he went to step on that runner board and his feet got caught in the spoke of the wheel and it carried him around and bashed his brains out.

The bread man who knocked my brother down was a Catholic called Burke. They had a son I used to play with. My mother made it clear to me we always had to be very respectful of the Burkes. I know now it was my mother's position was that it wasn't Mr. Burke's fault so my mother had taught me to be very respectful to the Burkes.

That was an extraordinary act of forgiveness on your mother's part.

No it wasn't.

Yes it was. People don't do that today. Forgive and get on with things.

Well my mother would have done that and she did do that.

Have I ever told you the story of when I was twelve years of age? I went to a motorcycle event. This was road racing in Port Stewart. I went to this motorcycle event when I was twelve and it was in a guest house. A bed and breakfast owned by some friends of my mother. And I remember they had this fortune teller coming to stay in the house visiting the house. He was a very well known fortune teller called Dolan from Vermalla. He gained a reputation, quite a reputation as a fortune teller.

At the age of twelve I had a skepticism which I still have to this day towards fortune tellers. And I told him so. And he asked me to see my palm and he said to me, 'You will toy with the idea of becoming a lawyer. You will also toy with the idea of becoming a professional politician. You will opt for the latter and become a politician.' So I went back and told my dad that. And my dad was a countryman which meant he wouldn't have believed in such things but he said, 'You should bear that in mind.'

So my father has seven strokes. And on the day I was elected as the M.P. from Derry he was completely bedridden. He couldn't speak, I remember I went upstairs to tell him I was elected as the M.P. and he said to me, 'Remember the fortune teller.' It was the most he'd been able to speak to me for a long, long time. And he was quite articulate in saying it.

CRAWFORD

Ivan and I work long hours. We drive across Northern Ireland and back again. We often end up in a hotel bar sitting, drinking, talking late into the night. Our periodic departures catch one or the other of us on the phone or in the loo but listening to the tapes on this particular occasion I hear Ivan being naughty.

We've spent the day driving my son around the North. Part work, part tour, over the course of the dark, cold, damp December day Wil developed a nasty cold. Ivan and I tucked him in with a hot whiskey and retired to the bar. We are well into our third round when I excuse myself.

As soon as I've stepped away from our table, the tape reveals that Ivan sits looking around. He taps his fingers on the table. He shifts in his seat. He checks his phone. He sends a text. He picks up the tape recorder and fiddles with it. He blows in it. He speaks in it: *"Check check check."* He taps it - tap tap tap. He looks at it again. Taps it on the table. Blows in it again. Seeing me returning, he sets it down and looks at me again.

Did you check on him?

No, I just went to the restroom.

You have to check a 13 year old.

Why do I have to check him? We're in the country. Where's he gonna go? There is a pause. My standing, Ivan sitting, us looking at each other is felt on the tape.

Should I go check on him?

Yes.

Once again, as soon as I clear the table Ivan picks up the recorder. He turns it over. Looks at it. He whispers into the recorder: *one, two, one, two, one, two*. His phone announces an incoming text. He puts the recorder down. He attends to his text message. He looks around and speaks to the barman. *Is there a night porter on Crawford?*

"No, not tonight."

Alright so I'll have to go then. You wouldn't phone me a taxi?

When I return, Ivan addresses me: *Now. There's no night porter on tonight. So, I am going to have to go.*

So, no one to stay up all night drinking with.

Well, you can stay up all night drinking. Crawford will stay with you.

I laugh. I don't think Crawford wants to stay up all night drinking with me. Ivan looks at me and I answer his question—He's fast asleep.

Go and get a good night sleep. That recordin device of yours is not workin.

I pick up the recorder. What did you do? It's working! What did you do?! You moved it to 8!

Nothing!

It went from 6 to 8 what did you touch?

Ivan puts on his coat and protests: *Nothing! nothing! I didn't touch anything!*

It's working fine. What do you mean its not working?!

Good night Jennifer. Good night Crawford.

"All the best."

HEATHROW

I hate Heathrow. The customs/immigration agents, like Chicago cops, are given power and permission to harass, harangue, and generally fuck with any one they like. Pass through Heathrow on your way to any other EU country and no landing card is required. No run of the gauntlet. Going to Stockholm? Paris? Greece? Estonia? "Have a shower, a bite to eat, do a little shopping." Going to Dublin? "Bend over we need to look up yer arse."

It is six a.m. I need coffee. There's a stand around Gate 90. I think they used to run cattle though here. Based on the smell, maybe they still do.

Terminal One is basically a Nisan Hut with stained carpet and plastic chairs. It occurs to me the BMI flight attendants wear those hats to protect their hair from the water and debris falling from the rusting ceilings. To get to Terminal One, you have to cross a suspended walkway over chic shops, a long bar, and a coffee shop that wafts up an aroma, signaling "this is the price of freedom!"

I hand over a pound fifty for two ounces of hot brown water and look for a seat near an outlet. The bodies are stacked three and four deep. I perch on a rubbish bin next to an Aussie who says, "I've been here ten hours. You might as well get comfortable."

These were the days before I knew about the "going any place other than Ireland' part of the terminal. If you took the escalator just past security down to the lower level there were a wonder of shops and eateries and the fore-referenced showers. Mecca. Mecca of Terminal One. But at this moment I am still green and so I am perched on a rubbish bin.

Over the years of traveling to Derry I fly through Heathrow for a time, then I fly through Dublin. I learn of a flight through Glasgow and that becomes my favorite route. The customs agents...actually everyone in Glasgow is friendly. There is a Starbucks. There are smiles. There is a feeling of good will as people pass through Glasgow. Traveling to Northern Ireland becomes a treat instead of a chore. Then American Airlines cancels their direct service to Glasgow and I am back to Dublin, Paris, Frankfurt. Any airport other than Heathrow.

Of course once across the Atlantic I still have to get to Derry. From Dublin I can sometimes fly to Derry sometimes not. There is a bus or train/bus to Belfast which then connects to a bus to Derry. Later there is a bus to Derry but you have to make sure you won't have to pee for four hours. From Belfast there is the train but to get from the airport to Victoria Station is a pain. From the airport to the bus station is cheap and easy and there I catch the Derry City Flyer. Flying into Derry is great but then there is the cab fare from the airport in to town. As all these trips are coming out of my pocket, I am always shopping the least expensive routes.

On this visit I find my way to Belfast. Ivan will be waiting at the City Airport reading his paper. Or he won't be waiting and I'll make my way to the Europa, catch the Derry City Flyer, and sleep my way to Derry.

On this occasion Ivan sits reading the daily news. A paper cup of coffee is placed on the table. I am pleased we are moving forward with his memoirs and look forward to making real progress on this trip. Upon spotting me Ivan folds his paper presses the palm of his hand against the table and hoists himself up. The ever-present blue blazer, colorful shirt, and flashy tie frame his face.

Learning about his life I believe Ivan has not changed since he entered the political scene in the mid-sixties. In his twenties Ivan was balding, grey-haired, and round. Today he is still balding, still greying, still round. Still fancying himself a ladies' man. *Well, Jennifer, there you are. Cheerful as always.* He kisses my cheek and takes my bag. *We're off. Late for an appointment. Car's out front.*

My father's family is from Pennsylvania. Rolling, winding, narrow roads, no street signs. Macadam covered cow paths. The Pennsylvania terrain is as similar to Northern Ireland's as the Pennsylvania Dutch accent is to the Derry accent. My father's family could get in the car and feel quite at home driving around Northern Ireland.

I was raised in the Midwest. A grid based on clear N-S-E-W directions and precise numbering systems with flat, unobstructed views. I feel very much at home in Northern Ireland, but left to my own devices, I am usually lost.

Nonetheless, I recognize my Hilton along the river. Is it a river or an inlet? The place Ivan and I eat burgers across from the open-air market they swear is open two days a week. I've never seen a soul. The opera house, the lovely pub with the mosaic tile, and yes, the Europa. Conveniently, the bus station is adjacent to the most bombed hotel in Belfast. It would be a simple thing to lug a big bag through the tunnel and into the restaurant or second-floor bar (I've done this many times). Then to leave the bag, walk back through the tunnel, board a bus, and disappear. BOOM!

In that tunnel is a bus-station restaurant that cooks up a fry that puts hair on your chest, which is why I prefer the bus-station fry, but Ivan opts for the hotel dining room breakfast. *Hello?* Ivan's mobile. Our constant companion. *Yes. I've just collected Jennifer at the airport and she's famished. Yes. We've got to feed her. She's American. She doesn't like the food here. But she's got to eat nonetheless. Aye, we'll be there then.* He's neglected to tell me the stop at the Europa is on the way to the appointment. Not the appointment itself. I can't get used to the time waits for all men mentality.

You have an appointment. Not here. Down the road.

Are we going to see the sheep farmers again?

Eat. Have some coffee. You look knackered.

What?! I like the sheep farmers. I would like to spend more time there. I bet I would like working on a sheep farm. No killing.

Shhhh.

Ivan drives. Ivan talks. I sleep. I am supposed to be listening. Taking notes for his memoir. But I snooze. Something about the seat in the Mercedes. The warmth. The rolling terrain. The smell of turf. It's all very very good. Relaxing.

You're sleeping.

Yes.

Mickey wants to see you.

Why?

Stop fussing and go. He's waiting for you.

We park in Derry's shopping center lot. Ivan ducks into a pub on Shipquay. I walk down to the bottom of Shipquay turn right between the building and the walls and slip in the back door. There on the stained second-hand couches sit members of the Bloody Sunday Trust. I perch on the arm of one by the door and wait quietly.

Mickey sits to my right in the Bloody Sunday Centre family room. Smoke circling, ashes strewn across the glass-topped coffee table, coats on against the chilly damp that always seems to seep out of the old bank's walls. I sigh. He smokes. We wait. One by one the members of the Trust file out. I know now the members of the Trust leaving before Mickey spoke to me was an omen. Not the good kind.

Mickey sits. Staring at me.

I spoke into the air. Do you want me to publish the names of the soldiers?

"Nah," Mickey said.

Do you want me to release the soldiers statements?

"Nah."

Then why do you look at me like that? Like you want something? You worked for six years to get the Inquiry. What else could you possibly want?

"They were alive you know. Before he was murdered, my brother lived. Do you think you could write about their lives?"

Sure.

I am saying sure. Like it's nothing. Mickey is saying he and John will get the members of the Trust on board. "It must be done." He repeats it several times. "It has not been done and it must."

In my time in Derry I learned much about Bloody Sunday. A big part of Ivan's story is Bloody Sunday so I spent many hours in the Family Centre reading material on the subject and talking with a few of the family members. Mainly Mickey and John. To tell Ivan's story I thought it was important to learn as much as I could about Bloody Sunday.

Even so, Mickey's request comes as a shock. But at the same time, I know Mickey. I know something about the families and the thought of getting to write their stories thrills me.

I am struck by only one second of clarity in the moment and I say, Mickey, no one knows me. Are you telling me they are just going to have me into their homes and tell me the stories of their loved ones?

"John and I will get them on board. It's important."

He keeps saying, "It's important. It must be done."

What happened to the voice in my head? It should have been shouting at me. I should have been saying, 'They hardly know me. How do you know I can do this? You don't know my writing. What do you know about my character, my dedication? Why not Eamon McCann? Roddy Doyle? Anyone Irish. Anyone else. Anyone who has ever written anything important. Anyone but me to write these biographies.'

But I didn't. I didn't ask. I didn't question. I leapt. I wanted to do it. I really did. From the moment the words came out of Mickey's mouth I wanted to write their stories. To do it well. To make the men and boys come to life. I had looked at their photos so many times. I knew every detail of their deaths. I wanted to know about the man in the roller skates, the boy with the guitar, the smiling face on the roof of the flats with the petrol bomb. Happy. Innocent. Hopeful.

I wanted it. So I leapt. I made the assumption that they wanted me to write these stories because I can be objective. I have no political or familial ties. I have few preconceptions. No one will question my motives. I can come in gather the information and write pure, true, objective biographies.

Then no one can say it was propaganda. I am an outsider and in this case being an outsider is a good thing. No one will be able to say I was preaching an agenda.

The leaping may have been a mistake. A crucial mistake. But it won't be the worst or the loudest or most damaging mistake I will make over the next year. Really, how many times has being an outsider been a good thing?!

Sure. I'll do it. I'll look at my calendar and let you know when I can come back.

"John and I will get the families on board."

Ten minutes. I don't think our meeting was longer than ten minutes. Omen. I was thrilled. Omen. I asked few questions. Omen. I was excited to get started. Omen. Not the good kind.

Ivan and I are in the car on our way back to Belfast before I realize what I've done. Fourteen biographies. Uninteresting people. Most of them teenagers. What's unique about a teenage boy? It began to sink in a bit. I didn't realize at the time that not being a journalist or an author might be a hindrance. I didn't contemplate the actualities of no one knowing me. I wasn't concerned about being Kermit-the-Frog green. It didn't bother me that I had no idea what I was doing.

Mum! Mum! Hello. Are you there mum? Yes, Mum. I'm calling from Ireland. I'm not coming home Mum. They've asked me to run for president. Well, I must. They've asked me! Ivan is teasing me.

What have I done Ivan? They hardly know me. They want to entrust their life stories to me?

I spoke to them about your writing.

I write you letters Ivan. We've hardly begun on your book!

They are good letters. You will do well. Stop fussing. I won't say a word on my book until you finish this. Then, I promise, we will write my book.

Omen. Omen. Omen. Omen. Not the good kind.

AMERICAN AIRLINES FLIGHT 91

Heathrow to O'Hare. My journey and my journal begin:

Today I made a promise. I promised the Bloody Sunday families I would tell their stories. Yes, much has been written about Bloody Sunday. Books covering the witness statements, the tribunals, and the events are all important but one piece is missing: the human faces of the tragedy.

Today I promised to give voices to the dead and to try to help surviving victims, family, and friends find some measure of peace and closure. I promised to share the human side, the human cost. The loss of more than 14 lives from gunfire on 30 January, 1972—the damage that radiates through families and friends and wounds generations.

Never before in my life have I made a promise so binding. Something I couldn't break or wiggle out of. Today I made a promise I must fulfill. And I will. For the next five months I will immerse myself so completely in the lives and memories of the Bloody Sunday families and victims that when I write, their voices ring from the pages. In my writing the dead will come alive for the reader. The pain of those left behind will be palpable, the injustice of the day will cry out in the hearts of the just, and the steadfast dedication of the campaign will inspire those who have lost hope.

Geez. I wrote that?!

My dad always told me I took myself way too seriously. So how do I go about this? I manage to support myself and three kids writing articles and informational materials other people put their names on. It's work no one else wants to do. But it is writing. I earn a living writing. Not a lot of people can say that. I work in my pajamas and am able to walk my kids to school and pick them up after. And I am still able to pay the bills. I do not, however, mind taking a leave of absence.

That was easy. What is next? Make a plan. I buy plane tickets and email Mickey I will arrive the 12th of May and stay for two months. Ivan arranges accommodation for me at the Beech Hill. I order recording equipment and a new computer.

That was easy. Their dad agrees to take my kids. Ahhh. Here we are: The tipping point. This man has never before and not since done a single decent thing where his kids or I are concerned. And so, this single act puts me over the edge. It makes me think GOD is involved. After all if one of earth's biggest assholes can do a kindness, GOD must be involved.

It leads me to believe I have found my calling. I grew up on a seminary campus. Being called by God was a popular thing. People were called by God all the time. Maybe I felt left out. Maybe I felt like I wasn't reaching my full potential if at some point, God did not call. But I felt it now.

If God was not calling, how could it all be going so well? I have the money to sustain me for two months. I have the equipment. My family is enthusiastic. My clients say there will be work for me when I return. My kids are looked after. I am writing something important. It means something. God must be calling.

Hummm, hummm, hummm. What to do next?
Begin research.
Learn everything I can about the victims.
Make notes. Lots of notes.
Create a file for each person. Start family trees.
Study the history of Derry and the Troubles.
Learn how to write biographies.
Make an excel spreadsheet for the interviews.
My organizational skills will impress them.
Watch films on the subject.
Travel to London and read Paul Greengrass' files for his film, Bloody Sunday.

Send letters to publishers describing the exciting project the Bloody Sunday Families and I are about to embark on together. They are under-whelmed. No matter. Moving on....

Write an introductory letter to the families and send to Mickey for distribution:

TO: Bloody Sunday Families
FROM: Jennifer Faus
DATE: 1 May 2003
RE: Introduction

I have been invited to assist in the process of documenting the life stories of those killed and wounded on Bloody Sunday. I am an attorney and writer. Samples of my writing are available from Mickey McKinney.

My role in this process is to facilitate the documentation of your life or the life of your family member. My preparation for our meeting includes notes from Eamonn and Joanne's books, reading other books, reports, and materials available about Bloody Sunday, viewing the films Sunday and Bloody Sunday, and reviewing the research materials gathered by Paul Greengrass in his preparation for writing the film Bloody Sunday. My singular goal in this process is to assist you in creating a meaningful document that contributes to the body of work and living history of Bloody Sunday.

The purpose of our initial conversation is to begin the process of writing your story or the story of your family member or friend killed on Bloody Sunday. Through this project we hope to present the human side of Bloody Sunday, sharing the lives, personalities, hopes, and dreams of those killed and wounded.

After our conversation is transcribed, I will write the first draft of the story. You are then invited to participate in the editorial process and will have the opportunity to review and comment on the story as the project progresses. A representative from each family and the people who are alive and participating in the writing of their own stories will have the opportunity to "sign-off" on the final copy before it is sent to the publisher.

I would like the primary family representative or individual who will be interviewed to commit to a minimum of four hours consisting of a two hour first interview and two hours of follow-up and review. I am committed to spending as much time as is necessary in the process of interviewing, research, writing, follow-up, editing, and review and we will not be constrained by time, but would like a commitment of a minimum of four hours from each person.

During our interview I would like you to feel free to speak about your family member, friend, or yourself in whatever manner your chose. Essentially, you are writing the biography/autobiography/memoir – how do you want people to learn to know and remember you or your family member or friend? Each story is unique and will stand on its own. Do not concern yourself with how others are approaching the process. Please speak freely and don't worry about moving in a particular order or how your words sound – all of our interviews will be taped and we will work to edit the transcripts to read just as you would like.

I will not give too much direction in the interviews but will ask questions from time to time and I am prepared to ask direct questions if that style suits you better. I request the following specific tasks during the process:

1. We will create a family tree.

2. I will view and perhaps copy diaries, letters, or other personal memories that you are willing to share (copies will be returned if requested).

3. I will view and help to select photographs for use in the end Product.

In our discussions/interviews, please be as candid and as detailed as possible. Many of the future readers of this document have never been to Derry and certainly never knew your family. Please describe things as vividly as you are able.

My sincere hope is to help you create a well-written document/book. Any comments, suggestions, and questions you have along the way will be welcome.

Hummmm...... what else needs doing?
Ask Mickey to line up a transcriptionist.
Practice using fancy new digital recording equipment.
Buy tri-band phone.
Learn to use it.
Pack an inordinate number of books and supplies.
Set off for two months in Derry.
On May 14th I arrive at the Bloody Sunday Centre, fit, focused, and ready to begin. I burst through the curtains of the family room. They look at me. I look at them. No one knows why I am there. Mickey slowly rises. His look of disbelief turns to a sheepish grin. He offers me a cigarette. I sit down, light up, look around the room smiling, and say, I'm ready!

A MOMENT TO PAUSE AND REFLECT

Goldfish do not pause and reflect. They just keep swimming. Here, in this space and time I will pause and reflect but then I didn't. It was quite a whirlwind. My dad died. I traveled to Ireland. I met Ivan. I returned to Ireland to help Ivan write his memoirs. I am suddenly now also writing the life stories of the Bloody Sunday victims. I am also, incidentally, working full time and still a single mother.

But I did not take a moment to pause and reflect. This would have been a good time. This would have been a good time to say to myself: I prepared for months to do these stories, sent my children off to live with their dad, and then on my own dime arranged to travel to Derry for two months and THEY DO NOT KNOW WHY I AM HERE?! This would have been a very good time to think about what I was doing. It would have been good to realize that even if he did call, God had called collect. I would really like to say that fucker called collect but I might alienate the more sensitive readers. All in all it would have been a very good time and frankly, very prudent to walk away.

Upon reflection I think Ivan set me up. I think Ivan wanted the stories of the Bloody Sunday victims written and I was all naive and dreamy and eager. Ivan saw in me an opportunity to do this thing. I can't put my finger on why he wanted this, other than he felt guilty. Maybe he just wanted me to keep coming over to Derry. But I was already coming over to do his story. On the other hand, if I was working on something else, Ivan could still have me come over and hang out with him but he wouldn't have to do any work. It is all speculation. I imagine Ivan will take the truth to his grave.

At any rate, I did not walk away. And so, for the next FOUR YEARS I will work on the blasted thing. To be fair I spend a year doing interviews. Another year writing and editing and two more years trying to get the thing published. It was exhausting. Infuriating. Exhilarating.

A PUB IN DONEGAL

Ivan is upset. He is raging. Ivan does not rage. I have been known to flare up from time to time. But Ivan is a pretty cool cucumber. Just not today.

Oliver Boyce and his fiancee Breege Porter were kidnapped, stabbed, and shot by three UDA members in Donegal on New Years Eve, 1973.

Why?

Cause they're Catholic!

Were they involved in something or....

No! Nothing! They were a courting couple! Catholics involved in nothing!

The Sunday ran a serial on it last weekend. They featured me in it because the guy who was responsible for having their murder carried out was a trigger man in at least four other deaths that I'm aware of. Three of 'em were innocent Catholics, one of 'em was involved in Sinn Fein. The shooter scampered off to South Africa.

I have very grave reservations that he was involved with British Intelligence and they got him out of the country. But this newspaper traced him to a guest house in Scotland where he's been for the last eight years. They didn't trace him. They were tipped off by an ex-UDA man called Glenny Barr from Derry who was once very prominent.

Ivan lights a cigar and orders another round. He fumes. He sits back and looks at the ceiling for a moment then sits up and leans over the table.

After Bloody Sunday the actions of the IRA became insidious, vicious, reckless. After Bloody Sunday it wasn't just shooting. The IRA started targeting Protestant businesses. Businesses were blown up and innocent people killed.

One particularly dastardly killing carried out by the IRA was of three Protestant men who worked in a local company called Robert Keys and Co. They were shot dead coming out of a coffee bar. None of them had any involvement with the security forces. But they had been mistakenly identified as members of the security forces and they were all three shot dead. There were many other Protestant people, innocent people murdered by the IRA. Bloody Sunday gave the IRA justification for killing people. They targeted Protestant businesses, assassinated Protestants, and created a general atmosphere in Derry that Protestantism was no longer welcome on the city side.

After Bloody Sunday, our non-sectarian city changed in character: the population movements of Protestants, evidenced by the closure of Strand Road Presbyterian, Claremont Presbyterian, the Glasgow Terrace, Glenbank Estates community churches, and the Baptist church. Christ Church, Church of Ireland, which was once the largest Church of Ireland in Derry, has only a shadow of its former membership. Today, the only major Protestant enclave in the City is Fountain Estates, and if your drive into the Fountain Estates today, there are a number of houses lying vacant in a city where there is a major housing shortage.

Our non-sectarian city changed in rhetoric: Sinn Fein has made use of the word Catholic. The great father figure of Republicanism in Ireland, Wolfe Tone, spoke constantly about Catholic, Protestant, and Dissenter. In my view, it is alien to traditional Republicanism to use the word Catholic in place of Irish, and to use it seven or eight times in speeches. So we now have a sectarian problem in Derry.

The IRA killed a number of members of the UDR which in turn alienated a large section of their relatives. The IRA said RUC and UDR men were part of the British war machine, and therefore legitimate targets. Acting on very bad intelligence they killed a number of innocent, unassociated Protestant people. The IRA pulled off some very dastardly killings of Protestants.

One that springs to mind is Tiban. In this case workmen were stopped in a mini-bus and questioned about their religion. One of the men on the bus was Catholic. He was allowed to go. The rest were executed. In a gospel hall in Darkley IRA gunmen entered and killed everyone present—all Protestant. A bomb was placed at an armistice service in Enniskillen and all those people were killed. All Protestant. Not one a member of the security forces. There has been evidence in Fermanagh and in South Armagh of farmers being targeted and shot who were Protestant. The objective being to drive Protestants away from those parts of the country.

I believe the reason why is because some local units of the IRA had lost the vision of Wolfe Tome. It must be emphasized it was a minority of the IRA not the general policy of the IRA. Some of the people who were in the IRA deliberately targeted Protestants and by so doing they were demonstrating that there are sections of the IRA that are right wing Nationalists. Not true Republicans. The vision of Republicanism was lost by large numbers of the IRA as a result of sectarian thinking. It wasn't militaristic thinking. It was sectarian. It was a marginal and minority group but it happened and they wreaked devastation and succeeded in creating an atmosphere of fear and hate and furthered violent sectarianism across Northern Ireland.

THE ELIZABETH HOTEL
4:00 AM

Ivan and I lay in bed. He in his t-shirt and boxers. Me in my red silk pajamas. We stare at the ceiling.

I can't believe you came humping that box in at one a.m.

Paul let me have access to his files at Granada today.

But then you made me go through all those photos. And video tape. And depositions.

It's stuffy in here.

The window won't open.

And we sigh. A collective sigh of two. Of exhaustion, exasperation, and resignation that we have lost another night of rest.

Ivan, do you believe that 1st PARA fired under orders on Bloody Sunday?

I don't know the answer to that. I have a suspicion they didn't. I have a suspicion they had a fairly open license. I believe they were ordered into the Bogside by Ford not by McClennan. Ford to Wilford. I think McClennan has lied that he gave the order. There was a major who gave evidence at Saville in which he was emphatic that the order came from Ford through to Wilford.

Do you think they fired because they were given free reign that day?

I think they thought they were being fired on. They were so hyped up by Wilford and by Ford and by their briefing before they came in. I think that some of the shots that came from the walls which in fact were shots from the Army gave them the impression that they were being fired on.

Why do you think they shot to kill?

I think they had been told beforehand that they had to pickup 400 of these Bogside young hooligans but they'd also been told that the IRA would be on the ground and the IRA would be firing and I think these guys were so hyped up at Magilligan and then in Derry that when they came in they were absolutely certain that they were going to be confronted by the IRA.

PARAs shoot to kill. It doesn't matter to them whether it was civilians or not. To them, people in Derry were all IRA. You know that. You've been interviewing the families and now the Brits have labeled you a terrorist.

In other words, the whole operation was a total fuck up. I have no doubt that Bloody Sunday was a watershed in Irish politics. It breathed life into the lungs of the IRA. We have since been subjected to thirty years of IRA violence. Thirty years in which the IRA carried out very dastardly deeds including the murders of many innocent people.

AFTER THE INITAL SHOCK THAT I RETURNED TO DERRY READY TO WORK

Mickey looked at me. I could see it in his face. The unreturned/not responded to email, texts, letters....I realized immediately I was an idiot. In a flash I saw I was green, ignorant, innocent, naive, guileless, and just plain dumb. Then as quickly as I had the realization, I quashed it. And I smiled.

Mickey slowly rose. His look of disbelief turned to a sheepish grin. He offered me a cigarette. I sat down, lit up, looked around the room, and said, I'm ready. Mickey looked across the coffee table to the facing sofa where Maura and Mary sat and to the chair Bernard leaned against. He began to explain to them why I was in Derry this time.

Maura Young, Mary Doherty, and Bernard Gilmour were the first to agree to meet with me. They recognized my face as the Yank who popped in from time to time to say hello to Mickey and John. The first families to volunteer, they willingly and enthusiastically gave interviews. They gave names of other family and friends to interview.

The first three narratives: John Young, Gerald Donaghey, and Hugh Gilmour are technically challenging. Without a transcriptionist, Hazel from Ivan's office and I spend our nights listening to interview tapes and transcribing as fast as we can. I am no typist, but Hazel is fast and works diligently. I race from interview to interview, trying to get as much information as I can. I want a complete picture of their lives. It is wonderful and exhilarating. I am thrilled! This is going to be great!

Despite their surprise at my arrival and their seeming unpreparedness I am not worried. Mickey is very enthusiastic and tells me not to worry he and John will arrange the interviews and we will get it done. None of the families has received my letter of introduction and my interviews start with them asking, "Who are you? What are you doing? Why are you here?" After four or five of these openings, I get the hang of it and my interviews begin with my asking, Do you know who I am or why I am here? Then I recite the story of Mickey asking me to do the project and I give them a copy of the letter as I paraphrase it. It's a real nice ice-breaker.

Nonetheless, people talk. For many it seems a chance to talk about their brothers, husbands, fathers, and friends in a way they were never invited to. I am surprised how many people say to me, "I've never talked to anyone about this before." I know that being a stranger and outsider has its drawbacks but I begin thinking maybe it is valuable as well. Could it be that Mickey is right and I am providing an outlet for people to talk about the lives of their loved ones where for thirty-one years they've only been asked about their deaths?

The weather in Derry is beautiful. For the first two months the sun shines every day and the air blows fresh and clean. It must be an omen. The good kind. I can't believe I am so lucky. This is the opportunity of a lifetime! I get to write about something that matters!

It might have been better for all of us has they refused right off to participate. I could have enjoyed a nice holiday and returned home unscathed. Maybe disappointed but with my bank account and dignity in-tact.

LONDON

London's public transport impresses me. Coming from Chicago where cleanliness, timeliness, and friendliness are not part of the mission of the CTA, it is nice to stand on a platform and know your train is coming in exactly two minutes and that it's not the noise that alerts you to it's presence but a whoosh of air. In Chicago we need be thankful for the noise, however because a whoosh of air would smell like urine and rats.

In the low season when the cold, the damp, and the rain keep the tourists away London is a lovely place to walk. Ivan and I plan to walk and talk so as not to be disturbed but it's not just damp today the rain is pouring down. We opt instead for the Paddington Hilton lobby.

What are you doing? People won't like seeing that sitting out.

Stop fussing. I thought about that. Which side do you want it on?

What?

The pen. It's a microphone. Do you want it on the inside or outside of your pen? After all your fussing about the bra, I've decided you can wear the damn thing.

Here, put it next to my pen. On the inside.

Now don't pull it out and hand it to someone.

I don't like that man.

Who?

That man over there. I saw him on the street today. I don't want him to come over.

Don't worry. Stop fussing. Go on then, we were talking about your childhood.

When I first decided to become involved in politics, in civil rights, I honestly didn't think there would be the ferocity of condemnation by my own core religion. People in Northern Ireland who spoke up on civil rights in those days were made to feel very unpopular by Protestantism. When the nineteen and seventy-two cabinet papers were released it was very significant because they shed light on the perspective of Faulkner's government at Stormont and the British. Those cabinet papers reveal that the Northern Ireland government and all of their memos to the British Government describe civil rights marches as Republican.

So despite the fact that you had people marching who had no time for Republicanism, people marching who were pacifist, people marching who were Protestant, people marching who were nothing other than citizens who felt strongly about the denial of civil rights, every one of us were lumped together as Republicans. We were categorized as Republican. We were categorized as IRA. We were categorized as communist. So every Protestant person accepted this message as delivered by the Stormont government. As a result, I spent a lot of my younger life being totally estranged from my fellow Protestants.

Ivan pauses and shifts positions. He looks around, out from under his eyelids. He leans forward and takes my hand. Holding the palm of my hand in his left he pats the top of it with his right hand. He sits holding my hand for a minute and says,

My mother had told me she wished to have an undertaker look after her remains when she died and that undertaker was a Catholic. And my uncle rang me up and said to me, 'Your mother's dead' and I said, 'Yes.' And he said, 'I hear you've got a Catholic undertaker.' And I said, 'Yes. That was my mother's wishes.' And he said, 'Well, they'll be none of us coming to the funeral.' It was very civilized.

And none of them came?

He releases my hand abruptly. Sits back in his chair. Puts his left hand to his temple, then, resignedly,

No.

And on that note, your phone. Our life is punctuated by your phone.

I am used to the phone. I know Ivan has to work but at the same time every time we get going on something the thing interrupts us and we are off track or literally off and running. I've taken to writing in my red leather journal during these times. If nothing else it keeps me awake. I am not used to the drinking and the late nights and the constant travel back and forth over the Atlantic and I struggle to stay awake on long car rides and through extended periods of Ivan on his mobile.

Go on, ask me something more.

Well, it sounds to me like you were caught in the balance.

Well, my immediate family supported me, totally, completely. But I had to cope with attacks on my family home and my family had to deal with the boycotting of our little post office, which Sam Evans organized, hold on – my phone. Hello? Well I cannot agree to that….No. No. Well then, ring me back.

Ready?

Cheer me up.

You're asking me to cheer you? You're all about the humor and we're not laughing!

We're just not getting it together. And it's my fault. I'm not happy on things that you've got to know about. It's not you, it's me. You know my mother was the driving force, with these two sisters. One who could neither hear nor speak properly. And the other who had these very strong views on things like cruelty to animals, pacifism, anti-war. Even to the extent that she had major questions regarding the Second World War. She was a pacifist with very strong views and she was very well read. So I did all this bubbling around and evolving, lots of telephone calls but most important of all lots of other things going on every waking hour and don't forget you had things like road blocks at night. It was very dangerous for me.

Road blocks?

Yeah. Loyalists: para-military organizations.

Once you started telling me about Lundy and the center. You want to share with people that you've had a difficult time? That it wasn't easy being Ivan Cooper?

Do you want me to tell you something? I think, even today, I feel desperately sad about what my parents had to go through on my account. My mother had a post office for thirty-seven years and served the community with integrity and decency for thirty-seven years. And these people organized this boycott. I want to name them in the book, who organized it.

Aren't you afraid they will sue you?

They're dead so they can't sue.

They have family?

They can't sue. It's all the truth.

OK. You're the boss. Let me get this down.

The primary organizers were... a large farmer called Jack Evans, a Welsh name. His brother Sam Evans, and a gentleman called Robert Nutt. Jack Evans' wife was my primary school teacher when I first went to school. She was a wonderful teacher and a wonderful woman. He used to beat her up and he was also openly unfaithful to her. His brother Sam was an ardent supporter of Ian Paisley and had a screw loose.

Wait, wait. When you say he had a screw loose....

He bordered on...

Stop. What was in his behavior that makes you say that?

He was absolutely nuts, shouting, this grown man, shouting. But on top of that, every one of his children had major defects in their character, sorry, major defects in their entire personality. But he himself had a major defect. He used to shout. He organized the Burntollett ambush against the civil rights marchers from Belfast.

Was Sam a farmer, too?

Yes, he lived in a place called Ness House. He was the brother of Jack.

What did he farm?

Mixed animals. You ask strange questions. You sure you're a reporter?

For the hundredth time, I am not a reporter. You know I am not a reporter. You've known that since the moment we met.

Robert Nutt was a totally inadequate little man who aspired to be part of this Protestant, what he perceived to be upper class, but what in reality was less than middle class. Was heavily dominated by Presbyterianism, and was based mainly on the snobbishness of, at that time, better-off farmers. So this inadequate little man who used to sell oil, who was making a valiant effort to maintain what he considered to be the public perception that he was part of this Protestant upper class, but what was in reality a joke. So they went around houses and the catchment area that came to our post office and they persuaded people to boycott. And the boycott was almost total.

None of the Catholics were part of it. There weren't many Catholics anyway. And I think there were either five or six Protestant houses that refused to have anything to do with it. That was number one. And number two was physical attacks on my home which comprised of petrol bombs and a more subtle type of thing which was anonymous telephone calls: death threats.

Your life or your family's?

Our life. They used to ring up and lie to my mother. If I was at a television studio in Belfast and I'd been on there, on television, as soon as it was over somebody'd ring up and say, 'We've got that bastard and we're gonna torture him to death before we finally execute him.'

Your phone is ringing.

And there were no mobile phones in those days! Hello? No. No.

Now then, they called your mother and told her....

Yes, they'd wait until I was off the air and they'd said to her, 'We've got him. We just captured him and we are gonna cut his throat from ear to ear.' It wasn't the time of mobile phones, so my mother couldn't telephone....

She had to wait.

Yeah, wait until I came home and that was terrifying, so, she suffered from angina and I used to find her in a collapsed state on many evenings when I had gotten home very late. So the anonymous letters. The anonymous telephone calls. The attacks on the house. The cruel disregard for many years of good service to the community. Thirty-seven years of good service to the community. The totally un-Christian attitude towards my parents who played a very prominent part of our local church. That still weighs on my conscious.

Was it always the Protestants behind this?

Oh, yeah.

Then why didn't they just kill you? Why did they have to go through all of this? Why didn't they just pick you off? I mean it wasn't like you were hiding or you had any kind of protection.

I was very careful.

I know you were careful. You told me about how you and John went different routes with people.

No, it was more than that. For example, when I used to come out at night to my home which was an isolated spot the dockers, the Derry dockers used to drag me out, get me into the house, and get me out in the morning again.

Derry dockers?

Yeah, you know the guys who used to tie up the ships or the boats or who dug the coal out of the coal boats or the grain out of the grain boats. Manual workers in the docks. They were loyal to me. I am very grateful to the Derry dockers who ensured I got home safely in the evening and came to collect me in the morning. It is because of the dockers I survived those years. They were very loyal to me and I've never forgotten their kindness and dedication.

What else?

Some of the most nauseating things. They used to send excrement through the post in these plastic bags. The anonymous letters. At one stage I was getting over forty a day from all over Northern Ireland. All sorts of pranks so we had to move to Derry. I remember we were only there a very short space of time and my car was parked outside my door in Derry. It was a little sports car called a Triumph GT. And these guys arrive in a car and threw it on its roof.

Flipped your car over?

Yeah, flipped it over. So that more or less continued for most of my early civil rights days and permeated right down to when I was first elected. There was a massive big heave to prevent me getting elected with a lot of smear campaign news. But I got elected. Would you like some more tea?

Yes. Thank you. What else would you like to say about that? How'd your dad deal with it? Losing the post-office and moving to Derry.

He had seven strokes. Some my father and mother's very oldest friends. People they'd known since they first came to that area as a young married couple. Some of these people just stopped coming. Close friends. And they just faded away.

Not long after we moved to Derry my father died. And that funeral was quite difficult as well because obviously some of the nationalist members of Parliament came along and they were well known television personalities at that time. And some of my father's family came along and they were right-wing Protestants so it was a difficult funeral. I remember it was conducted by the Reverend Brian Hammond. He went on to become a Church of Ireland bishop. He was a very kind decent man who I enjoyed a good relationship with and who I respected and admired. You know who I saw this morning?

I don't know.

I saw this morning a unionist member of the Northern Ireland executive. Called Sam Foster.

You didn't say hello, you just saw him?

I saw him on the other side of the street. It's remarkable how you can see people in the big city like this. I never ever come to London without meeting some people. So you've got all this a massive amount of stuff going on and then of course us young members of Parliament. We went into the Stormont Parliament and first thing that happened there when we were confronted by Unionists? We had a sit down protest on the floor of the chamber.

You and who?

John Hume, Austin Curry, Jerry Fitz, some of the Nationalists sat too. Sat on the floor and sang 'We Shall Overcome.' That *caused major problems for me. Major, major, mega problems. So we had all of this sort of thing going on. A great amount of television and working tremendously hard in the constituency and then we had that very bad year in nineteen and seventy-two. I think that thing is going to have be looked at in the archives for more detail.*

When you say the archives, you mean the thirty year period?

There was so much stuff going on, you spoke last time of getting some young person to do some research? There was a massive amount going on between nineteen and sixty-nine and nineteen and seventy-two. Nineteen and seventy-one we had internment. I spent a great deal of time visiting people in internment camps. I spent a great deal of time trying to raise money for them or chairing committees to raise money. I spent a great deal of time just with their families. And I spent a great deal of time walking with my constituents but I had all sorts of problems.

You were in that big geographic.

Yeah. But I also had all these problems like trying to balance time with the families of people who were interned. Trying to get these cases appealed of people who were interned. Flying back and forward to London. It was one big roller coaster.

Ivan's phone rings again.

Yes Chris. How you doin? Not too bad. Yes. He did? So the judgments are satisfied? Right. OK. No. I thought there were more judgments than that.

As Ivan talks on the phone, a man walks up.

"Excuse me."

Hello! Can't believe I'm after meetin' you here. That's one of the problems of being Irish, you can't have a little thing on the side here...*Jennifer, this a friend of mine from Letterkenny. Jennifer is writing a book at the minute.*

"Don't tell me yer doing another fil-um! Very good. You're writing a book about this man?"

Yes.

"Very good."

I am trying to explain to her all the turmoil. I'm just around to Blinny now....

"I'll tell her that one!"

All the best.

"All the best."

That's Hugh McGee. He owns the very nice Holiday Inn in Letterkenny in Donegal and three or four other hotels.

I am so embarrassed! I looked like a million bucks yesterday. I went to Granada films with my hair and make-up done. I was gorgeous. Today I am wet. I'm exhausted.

Your maroon dress was very nice yesterday. But you look fine. You're yawning but you look fine.

Have we passed that Holiday Inn? When we went down to Donegal?

No we didn't go to Letterkenny. That's for the future.

What is the name of that town where you.....?

Westport. That's something we have to do. When you come next time.

Yes. I have it written down on the schedule.

When are you coming?

I arrive in Belfast on the fifth.

So how long are you coming to Ireland for all together?

The fifth to the twenty-second. And then on the twentieth of the next month.

How long are you staying then?

Four to six weeks.

So nineteen and seventy-two was a very important year. It started off with a hangover from internment. To start off they interned a lot of the wrong people and in additional to that they then set up a review procedure. There were all sorts of difficulties about getting access to see these people. Then they set up a review procedure that was totally obnoxious to any lawyer or free-thinker. You are yawning.

Yes. I am sorry. I am.

You're a wreck.

I'm doing my best.

Well, will I get you a drink to pick you up?

I already had two cups of coffee.

Well, will I get you a drink to pick you up?

A drink to pick me up?

Will I get you a brandy?

Ohhhhh.

To pick you up?

You want to pick me up off the floor is that where you want to pick me up from?

I know I kept you awake all night, wallowing around like a beached whale. Created too much heat in the room. Bloody windows wouldn't open...I told you a joke actually and you kept on talking, you were on automatic pilot at that stage....

When I fell asleep and I responded to you I just kept talking? What'd I say? I think I do remember mumbling something, but I don't know what it was... '68 to '93?

What? For research?

No, when you were in Parliament.

Through '83.

And what committees did you serve on or what honors

did you have?

None. I was Minister of Community Relations for six months. Not even for six months. For five months.

Anything else? You just showed up for work every day?

I was on various boards and committees all of which are largely irrelevant. You know, it's funny how some things are coming back. We set up something called—after we withdrew from Stormont and we urged the nationalist population to withdraw consent—we set up an organization called The Assembly of the Northern Irish People. And this was comprised of elected representatives amongst the nationalist population. So we set up sort of an alternative talking shelf assembly which was set up in my constituency.

So here's this little Prod who's elected to Parliament and his constituency is reckoned the one place where this assembly could be set up without any interference. Now I reckon that was a great tribute to the strength of my representation because John Hume could not have it in his constituency. The officials would have disrupted it or some other republicans would have disrupted it. Austin Currie couldn't set it up in his area because he could have been disrupted as well. But I was able to do it in Dungiven.

I remember I made a speech at the first meeting of the assembly. John Hume had asked me, John Hume was president of the Assembly of the Northern Irish People, but he had asked me to make a speech. The political columnist for the Belfast Telegraph, a guy called Barry White, who wrote a book on John Hume. I remember he wrote that I put my head to the one side, 'and Cooper cocked his head to the one side' and 'this young one knows his oratory and has the confidence to express his civil rights opinions.'

Oratory was one of my strengths when I was young. The capacity to speak to large groups of people and to feed off them. Some people say I was groomed to become an actor. I don't know. I don't know if Cooper is a better actor than Jimmy Nesbitt, or Jimmy Nesbitt is a better politician than Ivan Cooper.

I have the ability to be a politician today. But I happen to believe that young people must have their part. One of the things that has happened in Ireland is all of them have sat on the job and refused to move to the side and the effect of that is that people of ability—young people have become frustrated and disappeared. We have to make way for young people. People ask me, 'Why are you not putting your name forward for a seat?' Because I am too old! Because I want to see young people come through.

THE BEECH HILL COUNTRY HOUSE

There doesn't seem to be a transcriptionist anywhere in Derry. Hazel and I continue to spend our nights and weekends dividing up the interviews and transcribing as fast as we can. I lock myself in my room at the Tower Hotel trying to transcribe interviews and write draft narratives. The management and staff continually ask if I am OK. "Do you need a doctor?"

The poor Tower Hotel personnel are perplexed. The maids are irritated that I don't leave my room and refuse to give me my daily supply of tea and biscuits which I see as vital to my survival so I liberate some from the cart (bad decision). In an attempt to communicate I hang a sign on my door that reads, "I'm working, feel free to knock if you need in!" Apparently in Derry this translates to fuck off and I am treated in ways appropriate to their interpretation.

I flee to the Beech Hill Country House Hotel in Ardmore, on the Waterside. It is a six mile walk every day but the weather is fabulous and I would otherwise have spent the time on the treadmill, so I am happy. Patsy at the Beech Hill understands me. She sees to it that I am regularly fed and watered but otherwise left to my own devices. She points to the laundry facilities telling me I am free to wash clothes. She gives me my choice of rooms. I couldn't love my own mother more.

I will eventually get over my American self, return to the Tower Hotel and even become a loyal customer to them as well as the Beech Hill. But for now I am alone in Derry and the Beech Hill feels like home. So I take refuge.

***

John Young is keeping me awake at night. He taps his finger on my desk at the Beech Hill. Tap tap tap. He wakes me, "You are not here to sleep. You are here to write our life stories." He is restless and his restlessness infects my life.

I first met John through his brother Leo and his sisters Maura and Helen. It wasn't long before John and I became personally acquainted. Everywhere I went, there was John. John is very present in Derry.

Yes, it sounds crazy but the more I tried to convince myself I was throwing myself too deep into the project, that John was just a voice in my head, the more insistent he was. And he was right to be so.

I was in Derry to write Ivan's memoirs but now I was also writing the the stories of the Bloody Sunday victims. My goal was to tell the true stories of the innocent men and boys murdered at a civil rights march as they fled for their lives. Their names had been smeared by the British Government and I wanted to be part of the process that righted that wrong. I am not a journalist. I did not plan to write an objective sterile account. What I did not anticipate was how profoundly the experience would affect me.

3FLOWERS BAR

From the moment we meet, it seems John Nash's mission is to get me transported from place to place. If a thing needs doing John is your man. In his car one day I mention I'm trying to contact Gerry Doherty. I'd left him messages at his work and wasn't hearing back.

"Gerry who?"

Doherty. They call him Mad-Dog?

In a flash John makes a u-turn and is on his phone, "Mad-Dog. I'm bringing someone to meet you."

About three minutes later we are pulling into the 3Flowers Bar and Gerry is still standing outside on the phone trying to get John to give him more information. He'd heard some Yank was leaving him messages and he had no plans to talk to some fuckin' Yank. Inside, John introduces us, then says, "I've gotta dive. I'll be back for you in an hour."

Gerry scowls at me. He pulls me a stout. He takes his time walking around the bar. He sits across from me at the corner. No more than six inches between us. He leans in, cocks his head, and looks at me with big, brown puppy-dog eyes. And then, he smiles.

The hour is filled with tales of his and Hugh's exploits. True tales of boyhood. I'm amused when Gerry—big, bad, crazy IRA man who bombed the Guildhall—twice. Who spent time in Crumlin road for attempted murder and sports tattoos covering his gun-shot scars becomes misty thinking of his fallen friend, "He was fearless. He woulda made a great IRA man. He'd been great. We coulda used a man like Hugh Gilmour."

After the interview it seems to me that Gerry and I are now buddies. He introduces me to the cheap lunches at the Pilot's Row and Gas Yard community centers, which now enable me to survive on £3 a day. In grand Yank style I complain about my transcriptionist issue. 'I asked the Trust to find someone for me but they've not gotten to it.' Rather than listen to me whine, he practically frog-marches me around the Bogside rounding up women to transcribe the hours and hours of interview tapes I desperately need completed. Two weeks later, the girls quit the project having accomplished exactly nothing. "It's too hard," they complain. Months into the project and still no transcriptionist.

I find a transcriptionist on the Waterside but she can't support the CD's onto which I've been downloading my digitally taped interviews. I am really enamored with my fancy equipment but I am also desperate so I re-tool. Two hand-held tape recorders and a million or so mini-cassettes and I'm back on the interview trail. She cost a fortune but she was fast. When I went to collect the transcripts she only provided hard copy! Of course! Who, in the 21st century would fail to ask if there would be a digital copy?! Now Hazel and I are typing the hard copies onto our computers. The always cheerful Hazel saves me again!

I finish Hugh Gilmour's narrative and Gerry sits up with me all night reading and editing every word. Until that night, I'd always stuck with Mike Royko's maxim: "Never drink until the column is finished." But Gerry and I drink and chain smoke for a solid eight hours. Hugh Gilmour's story is the only one that never needs editing. I will re-write Nash thirteen times, McDaid eight times, and Young six times before they are finished but when Hugh's brother Bernard reads Hugh's story he says, "I cried through the whole thing. Don't change a word." Gerry Doherty becomes my hero.

WESTPORT

I never really get used to the heavy drinking in Ireland. Ivan and I drink in the late afternoon at pubs all over the North where we meet his clients for meetings. Late afternoon turns into evening. There is a meal and then more drinking often until two or three in the morning. Red wine with dinner then whiskey, then Irish Coffee, then Baileys. Then it's off to bed and we are up and going again at eight in the morning. It is not a diet or schedule I am used to and I struggle with exhaustion and the tendency to talk too much when I am drunk. Which seems to be about twelve hours of my day these days.

A time will come when Ivan and I are not constantly on the road and I settle into a routine that includes running every afternoon. It helps me think and sweats out the alcohol and I am finally able to shut my mouth and listen. But today I am steeped in alcohol and in the middle of Ivan's pontificating on his childhood I say, I've been wanting to ask...............

............because this plagues me............. Why is it? .... Why is it..............you don't speak.........out strongly.......... in favor of integrated education?

I never miss an opportunity to talk about integrated education. It is such a fragile movement in Northern Ireland. There's an integrated education organization that invited me to come and meet them after I had been heard on television and radio. I couldn't make the day I had arranged to go so I got Hazel to call and apologize. I haven't heard from them since. They are so fragile.

Look, a lot of people in Northern Ireland lend lip service to integrated education. But you need to look at the history of Ireland of Republicanism. Wolfe Tome, the father of Republicanism spoke in terms of Catholic, Protestant, and Dissenter. Look at the great Protestant leadership with allegiance to Ireland. Protestants who believed in Ireland. Ireland is dotted with Protestants who did not believe in Catholicism who nonetheless believed in Ireland.

We don't have an Ireland today of Republicanism. We have right-wing Nationalism and that is different. The great philosophy of Ireland is the philosophy of Republicanism. We must have an Ireland for the Irish: Protestant, Catholic, and Dissenter.

Right wing nationalists talk about Catholic. That Catholic ideology is very demeaning to the Catholic church. You have priests opposing integrated education. Martin McGuinness gave eleven percent of his budget to integrated education. He should be giving forty percent of his budget to integrated education.

I'm an Irishman and I'm not a Catholic. I'm a nationalist. I don't have to be a Catholic to believe in Ireland. I am part of Ireland. I am part of Europe. I am part of a wider world. I belong to one of the two great Diasporas of the world: one is Jewish the other is Irish. We flung our people all over the world.

When I go to the Catholic church—and I have no problem going to a Catholic church—no matter what church I go into I belong to a family and it's called the Christian family. I am quite comfortable worshiping in any church but when it comes to the taking of the sacrament I do not get down to my two knees. I sit there on the seat and the reason for that is I do not recognize transubstantiation. I do not kneel down to make a confession because I don't recognize the role of any priest to give me absolution. I am not part of that religion and never will be and the reason why is ideologically, doctrinally, philosophically I can't.

I can't take communion at a Catholic church for two reasons. First of all, because I am not a Catholic the priest is not supposed to give it to me. I am a man who believes that everyone, no matter your creed, your class, your color—it doesn't matter how important you think you are—all of us can share at the Lord's table, rich, poor, Jew, Gentile. The second reason is if a priest recognizes me he would like to give it to me because although I am not a member of the Catholic church I am a member of the Catholic community. Priests at funerals I've been at have apologized for the fact that Protestants can't participate. So what he does is give a blessing which I regard as false.

I went to a funeral in Dungiven about a month ago and 95% of the people went up to the altar and took communion. After the funeral I spoke to the local counselor who was a Sinn Fein counselor and his father was my election agent many years ago. I happen to like this guy a great deal and I respect his views and his opinions and I said, 'I can't believe how many people went up and took communion' and he said, 'Yeah that is a feature of this parish' and I thought about that and you see the Catholic church has still got a very strong appeal to families. A lot of women believe that in bringing up their children it is essential to have the support of the Catholic church. The other thing is the Catholic church has been unhelpful in relation to children attending integrated primary schools because in most circumstances the church has refused to allow it.

You see for a lot of women their ideal life is a good education for the children and fidelity from their husbands. Secondary to the great education for the children is fidelity from their husbands. The other thing is adherence to the church. Almost servility to the church. I think you have to envision beyond that. That vision is a vision of reconciliation of breaking down barriers and all the rest. If you live in a totally Catholic community you're quite happy with your existence in that community and so many women who might well believe in a good education don't necessarily want integration.

The integration that I talk about is for the future of Northern Ireland it's not for the preservation of little polarized communities. This is not a historical feature. This has taken place since the bombing campaign. Because of the bombing campaign and the Provos and the IRA. Before that there were Protestant villages and Catholic villages and there was always a smattering of integration even in those so-called Catholic villages and Protestant villages. The provisional IRA campaign created that situation. The IRA created polarization because people wanted to feel safe. They wanted to feel safe within their own community. They are quite happy to remain in those communities.

I am a strong believer in forced integration at the primary school level and that means you bus kids. You've done that in the United States of America and I believe you do it here. All I can do is continue to preach the philosophy at every opportunity I get and I do it. Now, the SDLP believes in integrated education but they don't passionately believe in it. They don't see it as a way of bridging the gap amongst the two traditions.

A pause. A sigh. A slumping of his shoulders, and Ivan says, *You know we've jumped from my twelve years of age to this here.*

I know. I know....we're doing that....

Ivan and I are not focused. We are not following a structure. Every time I try to impose any rigor to the interview process. Every time I bring out the excel spreadsheets and note cards and suggest to Ivan we need to follow a process he agrees we must. Then he subverts the plan. I try the formula that is working with the Bloody Sunday families—make a family tree; complete interviews; write chapters; review chapters. But Ivan is rebellious. He is going to talk about what he wants to talk about and there is no directing the conversation. He refuses to review anything. He will not stick to a topic agreed upon, a schedule, or a format. This is why I say he spoke to me under the guise of writing his memoirs. I don't believe he ever planned to put down his memoirs. He needed to talk about Bloody Sunday. He needed to talk and I was willing to listen. Except when I talked and so, rather than take advantage of Ivan recognizing we were off track in saying, *You know we've jumped from my twelve years of age to this here,* I join the chaos and respond with:

There is so much more. I reserve the right to change my opinion as I get more educated about Irish history....however, it seems that Britain has done a horrible job and failed miserably at governing a country they claim to be their own and what you are describing to me now is a continuation of that failure despite the fact that your own Parliament has become more integrated and more diverse. The failure is being passed on from generation to generation despite the fact that you have SDLP, that you have Sinn Fein that you have the labor party, the green party, and the purple party and the orange party and the grey party and everybody else who is involved and yet - Britain - utter failure.

The other day I was involved in a television program involving the release of the cabinet papers of nineteen and seventy-two. Dr. Eamon Phoenix was the man who revealed the basic outline of what was the content of those papers. The more I heard what he had to say, and I was part of that history, of that history making, the more I said to myself, 'Jesus, what type of government did Britain have?' How stupid were they in dealing with Ireland in the context of Irish history and the truth of the matter is, Britain doesn't have any idea how to govern this place with all its divisions, polarization, eccentricities, and don't forget that even the wildest enemies in Ireland can become friends in a short space of time.

But the British sit by and pontificate. So yeah, I agree, I think the British have made a terrible mess of dealing with the Irish. They've totally totally failed to understand it and the more they've used their generals and their armies — allegedly at keeping the two polarized sides apart — the more mistakes they've made. They have also been engaged in Machiavellian behavior like assassinations and that type of thing which brings no decency to any political cause. So yeah, I agree. I think Britain has made terrible mistakes.

Are you repeating the mistakes in your own government?...or...do you not...or...wait………..I have three questions. Are you repeating the mistakes that Britain made? Or are you trying to find your own way and making mistakes along the way yet making progress? Or has Britain so impeded the process of self-governance that you're unable to make strides in self-governance?

I think it's the second one. I think we've got to make the mistakes ourselves. We've got to do what we can and build the wee bridges that we can build. I think that Britain now is largely irrelevant. We have two distinct communities. You are best making your own wee mistakes and make what progress you can. Recognize the failings of each other and do the best we can without the British trying to point us in any one particular way.

Do you think they can keep their hands off long enough to do that?

Yes, because the British have made so many blunders and mistakes. I think they'll let us get on with it. They've made very big mistakes. Bloody Sunday is a good example of that but there is a whole catalogue of things. You sound like a formal interview.

These are just questions that keep me awake. I know. I know we need to go back and build this from your childhood....

I thought these were the questions of my friend.

These are the questions of your friend.

These are the questions of a television interviewer.

These are the questions of your friend....who....you know a little knowledge is a dangerous thing.

Who's been filling your head full of the Republican stuff?

No one.

Oh yeah....you've been spending too much time in Cork. We've got to go back around. We came from when I was twelve years of age to integrated education to here. I used to play in the town market in Claudy. I used to play Cricket which was traditionally a Protestant game. I used to play Gaelic football which was an essentially Catholic game. I used to play every sport because I lived in an integrated village. I loved the Catholic boys who played with me. I respected them.

When it came to the twelfth of July and the local band marched I knew that they couldn't participate in that and when it came to the Catholic march on the fifteenth of August I knew that that wasn't part of my tradition. When it came to sports, our sports were held on a Saturday their sports were held on a Sunday. I used to peek out the window and watch their fancy dress parade and marvel at how good their fancy dress parade was compared to our fancy dress parade.

So we recognized those things which didn't divide us but we also recognized our diversity which did divide us. We also recognized some of the better and positive aspects of what they had and I would like to think they recognized and respected some of the better things we had. So I was brought up in the perfect way. There was no IRA. People mingled together. It was nothing false. It was normal.

I think you've got to play together as children and be educated together as children to understand it. I left Claudy and came to Derry full of my Protestant attitudes and I went to a school were they played rugby and I hated rugby. I didn't play rugby. I didn't hate rugby because of the sport. I hated rugby because the bloody school I was at was full of people who were better off than I was and who had very snobbish attitudes. Many of them didn't pass any exams to get there. I had. But their parents had paid.

I loved soccer. My dad used to be a supporter of the Derry City football club which had its pitch in the Bogside and I used to go along with my dad to the matches. I dreamed of the day that I would be able to play football in the Brandywell. The team that I supported was a very interesting team. The goal keeper was Charlie Hapburn who was a Catholic. It was a totally mixed team: Tommy Hershberg, Tommy Pearson, Digger Smith, Barney Cannon. It was a mixed team and we cheered for Derry City. When Derry City played against the Lindfield team from Belfast, an exclusively Protestant team, we cheered wildly for Derry. All the supporters of Lindfield looked at all supporters from Derry as Fenian and looked at all the players as Fenian even though it was a mixed team.

It was the same with Glasgow Celtic. Half the Glasgow Celtic team were Protestant. The Ranger supporters categorized all of them as Catholic. The captain of the team, Bertie Peacock came from Colraine. He was a Prod. He lives in Colraine today as a Prod. A lot of that is about people's perspectives. I was mad about becoming a footballer someday. I wasn't any good. I was useless. The only place I could play superior football other than the town market in Claudy was in the Bogside. So I met this guy from the Bogside called Dermott McCleneghan. He was two years older than me.

His mom and dad lived in the most atrocious housing circumstances. He was a gentle, kindly, lovely young boy and a very skillful footballer. Much more skillful than I. Then I met these other friends of his. They didn't care if I was a Protestant or not. I told them I was but they didn't care about that. We all played football together and I started bringing some of my Protestant friends. We all played together in the Bogside. As our friendship grew I became interested in other viewpoints which were held.

I spent a lot of time in the McCleneghan household. They lived in such poverty. There were poor Protestant families in my neighborhood, but I had never seen such devastating poverty in my life. These people had nothing and yet they were a kind and generous family. They would share with you whatever they had. Just as I'd never known such poverty; I have since never known such kindheartedness and warmth as I received in the McCleneghan house.

I was confused. Very confused. To be fair, the structures of Protestantism seemed more accommodating than the structures of the Catholic church on the issues of civil rights. But I was confused. Troubled. Fighting with myself. But I was there because of football. I liked these guys. They were lovely. Simple. They had little. Lived in poverty. Had nothing. One of the finest people I know is Dermott McCleneghan. He is a very fine man. He and Eamonn McCann. Two bollocks but I love them.

I was confused. I recognized the importance of power. You can only administer change through the acquisition of power. But if you've already got power then you've got to try to change from within. So I went through all that trauma and all the rest of it.

Then I wrote the letter. I didn't write the letter because I wanted to change the world or I wanted to change Ireland from a political perspective. I wrote the letter because I was outraged by the behavior of people who, like me, claimed to be Protestants and who could abuse Catholic nuns by spitting on them and being outrageously sectarian. I felt disgusted and ashamed to be a Protestant. So I wrote it. I wrote the stupid letter that had no relevance at all as far as I'm concerned. But I wrote it.

McCann and Dermie think it was the most significant letter written in that period of history. But even today I just don't believe that. But anyway, I wrote it. I was so disgusted at these football supporters spitting on nuns. I was brought up in a tradition to respect the cloth.

That cloth was the cloth of clergyman and priest. A man who was—call him good or bad—wearing the cloth of Christ. I don't believe that today. But I did in those days. My mother and father had taught me that when you passed any clergy man you did that —a small salute with your right hand—sort of a tipping of the hat. It was a show of respect and so I did that.

I remember when I used to go to football matches and I walked to the Brandywell there would be priests and I would salute them.

I was brought up to respect the cloth and here were these little assholes spitting on nuns. They were coming down from Belfast and desecrating our city. Our city which wasn't sectarian and they were desecrating it. So I wrote the letter and that then took me into it.

Immediately after I wrote the letter, I was banished from Derry. I couldn't get a job because all the shirt factories were owned by Mason and Protestant leadership who were fronting for the Brits. So I just couldn't get a job. I had no work so I saw an ad in the paper and I responded to it. I was interviewed in Dublin and the guy who interviewed me is still alive. He is living in Westport. He must be eighty-five or eighty-six. I would like to see him again before he dies. He said to me, 'Ivan I would like to offer you the job,' and I said to him, 'Hold on, I have a problem, I haven't told you I'm not a Catholic. He said, 'I don't give a shite what you are. I'm offering you the job, I don't care what religion you are.' So I went there. Everyone knew I was a Prod.

In Westport I was very much a part of the community. I helped found Junior Achievement and then we had this big debating competition in Ireland. We won it. These guys from Westport, County Mayo. Three of the four person team became politicians. One became an European Community Commissioner. I am no longer a professional politician—a has-been. The rest of them are gone as well. The forth guy was better than the other three of us but he ran off with another man's wife.

I got involved in television and I got involved in various things and though far away from Derry my three years were lovely. Amongst lovely people. Really lovely. But, the call of Derry was there. One of the very difficult things is someone like me who is constantly plagued with the cause. It never goes away. It means you sacrifice everything because the cause is all important and *even though I was happy there—I was very happy. I had a good job with a good salary. A company house and company car and all the rest of it. A wonderful life.*

It could have continued. I had this work ethic. Getting up very early and being at my desk early and the bloody place didn't go to their desks until about ten in the morning. I was at my desk every morning at eight. The summers were idyllic. We used to play football out on the beach in Mayo. I was happy when I was there. But I wasn't happy. I kept thinking about this bloody place up here. Discrimination and deprivation and all the rest of it and even though I had a good salary and a good job....wait, my phone is ringing.

Is that Glen? What is it? It's 2 am. Is everything OK?

It's Glen. He wants to know if we'd like to play Monopoly.

TEXAS, USA and DERRY, NI:
Two places in the world where it's OK
to carry your beer into the loo.

This is the hard part. This is the part that keeps me from publishing this book. The manuscript sits on my computer for years because I cannot write about this. I don't want to think about it. I never talk about it. I don't know how to write about it as I reflect upon it—eight years after the events I am trying to write about—I know this experience changed me. And I cannot say I like the person I became.

It started with..........

Well, remember how Gerry Doherty helped me with Hugh Gilmour's story? OK. So now I think I understand that Gerry helped me because he wanted to control the content. The truth of the matter is that many of the Bloody

Sunday families had affiliation with the IRA before Bloody Sunday and even deeper connections after. Gerry sat with me and edited every word so he could control what I wrote. For example, my draft contained specific information about the numbers of IRA members and information about the weaponry in the time before Bloody Sunday. Gerry asked me to change that language. I didn't think anything about it at the time. I am so naive, I thought his interest was genuine in the sense that he really cared about Hugh and wanted Hugh's story to be true to who Hugh was.

At the time, I was grateful to Gerry for his help and I wanted to express my appreciation so I invited him to dinner. I made a reservation at La Sosta because I really love their food and Ivan and I had had several lovely dinners there together. I thought it was a nice place to take someone for a thank-you dinner. Gerry accepted my invitation and insisted on collecting me at my hotel. He knew that I was walking into town from someplace on the Waterside every day. I did not think Gerry was spying on me when he asked to collect me where I was staying. I thought he was being a gentleman.

Upon meeting me at the Beech Hill, I think we had a drink in their bar, but I am not clear on this point. I do know we walked around outside while waiting for a taxi. I showed him the gardens and the gatekeepers house I admired. We walked around the cemetery and peered over the wall to the grand house next door. I told him that I often wondered who lived there. That to me the house had both haunted and romantic qualities. That I would love to see the inside. Gerry sniffed and snorted about how it was certainly owned by some uppity Prod. How it was probably not come by honestly, etc., etc.

This was not the first time and it would be far from the last that people would make derogatory comments about Prods and Americans in front of me even though they all knew I was both Protestant and American. In explaining this phenomenon to people I eventually likened it to a dinner party where people talked about 'those niggers' with an African American sitting as a guest at the table. Gerry's visceral response to this house in the country confused me a bit. Perhaps I should have been more sensitive to the deep-seated historical hatred that keeps people from crossing the Foyle, but at the time I was just not aware. Clearly not as aware or savvy as I should have been.

So Gerry and I went to dinner at La Sosta and we had a nice bottle of wine and I told him how very grateful I was that he helped me with Hugh Gilmour's story and he basically said, 'No problem, happy to do it.' We finished dinner and we left and I thought that was it. I was completely unaware of the tsunami my actions were stirring. I really innocently thought it was a perfectly honorable thing to do—to take someone to dinner as a thank you.

We went to the Oak Grove after dinner and Gerry spent the rest of the evening talking about well, to describe it, how uppity I was. That I was staying at a fancy hotel. ON THE WATERSIDE. That we went to a snooty restaurant and had a BOTTLE OF WINE. That the place had table cloths and napkins was now a really big deal. He went on so long and so loudly about it that I am embarrassed to this day. I am embarrassed I was so naive, so stupid. I am so embarrassed and ashamed I can't find the words to adequately describe my feelings. Embarrassed and ashamed don't quite touch the depth of my feelings about all of this night and what was to happen after.

While staying the the Beech Hill, I got in the habit of going to Mass every morning. I did not hide my Protestant affiliation, it was just that every morning the church bells rang and I got up and I walked across the street to St. Mary's of Ardmore. It was important I thought to have a routine in Derry and the services really seemed to ground me and get me ready for the day. I also thought it helped me in writing the stories. The Catholic church and Mass was such a part of daily life for people in Derry that I thought being in that routine and getting some exposure to the Church would help me my writing. Perhaps make it more genuine? So many people talked about having to get up and go to Mass before school every morning that I did so too. St. Mary's was unassuming. It was a welcoming church and no one seemed to mind that I was new to the structures and dialogue of Mass. I showed up. I participated. I did the best I could and they seemed perfectly OK with that. After the difficult time in Derry I stayed in town. On the city side. But on the few times I went out to the Beech Hill after that, if a taxi took me, I always had him drop me in the car park of St. Mary's.

After my dinner with Gerry, my choice of home in Derry becomes an issue. The Beech Hill is on the Waterside and suddenly it seems my loyalty is being questioned. In all the interviews I conducted, and the life stories I had written so far, only a few people seemed to notice I was human. That I was a woman living in a foreign country alone. Mona Bradley offered me a meal when I went to visit her husband and Maura Young took me to lunch and walked me around the city and the Bogside. She showed me where the events of Bloody Sunday happened. She trusted me with John's personal possessions.

Beyond this, despite the fact that I am now a fixture in Derry, no one asked if I needed any laundry done, or enquired into my accommodations, or if I was in want of a meal. Not even one, "How are you getting along?" This is fine. They don't really know me. I am not worried about the level of hospitality. It is not the midwest after all and really, I am here to work and the way I see it, I am here to work for them, so it doesn't occur to me at the time that no one is enquiring as to my comfort, etc. I am only saying this upon reflection. It was not something that bothered me or occurred to me at the time. Then the story that I am staying at the Beech Hill breaks and everyone has an opinion about my living situation.

I want to pause here and say, to be fair, later, after I weather this storm, I will meet people I still regard very highly. People I really grew to love. I don't know who was behind what happened during this very hard time but I can tell you I found something to love, something to connect with with nearly every one of the Bloody Sunday families.

After our dinner, Gerry informs me that living at the Beech Hill on the Waterside is absolutely unacceptable. He insists I move to the city side. I am confused. No one had enquired into my well-being, where I was staying, nothing. But I cannot stay on the Waterside? It is again implied that staying on the Waterside means that I am not loyal to the families. It is implied that if I stay on the Waterside I cannot be trusted and the progress we have made on the Bloody Sunday book will stop and I will be out of luck. Close to the publishing of the book, I receive several emails making the same accusations and I believe I now know who was working behind the scenes. At the time, I believed that the life-stories I was producing were proof enough of my dedication to the project and my loyalty to the families. I interviewed them, I wrote drafts, I edited the drafts, I took out and put in content they wanted removed and added, and every story in the book had a final approval by a representative of each family. I even made a special trip back to Derry just before the book was published so each family could make sure the story going into the book was the story they wanted told.

Gerry not only insists I move he installs me in a strange back-alley apartment that belongs to a 'friend of a friend.' I was allowed freedom of movement. If it can be called that. I was instructed to leave the apartment in the morning and not return until dark. Essentially I was only allowed to sleep there.

They always watched me. It was not a creepy black car or shadowy figure following me. They just let me know they always knew where I was. That they were watching me.

"How was coffee at Java today?"

"I saw you running along the river. You were not running very fast."

"You were sure huffing and puffing as you walked up Beechwood today."

"I always see you with that backpack. You look like Edmund Hilary."

If I wandered into an area that was taboo, for example, walking over the bridge to the natural food store on the Waterside, a taxi would pull up and someone would say,

"Gerry thought you might need a lift. Where can I take you?" Once, one of these drivers said, "We don't need to know why we are doing something. We never know ahead of time. Gerry tells us what to do and where and we go do it." His statement unsettled me. It was expected that I turn up at the Oak Grove at 4:00 pm every day. If not, someone would come looking for me. It all seemed so innocent. Like a concerned friend. But there was not a second during which my movements were not tracked.

 I had to leave the key to the apartment at the Oak Grove every time I went out. I was told it was because there was only one key. But men entered the apartment when I was there and followed me around even talked to me when I was in the shower. There was no light in the bathroom. They said it was broken. So the door had to remain open. My clothes and my files had to be in certain places. And there were times when they showed me I had no power and that I cannot talk about. I can only say that I did not sleep. I sat awake every night. Listening. Waiting.

 I was alone. I did not know how to leave. I had no one to go to for help. I was not a journalist with an editor back in the states keeping tabs on me. Who was I going to call? My kids? What would I even say? I felt ridiculous and powerless. I wanted to be rescued. I went into what I can only describe as a state of suspended animation......I felt.....caught in a vortex? It is logical to say that when faced with a situation like this the best thing to do is pack up your stuff and get on a plane and leave. But I could not.

 I thought that what was happening was a test of loyalty. I can say today if what happened during that time was a test of loyalty they have a fucked up idea of loyalty. During that time and in that apartment I learned I am weak. My whole life I prided myself on my strength. But they broke me. Nonetheless, and much to the dismay of people close to me, I defend Derry vigorously. I do not let anyone say a negative or even perceived negative word about Derry or her inhabitants.

I feel betrayed. I start to realize that I am trapped and sinking into depression. I begin to try to figure out how to get the hell out of Derry. I want to be rescued. I feel broken and I keep thinking I need to be rescued. It is foreign to my personality—to my life experience—to have this feeling of victimization and it is humiliating to say this feeling will travel with me for years after I leave Derry. I try to find refuge at Mass but the Long Tower feels remote, foreign, and cold. Not the warm, welcoming St. Mary's in Ardmore. Interviews stall. Transcripts wait in queue. I abandon my Protestant work ethic, my belief in God, my work though the day, get a good night sleep, eat well, exercise, and you'll get on way of life and I decide to quit the project.

I am today confounded by what I did next. It is not the action of a stable person. I go to the city cemetery, walk past the garden, along where the bunnies play above the football pitch, past the old house that looks like temple ruins, and climb the steep hill through the rows, to lie in the grass by his grave. I ignore the disapproving devoutly Catholic stares of the people tending graves. I lie in the grass next to John Young watching white clouds float across the blue sky. I marvel at the beautiful weather. The fresh clean air. The soft green grass supporting me. I talk to John. As the sun sets behind us, shimmering on the Foyle, illuminating the green pastures of the Waterside, I spill out all my pain, frustration, and sorrow. John listens and I feel he is assuring me that he will stay the course with me. And this, for better or worse, weds me to the project. After I speak to John, I never talk to anyone about this period of time in my life. In a sense, I leave it there with him.

I start interviewing people as fast as possible. Packing in interview after interview. Prior to this I was working on only a few at a time. I would interview, transcribe, then write the story. Now, I am just getting interviews on tape. As many as possible so I can get the heck out of there. I can do the rest at home.

I was never a drinker. Now I drink. A lot. If I ignore everything else. If I block it out. I can get this done. And then I am attacked in the apartment in the middle of the day. It is brutal. The alleged apartment owner is furious that I am there is the middle of the day. I just came back to collect a file. It came out of no where. I can only describe the rest of that day as blind. I learned the point at which I mentally break. I knew I was physically strong. That I could physically withstand about anything. I had always had a very high tolerance for pain but I never gave a thought to the tolerance of my mind. Skin rips, bones snap, soft tissue bruises. We all know this. We all know these things can happen to us. We never think about at what point will I not be able to mentally take it any more. This too follows me. Stays with me for years after and I wonder if it influenced later decisions.

I had no plane ticket home but I had to go and I had to go now. Why was no one coming to rescue me? I needed help! I bolstered the courage. I know now it came from outrage but the origin didn't matter. I needed to escape.

Derry to Belfast.

Belfast to London.

London to Chicago.

Once in Chicago I board a plane to Miami.

My dear friend Vanessa dries me out, fills me with Cuban food, sees that I sleep, sun myself, and most importantly—laugh.

Back home in the States my house was invaded. Not ransacked. Not broken into. Quietly invaded. One would not know someone had been there. A picture was moved. Files re-arranged. Keys removed from their hook. A pile of unfolded clothes would be folded. The back door left standing open. The refrigerator door left open. A book flopped over the back of a chair. The rocking chair moved to the other side of the room. A line of dust cleared from the dresser, just the width of a finger. A file you are working on disappears, then returns to the same place a week later. All things about which one could say, "did I leave that there? Did I move that? I don't remember doing tha." Things to make you think you are going crazy. Things that if you tell people, they will think you are going crazy. Things that make you take an inventory before you leave the house. That cause you to leave the lights on. That make you look over your shoulder and suspect everything and everyone. These things are not happening over time. They are happening every day. It goes on for months.

The local coffee shop phoned one morning from my mobile saying I left it. Retuning to collect it that evening, I was told there was no phone left. The next day, I was told I collected it. I did not. Two weeks later, the phone turned up under a pile of papers at my house. All the contacts erased.

People don't want to believe these things happen. They say "You must have misplaced it." Subtle terror. Intimidation.

At one point I was followed. For weeks. Not quietly. A man in a plaid jacket followed me. He followed me so closely, when I once turned back, I ran straight into him. Plowed right into him. I wondered, "Why didn't I say something to him?"

"Oh, it must have been your imagination," people say. "Why would anyone follow you?"

"You are just being paranoid."

The mug's color is spring grass green on the bottom and cream the top third. When I bought it the British Army bases were still there. Remnants of checkpoints, surveillance cameras, fencing, and razor wire. On the back wall of the Oak Grove, behind the bar, over the mirror, hung a row of coffee mugs. Next to the cracked and stained mugs of the locals, mine was clean, in-tact, pretty. I signed *'Jennifer'* on the bottom in permanent marker. Years after my last drink at the Oak Grove Gerry tells me, "It's still there. I drink my tea from your mug."

THE BAR AT THE BEECH HILL

Everyone in Belfast was pulling my leg about having to come to the airport on Boxing morning. No one here gets up out of bed on Boxing morning but I was delighted because on Christmas day I went to the home of this elderly couple. They're very old and I don't think they'll have another Christmas. It was a very quiet day.

They don't have a TV or Christmas decorations or Christmas cards or anything like that. I had a very nice quiet day.

So yesterday morning I was at Belfast City at 8:30. In good time. An hour early. I had breakfast at the airport and there were papers at the airport, so I read the paper. There was no Jennifer. So I thought maybe you had flown into Belfast International so I had the people at Belfast International paging you. All morning.

I forwarded you the email from the airline.

You know, no matter where I am in Europe I can use my mobile. You get here and you can't use your mobile.

I know and last time I was here I actually spent a lot of time trying to get a mobile phone.

I sent you an email after you didn't show up at the airport and that's two emails now you say you haven't gotten from me.

You said you sent me an email the other day and I checked my email yesterday and I don't have any email from you.

I sent you an email about what time I was going to meet you at the airport.

I would have responded if I had gotten an email from you about that. You know what, I want to to see the email you said you got about the plane because you said the time was incorrect.

It was incorrect.

I sent you three emails about my trip here. The first said, 'Here are some possible times but I need to confirm. Let me know if any don't work for you.'

Jennifer, You messed up.

No, I didn't mess up. The first email said....

You got the times wrong.

No. I forwarded the email from the airline. The email the airline sent me. So how could I have screwed it up? I didn't alter it. The first email I sent said there are a couple of different times but I haven't bought my ticket, I'll email you back when it's firm. The second email I sent you asked you to confirm that the time I'd chosen was alright. The third email was the confirmation from the airline. I never heard back from you after the first email or the second email or the third email. I haven't gotten anything from you.

Jennifer. Hazel sent you the email.

This is concerning to me. You and I have to have private communication and there is a third party involved and now I am starting to distrust this third party.

You are not checking your email.

Why would I not check my email? I am telling you, it's not getting to me.

I know you messed up because you rang the wrong number from Dublin.

You say you've left messages for me and I've never gotten them, so how can you say I rang the wrong number?

Jennifer, I know you rang the wrong number.

Well how did I get a hold of you this time if I rang the wrong number last time? Am I smarter today?

Well you weren't thinking.

Well we have to fix it because look at it. I send you messages that you never get and you send me messages that I never get.

That's one thing I am very good at. I am a very efficient person. I am very responsive.

Both of us are smart. Both of us are efficient. Both of us are responsive. Both of us are honest. Both of us know how to use the technology to communicate yet neither of us is getting messages.

I don't know how you can say that.....

I'm not stupid. You're not stupid. If I say I've emailed you then I have. If I say I've rung you then I have. And if you say you've done the same thing for me then I have to believe that. You aren't even sending your own email. You have Hazel do it. Men are always taking credit no matter who does the work! Did you know male reindeer drop their antlers in early November? Female reindeer do not drop their antlers. All of the reindeer that pull Santa's sleigh have antlers so they are all female. Yet they are always referred to as male. Men! Always taking the credit.

You know who came up with that whole reindeer story?

It's from The Night Before Christmas.

The Irish.

It was Clement Moore from New York.

Nope. The Irish. And Valentine's Day.

And did they come up with St. Patrick's Day?

St. Patrick's, yes.

And 4th of July and Thanksgiving and…..Bastille Day?

No. Not Bastille Day.

WORK ETHIC

It is hard going back to Derry. I am afraid. I consult someone who calls himself a 'personal protection specialist.' He coordinates security for yachts, moves billions in cash through Afghanistan, and makes sure supermodels don't chip their nails. I change my mind about where to stay.

Three times. Then I change places two more times after I arrive. I feel uncertain and unsettled but it is only about me. My personal safety. I actually feel positive about the project. Reflecting now I wonder how on earth I managed to feel positive about writing the Bloody Sunday book.

At this point, all the people working on and volunteering for the book are Protestant. Makes ya think about the work ethic thing, huh. I am still looking for a transcriptionist. I am obsessed. The transcriptionist is key. Without someone to transcribe all the interviews it's a bust. Everyone I meet hears the same refrain, 'Do you know anyone who could use work as a transcriptionist?'

Then one day, my American tendency to complain pays off. I complain at the right time, in the right place, to the right person and 'Gerry from Derry,' Jackie Duddy's brother, introduces me to his daughter Catherine who becomes our official, paid transcriptionist. In my opinion, Hazel and Catherine should be sainted for their dedication to the project. It could be the first joint Protestant-Catholic sainting in Northern Ireland.

When writing about the project in 2003, I wrote "our" transcriptionist. But there was no "our." I paid her. With my money. I bought the plane tickets and paid the hotel bills and covered all the expenses associated with living on the road—food, laundry, all the recording equipment, a laptop computer, bus, train, taxi, and an astronomical childcare bill. I kept repeating the idea, and I do still when I talk with people about the book, that it was a joint effort. But the only sense in which it was a joint effort was that people granted me interviews and read the drafts of their stories. There was no unified effort to write the book. It was me. I did it.

Pushing boulders uphill in a storm. Remember I said I changed? Well, I can tell you I was carefree before Derry. Now, I always seem to choose to push boulders uphill and I can't seem to change that behavior.

When I left Derry after that first go-round, I had only three narratives drafted and was having a terrible time getting people to agree to be interviewed and participate in the project. I don't do the right thing: cut my losses and bail out. I must be the most hopeful or stubborn person on the planet. I didn't realize what a very lonely activity it was. I was singularly focused. I remember holding my hand up to stop my children from talking to me when I was writing. I held that hand up too many times. I also lost touch with friends. In their wise words even as they faded from my life:

"If after they asked you to do the project and you put all that time into preparing and they did nothing why didn't you just turn around and walk out?"

"Screw them! It wasn't your idea and you are doing all the work and paying for everything?"

"Don't be stupid."

Yes, well, I come from a Protestant upbringing, which means I have the worst of two afflictions:

1. Work ethic. "If you work hard enough you can achieve anything."

2. Belief in people. "Fundamentally, everyone is good."

The first quote comes from my parents who, no matter how hard you worked, always believed you had a little bit more to give. The second quote comes from Anne Frank, who because of the number of times that belief has gotten me into trouble, I've never really liked.

KILLALOO

I wasn't born a non-violent civil rights activist. I used to fight with my brother. We battered each other frequently. Everyone was half-terrified of us because we could defend ourselves. Not very non-violent. But there were influences all around me. Talk at the tea table was often about injustice. Of course there was plenty of gossip and humor there as well.

As I said, I wasn't born a civil rights activist. It wasn't my goal as a child to align myself with what has been seen as a Catholic position. I didn't know then that my involvement in civil rights would cause my family to be ostracized by their community, my parents business boycotted, their lives threatened. I didn't know when I was a child that my career would cause my parents to lose lifetime friends who simply dropped and deserted them, that my father would suffer seven strokes and my mother worry herself sick waiting for my safe return from an ordinary day's work. I didn't know my parents would be forced from their quiet country home to the relative safety of the city. On the contrary, I had quite an idyllic childhood.

The area I was born into was very Protestant. Our family church was just up the road. A mile down the road was a Presbyterian church. A few hundred yards up the road was another Presbyterian church. There were children in my school who went to the same Church of Ireland my family attended and there were Presbyterians and Methodists.

At that time, we socialized together but we certainly didn't know much about each other's religions. Each clergy came to the school and educated his flock individually. The chairman of the board of governors of this school was a Church of Ireland clergyman so periodically he came to the school and talked about religion to his flock. The Presbyterian clergyman also came and he talked only to his flock and so on. So there were very clear lines of demarcation within the broad umbrella of Protestantism.

We went to each other's social events which took place in our respective church halls. At one of the Presbyterian churches I was a member of the table tennis club and the amateur dramatic society but I never set foot in the sanctuary. As a child I knew no more how my Protestant neighbors worshiped than I knew about the worship services of the Catholic boys I met in Claudy when I went to visit my sister. My sister Leticia was twenty-three years my senior and had a home in the village of Claudy and when I went there I met boys who were both Catholics and Protestants and we played each other's games.

In other words, the Catholic boys played cricket and the Protestant boys played Gaelic football and each of us knew that we had our own days of celebration. The Protestant boys had the twelfth of July and the twelfth of August was the Apprentice Boys parade. On the Catholic boy's side we knew they had a celebration on the fifteenth of August. The respective bands marched through the village without giving offense to anyone. So, my upbringing was egalitarian without really strong feelings of religious separatism on either side.

I have never looked at myself as a Protestant because the church that I belong to was founded by Saint Patrick in 432. The Church of Ireland is an all Ireland church encompassing North and South. It has always been looked upon by the broader Protestant community as a church that is like Rome because of the similarities in the liturgy between the Catholic Church and the Church of Ireland, which is in communion with the Anglican church, which is the church headed by the Queen. Nonetheless, the Church of Ireland has its own independence, its own individuality, and was founded by St. Patrick. One thing that I can never fully understand about large elements of Protestantism is that they want nothing to do with St. Patrick. Yet a large part of the Protestant community believes St. Patrick founded their church.

As I said, the community where I grew up was largely Protestant. So much so, there were two Orange Halls within walking distance of my home, and the one just a couple hundred yards down the road had a band. I never had any particular interest in that band but I did have in the Claudy pipe band. They played Irish pipes called Brian Boru pipes, which have nine pipes as opposed to the traditional seven pipe Scottish band. I learned to play the pipes but I wasn't very good, so they let me play the drums, which I wasn't very good at either. People used to say we were a Fenian band because we wore green kilts and green shawls fringed with orange and purple. We were know as the Claudy Brian Boru pipe band. I did not wear a kilt. Drummers wore trousers. I suspect you were relieved to hear that.

So I had an interest in that band and the leader of that band, known as a drum major in those days. He is a friend of mine to this day. In fact, throughout all of the civil rights movement activities whenever Protestants boycotted my family's business, criticized me, maligned me, character assassinated me, he remained a friend to me. These friendships buoyed me through the years when my involvement in civil rights was so hard on my family.

The person who really held my family together was my mother. She married my father when she was sixteen. She was very outward going with a big personality. She had been a nurse, postmistress, and forensic science teacher all at the same time. So she was well known and very energetic. And she was born with *incredible leadership skills and through that became strongly associated with the church.*

My mother was very resourceful. Her home always had good heating cause she would have always bought a ton of coal and stockpiled. Nothing was bought unless you could pay for it. There was no financing of anything. But the provider was my mother, the money manager was my mother. She bought everything for the house and the children and my father. She was a wonderful gardener. She had green fingers. She was also very fond of buying things. Particularly furnishings. She used to go to auctions and buy second hand furniture very cheaply. Some of her grandfather clocks and her chairs are still with my sisters in Donegal. She was very resourceful. I don't think there was anything my mother couldn't do.

My father tended to be a rather quiet man, well respected in the Catholic community with a reputation for fairness. He employed several Catholic men at the post office and did not fly the Union Jack in respect of his Catholic employees and customers. He was well known in our surrounding Catholic areas where we used to stop for tea in houses and that sort of thing. One thing that sticks out in my mind about my father is he was a dreadful driver. He didn't take up driving a car until the latter part of his life and then drove around at 30 mph. My mother had a license but never drove. She was the perennial back-seat driver.

Robert Henry and Mary Jane (Bob and Jeanie) Cooper were the parents of Leticia Maude, Violet, Ralph, Ivy Mae, Billy, Ivan, and Robert Lynn. Violet died of diphtheria at three years of age and my brother Ralph was killed tragically by a lorry when he was just seven. My mother had an old uncle and aunt, Thomas and Elizabeth Averill. They never had any children so when I was born I was called Ivan Averill Cooper. That caused me some problems in primary school because Averill is a well known girls name and the other boys used to pull my leg about having a girl's middle name. Having a girl's name didn't concern me. The only other person I knew of who had that as a Christian name was a man called Averill Harriman, the US ambassador to the UN.

Averill came in handy later when I opposed a man named Douglas Cooper in an election campaign. It is well known in politics the higher up the ballot paper the better. I was concerned people who intended voting for me would vote for the first Cooper to catch their eyes and Douglas Cooper would have had a number of my votes. I changed my name round to Averill Ivan Cooper, putting me further up the ballot paper.

My mother had two sisters and two brothers in Scotland and so my childhood holidays were spent in Scotland. She was very close to her two sisters. One of those sisters used to send us parcels every Christmas. We looked forward to those parcels very much because they normally contained little toys for my brother and me. Our journey to Scotland was always by ferry. We traveled from Derry to Greenock. The earliest ferry I remember was called Laird's Loch. I remember that boat because it also carried cattle. Because of that, my mother would save to make sure we were able to travel first class. Third class was in steerage, which was not only close to the cattle it was where the working men traveled. These men used drink all night and were quite drunk around the ship. They used to pee in the wash basins and things like that so my mother was always certain to save the money so that we all could travel first class.

The journey was horrific. The journey in my childhood from Derry to Glasgow took ten to twelve hours. A journey of five hours today. It was simply dreadful. Arriving in Scotland was so much looked forward to, not only to be free of the boat, but to enjoy a way of life quite different from our own.

I was brought up in the country with green grass and open fields. My mother's sister lived in the town. They had parks, which we had no experience of, and slides, swings, and ice cream wagons that came around and sold ice cream, which we never had. It was a wonderful world. Each year for two weeks we enjoyed carefree city-living. Our playmates were Catholic. They were lovely kids. Very friendly. They used to take us to the park where we sailed yachts. Another thing that was entirely alien to my upbringing.

There were no yachts where I came from. There was a river at the bottom of one of our fields where we used to fish after a flood and catch salmon. Well, truth be told, there were very few salmon and we really weren't good enough to catch them so mostly it was white trout. But this experience of sailing these yachts wasn't something we normally experienced and it was tremendous fun. My mother's sister had been married twice. Her first husband was killed during the war. He had been in the Royal Air Force.

So the civil rights movement started in a gentle sort of way. You've got to remember at that time on the outskirts of the city there was an abandoned camp. The American Army had abandoned a camp after World War II and left all their huts behind. As soon as the Americans moved out, Derry families moved in. The living conditions were somewhat improved but infant mortality rate was about forty-four percent and families that lived there were very stigmatized. If you said you lived at Springtown people would look at you as if you had two heads. I remember when I went to work in the shirt industry there was a girl named Rosie Sweeny. I remember people saying she lived at the camp. So I got involved with squatting people.

Then I was involved in discussions with Dermie for hours and *hours in his front room and we were talking about conditions people were living in so we were going around looking at people's houses. I wanted to do something about that because I couldn't bear the thought of human beings living in huts and terrible housing conditions. Many of the landlords operating in Derry were rack-men: private landlords who were charging rent and doing no repairs.*

I used to walk along the Lecky Road past all this bad housing. Abominable housing. Owned by Raymond Saville DeConnely Mt. Morency Lecky Brown Lecky, an English gentleman, these little slum houses in the Bogside had two bedrooms, outside toilets, and no proper plumbing. The residents suffered from tuberculosis, which ran rampant due to overcrowding.

Dermie's father had tuberculosis and his doctor had said his tuberculosis could be improved on if he was taken out of the horrible housing circumstances he was living in. I went with Dermie's eldest sister to see the mayor about getting their father out of the terrible housing conditions. His doctor had written a letter saying his tuberculosis could be arrested if he got out of that housing situation. Today Dermie's sister is a PhD, a lecturer at the University of Redding, but back then I saw that girl getting battered about in her efforts to get her father and mother a house and I had to do something.

LAKE GENEVA

I am particularly excited about this trip to Derry to work with the families because I've been invited to meet with the Bloody Sunday Trust! Finally! I want to share with them what good work we are doing. I prepare my progress report, print up handouts, and rehearse my speech. I am excited to tell them all about the project, the progress, interested publishers, and the hope I have for our efficient completion. I don a suit, put on makeup, and arrive on time and ready. No one turns up. 'Hey,' they seem to say, 'maybe next month.'

Mickey and I talk about submitting a grant proposal to fund the project. At the time Mickey told me about one that would provide £10,000. Enough to cover half our anticipated expenses! On my last day in Derry on this trip I turned over the fully drafted proposal to the Trust for their documentation and submission. I never heard what happened with it. Did they submit it? Did they get the money? My friends ask me why I don't recognize when I've been set up.

I was starting to notice things but I wanted to remain positive. I needed to stay focused. By the time I met the Nash family I was beginning to be wary. I was starting to take a more cynical view of well, the whole thing. Bloody Sunday, Derry, the families. I thought if ever there was a place that could cover up an incident for over 30 years, any place that could manipulate the facts, it was Derry.

And so, struggling with fear, suspicion, and a growing feeling that I really was being set up, I met the Nash family. They talked about love and devotion and steadfast commitment and forgiveness, but always, just under the surface, I sensed anger, rage, hurt, and distrust. I didn't understand it. I couldn't touch Bridie and Alex's love. I couldn't feel Willie's playful spirit. I couldn't hear his boisterous happy laugh. But I was close to the pain. So close it touched me. It thrust into my bones, chilly and damp, and it ached. I didn't know how to deal with it. It was unrelenting. I became angry and frustrated. The sadness and betrayal seeped from the positive façade of this vibrant vital family.

Meeting members of the Nash family I was confronted with their seeming extremes and contradictions. I first encountered Linda through a narrative written by Joanne O'Brien in her book 'A Matter of Minutes.' The narrative is prefaced by a photograph of Linda, Willie's sister. Taken near the place where her brother and father were gunned down on Bloody Sunday the photo is raw and gritty. In the picture, Linda looks hardened and tired. A contradiction to the passionate energetic woman I met in Derry the summer of 2003. Did the stark photographic image reveal a truth Linda would not? In 2004 I met Linda again. She remembered neither me nor sitting with me for over three hours talking about her family.

I met Patrick, Willie's brother, just weeks after his dear wife's death. Deep in grief he nonetheless sat with me for several hours sharing his life and telling me, a stranger, his family's stories. Seemingly without reservation. I found Patrick to be a kind, gentle, jolly man, and yet he told me of incidents of internment, harassment, insult, and deprivation. How could he not be angry? I seethe when people drive slowly in the passing lane. How could he be so calm and forgiving? Was he hiding something?

Mostly I learned to know Willie's brother John. 'Banty' to his friends. As the months passed, he reinforced my perception of extremes and contradictions. John seizes every moment. He is patient and steadfast. He acts quickly, decisively, impetuously. He is angry, ferocious, and kind. In his day of a thousand errands and details he shuttles me, too. He expects me to be prompt. Ready for anything.

He rages at me. He listens to me. He works with me in the sitting room, across the kitchen table, or at the bar. He pushes me away. He answers every question. He looks for every detail. He finds me when I am lost. He gives me direction to go on my own. He's impatient with me. He takes the time we need. How could I trust someone who seemed to change at every turn?

When I met him in the spring of 2003 John had dedicated much of the previous thirty-one years of his life to telling the truth about Bloody Sunday and clearing his brother's name. He and other Bloody Sunday family members dedicated six years to supporting their solicitors' investigation. Entire rooms in their homes are consumed with the effort: shelves of documents line the walls; cabinets burst with files; cd-roms litter computer desks.

When I returned home, I sat at the edge of Lake Geneva among the red, yellow, and brown leaves, the last of the summer sun at my back and I puzzled. Having a brother murdered and father shot in cold blood by the Army would probably be motivation enough, but for thirty years? I wonder. Would I possess that kind of drive? To get up every day for three decades to unearth and proclaim the truth?

I can't answer. I've never been the sister of a murdered brother. I've never watched a friend gunned down in the street in the prime of life. I've never had to watch my parents grieve over the loss of their child. I've never been the victim of a house raid directed by my government. I can't tell you where the Nash family gets the determination, the stamina, the dedication to give themselves wholly to the cause. In spite of my friends and family imploring me to give up this folly, I tell myself the only way to learn to know people is to take the time to learn to know them. I resolve to be more patient.

THE GLENSHANE PASS

Without fail, Ivan recites hymns when we travel through Glenshane Pass. I don't blame him. It's a beautiful unspoiled area. Grass-covered slopes rise up the wild rugged Sperrin mountain summits with only sheep to impede the view. There are no other roads. There are no dwellings in the area save for a few old barns. On one side the grasses, heathers, and rushes vary the color and texture of the landscape. On the other side rolling hills divided by stone walls and hedgerows harken back to days of tiny farms with altitude-loving fields of potatoes, alfalfa, and barley.

'There were ninety-nine safely lain in the shelter of the fold. One was ide in the hills far off, far away from the streets of gold. There were ninety-nine safely lain in the shelter of the fold, but one was ide in the hills far off, far away from the streets of gold' That's the lost sheep. One lost sheep. And ninety-nine were in the fold.

Did you ever read The Hymns of Mrs. C.F. Alexander from Derry? She wrote 'Once in Royal David's City.' Have you heard that? What about 'Son of Christmas,' or 'All Things Bright and Beautiful?' All creatures great and small. Mrs. Alexander wrote that. She wrote another hymn: 'There was a green hill far away beside the city wall; Where the dear Lord was crucified, who died to save us all.' That hill is a hill that she used to look out on from her window just outside Derry. I think that is very beautiful hymn. There was a green hill far away beside the city wall. Did you ever hear the hymn 'What a friend we have in Jesus?' All our sins and grief to bear. What a privilege to carry everything to God in prayer.

I was at a funeral, a eulogy a few weeks ago and that was one of the hymns that was there. And it's remarkable after all these years I can still quote all these hymns.

Didn't you say you wanted to be buried by your parents?
Yes.
And where are they buried?
Glendermott.
Anything else?
No.

OK. You told me that and then I couldn't remember and then I was concerned because I was the only one that knew. You would never forgive me if I screwed that up. You might drop dead on one of our adventures and then what would I do?

You'd call Hazel. The guardian.
Does she know?
No. No, her partner's mother died recently and they buried her out at that graveyard where my brother and sister are buried. And the grave partially caved in before they got the coffin in. They dropped the coffin and then the coffin was... because it was partially filled-in they put it in at an angle and the top of it was less than two feet from the surface. So she was extremely distressed over that.

So her head was up? And her feet were down? Wouldn't it be worse if her head was down and her feet were up?
You're dead!
I know, but for all eternity you're standing on your head!

Yeah, well, that's the other thing. They put it in initially upside down.

Oh, that's awful! The body bounced around in there?

But what would it matter for all eternity?

It wouldn't matter. But it's just knowing. It's not for the dead person, it's for the person left behind them. You know it occurred to me the other day that I've never been to my grandparents' grave. My mother's parents. I've never been there. Not since we buried my grandmother.

Why haven't you been?

Well, I haven't been to Pennsylvania. Not that if I went to Pennsylvania I would go, but…

Would you pray at the grave?

Why would I do that?

I'm asking you a question.

No. I don't know. I don't think so.

Cause Catholics pray at the grave.

To God and the saints?

To God and the saints. They believe that even after death you can influence the future destination of the soul by praying to the saints. They believe you can influence that. I don't pray at graves.

Well, my dad is buried. He was cremated. They put his ashes under a tree at the seminary where my mom teaches.

Under the ground?

Mm-hmm. They dug a hole for the tree, they put the tree in, and they left all the dirt around. And then we took his ashes and put the ashes all around the tree and then put the dirt in over it. We kinda mixed them together.

Is that what he wanted?

Uh-huh. You know, that's a good question. Wanted. I mean….

Well, some people decree that sort of thing. Or request it or put it in their will.

I don't know. Once he knew he was going to die he had to decide what would happen with his body. He donated whatever organs they could use for their research into his cancer. And then wanted to be cremated but then, you know, then what do you do with the ashes? So I guess the tree seemed as good a place as any. Answer your phone.

Hello? Yes Pat, how you doin? Hummm....If Eurotrack were to place an order, it would be an order all together stretching over three years. I must tell you Pat that at this point and time the discussions with rail track are not providing a great basis for hope. Now this particular sleeper is what's known as the G-45 and the metal elements and the steel elements in it are manufactured by a German company.

The German company have been involved in discussions over the last week but it looks as if they may well place the order with Redi-mix concrete rather than Keith Carson. My confidence doesn't hide my...I have made an appointment with Keith Carson next week to see a lawyer in connection with...if he doesn't get an order, to discuss the possibility of him looking for compensation for a quarter million pounds that he has spent in developing and researching the G-45 sleeper. Pat, can I just tell you that in this particular case there are like four or five creditors who are badly affected including the people you just mentioned? I feel very badly for them. There is a wee man called Des Lockrey. I don't know if you remember a case with you and Gerry McMannis where at the meeting with creditors you had a bit of fun at his expense. Don't know if you remember that case. Well McMannis behaved deplorably.

I am writing a book at the minute and that is one of the things I am putting into the book. But this wee fella Lockrey completed his IDA to the last letter of the law but he is caught for about $38,000 in this case. And I feel very sorry for him. There is a fella called Vivian Fraser who is badly affected as well. They're badly hurt you know. I feel very sorry for them. I really do. I feel very very sorry for them. He's caught about half a dozen small people. He's going to see a lawyer on Wednesday to see if he has any basis for…what we were going to do is see if we could leverage an order by threatening legal action but rather than paying compensation they might place an order. Alright Pat, thanks very much. All the best to you. Thank you now. Bye

That's nastiness in my part. Vindictiveness. He appeared at the meeting of creditors and he gave a little client of mine an awfully hard time. He was digging sand out of a mountain and he was working seven days a week and these two guys in their fancy suits put him through a bashing machine and I don't think I'll ever forget it. It was five years ago but I'll worry about that all night now.

TRAVEL WEARY

At Heathrow the gate to Belfast is at the very end of a long corridor deep in the smoking section. It's not labeled. It is behind a rope and two sets of alarmed doors. When you check in, they say to go to Gate 12 but there is no Gate 12. Well, OK. There is a Gate 12. It is behind the rope and the two sets of doors. There is no sign to indicate that the gate is back there. The hallway looks as if it comes to an end.

At Stansted, gates 81-82 and 84-88 have large signs like "GATE 81," which has flight times displayed on TV monitors, vast comfortable seating areas, and smiling staff behind large desks. The gate to Derry is marked by a small single "83" over double doors that read, "Do Not Enter."

At Heathrow, they don't announce the Belfast flights. There are no check-in desks or airline personnel. In short, if you are new, you have to ask the other passengers sitting around smoking, drinking coffee, and scowling if you are in the right place. At the appointed time. Or thereabout. The rope is removed, the doors open, and the passengers file through and onto the plane.

On my boarding pass at Stansted it says, "Boarding announcements may not be made for your flight. Please check the departure boards and/or TV monitors for boarding information." That's grand except there is no announcement, no board, no proper gate, just 83 and "Do Not Enter."

Tenth flight across the Atlantic this year. Seated next to snot-nosed teenager on group holiday with other snot-nosed teenagers. This because I was greedy and hopped an earlier flight. This because I gave up my perfectly good seat to another snot-nosed teen so she could sit with her snot-nosed girlfriends and snap flash-photos and giggle loudly for the entire journey. Punishment and reward. I'm tired. Have I gone mad? Only seven more hours. Just breathe.

It would be fair to ask, "What were you thinking when you said yes to this project?" I guess I was thinking it was an honor to be asked to participate. The only excuse I have for keeping at it, I suppose, is it is not in my nature to quit.

My last trip to Derry was with mixed emotions. It was to be my first interview with Tony Doherty. After hostile words from the McGuigan family, I wasn't sure what to expect from Tony. I knew the politics between the families meant I had to please Nash to get Wray and please Wray to get McGuigan, but I didn't know which camp Tony was in. Did I need to go through someone specific to get him to participate? Was he the key to another family?

By this time my frustration at the seeming lack of interest from the families in documenting the lost lives was mounting. Every trip I made to Derry I thought, "This time they will be excited!" I now had six narratives in the bag and I felt since they seemed pleased with the results more families would become active in the process. I had hope and things did go well that trip. Catherine, my wonderful transcriptionist, scheduled interviews for me. This was the first time I heard before I arrived that yes, someone would meet with me. Ivan booked a room at the Tower for me and Rhondalee Nash was doing background research that would save me loads of time. I was elated.

Tony Doherty was hesitant but gracious. I met with the McDaids as we were nearing their final version. John Nash was feeling satisfied with Willie's story. John Duddy told me more about Johnny Johnston and we spent several happy hours looking through photos. Mrs. McKinney tolerated me sprawled on her living room floor and patiently told me her stories of Willie.

YES! I had hope. Could it be that I hadn't accounted for the time it would take for them to trust me? I felt good about our progress. I felt that now we were moving efficiently and more people would participate. The inquiry was coming to a close and we would finish the book as well. However, I soon learn that being trustworthy doesn't mean people will trust you. Making good on your word does not mean others will make good on theirs. All this healthy progress and cooperation was a blip.

The next two trips were back to the old routine. Little cooperation. No communication. My first trip to Derry I spent the better part of a month just trying to find a transcriptionist. Most of the families didn't even know why I was there. I showed up countless times to interviews and they didn't have a clue, "Who are you? What do you want? Why are you here?" I wrote letters of introduction. I sent regular updates and progress reports. How can they not know?! I wonder. Am I the problem? Or are they?

I suspect it is a bit of both, but I feel like I am working hard to produce a quality document and they don't give a shit. Isn't it in their interest to give a shit? Then I realize maybe it is a cultural thing. Maybe I just don't speak the right language. After all, I have learned some things about the cultural differences in our language.

For example, when Paul Mahon testified before the Saville Inquiry that Liam Wray threatened him, I knew it was just a matter of cultural misunderstanding. I don't know what, if anything, transpired in the bar between Liam and Paul, but I have learned that in Derry, "I am going to kill you" is typically just polite conversation.

If your house is firebombed. If you receive a beating that puts you in the hospital. If your wife is run over by a car. Then, and only then, you can figure you've been threatened and most probably something terrible is on the horizon for you.

I know this because I was confused for so long. When people said,

"I will find money for the project."

"I will line up your interviews."
"I will make sure the Trust understands the project."
"I will find a transcriptionist."
I thought they meant,
"I will find money."
"I will line up interviews."
"I will find you a transcriptionist."

"I will make the Trust understand." After all, in my neighborhood, if someone says "I will do it," that typically means, "I will do it." Not in Derry.

See?! It is a simple cultural difference. I just didn't realize it and I let it frustrate me. When a person in Derry says they are going to do something and they mean it, it is done immediately. All you have to do is wait 24 hours. If that time passes and it's not done, whatever they said, they didn't mean it. They were just being nice.

Therefore, if Liam said to Paul Mahon, "I am going to kill you," and that is what he meant, I have every reason to believe Paul would be dead now and clearly not able to tell his confused story to Saville. Since Paul Mahon is indeed alive and kicking and running his mouth—I can only conclude that Liam Wray did not threaten to kill him.

See? I finally get it! Now I can stop torturing myself with, "How many times to I have to turn up? How many documents do I have to produce? What do I have to do to get them to trust me? To get them involved? To get them to do something? After all, THEY ASKED ME!" and just get on with the project. This time I tell myself, if you are going to do a thing, stop complaining and just get on with it.

Despite finally understanding the cultural differences in approach to the project, I've now charged over $15,000 on my American Express to support it, I owe hundreds of favors to friends who watch my kids so I can travel to Derry, my clients are amazing and totally understanding but a week away every month is causing them to question my commitment to their work, and so I am starting to feel a little taken advantage of by my Derry friends.

On this particular day I reach my ATM withdraw limit paying our (our....again with the our) research assistant and transcriptionist. I walk into the Bloody Sunday family center where half-a-dozen people are hanging out and ask, "Could I borrow £20?" Everyone looks around. I swore on my life I'd return the money the next day. I wasn't out of money, I'd just reached my daily withdraw limit. Did I mention I reached my withdraw limit paying "our" transcriptionist? For the book they asked me to write?! Did I mention the transcriptionist was related to them?! I thought with so many of them sitting around they could all chip in a few pounds and get me where I was going. Nope. They made me sign an I.O.U.

MAGILLIGAN BEACH

Ivan and I drive out the winding road to Magilligan Beach. I can't see the prison/Army barracks. It is hidden among dunes and reeds. Next to the car park stands a white building which houses a pub. A place to wait for the ferry that crosses Lough Foyle to the mountains of Donegal. Along the quiet inlet runs a narrow stretch of sand the end of which turns sharply right. On the day we visit it is cold and blowing. We spend our time indoors out of the wind but I make a brief sojourn down to the beach and attempt to walk around the corner. Met by the sight of a military tower I stop in my tracks. I see no activity or personnel but it is ominous enough to turn me back. Over drinks at the wee pub by the water Ivan tells me about the civil rights march at Magilligan.

Magilligan was an auxiliary base where members of the Territorial Army went at weekends to engage in maneuvers and target practice. It was augmented as a regular Army base in about 1970.

The intention of the Magilligan march was to march towards the internment camp that was close to Magilligan beach. We planned to march straight through the camp as a demonstration not only against internment but as a show of solidarity with and support for the interned prisoners. The march started off and was almost immediately rerouted by the Army down onto the beach at Magilligan.

I had actually insisted that the march proceed on the beach specifically to avoid any violence and any rioting. There were no stones on the beach and I felt that by marching on the beach we had in effect removed the risk of trouble. It was therefore much to my astonishment to find that the PARAs had set themselves up on the beach behind barbed wire.

The PARAs were much more belligerent than the soldiers who patrolled earlier demonstrations and it was very obvious to those of us who had been involved in many civil rights demonstrations that they were going to take an offensive position and use a very heavy hand.

The meeting point was a ballroom up on the main Limavady Castle Rock Road. We then marched from the ballroom down the road where the Army forced us off the road and onto the beach. When we got to the beach, we decided to march along the beach and back up to the camp. The PARAs had erected timber and barbed wire barricades on the beach to prevent us from reaching the base. So, with hundreds of people milling about, we were faced with the decision of where to go next.

I was speaking to Sharpe, a senior police officer, regarding the march being rerouted and prevented from getting near the camp when one of the paratroopers fired a rubber bullet at point-blank range, which hit me by my temple. I was knocked unconscious for about 7-8 minutes. When I became conscious, the violence had begun.

I did not know at the time what precipitated it but what followed was very violent treatment on the part of the Paratroopers toward the marchers and quite a number of marchers received head wounds as a result of being struck by the PARAs' very long battens. We realized that this was a heavy-handed regiment who were anxious to be cut loose on the civil rights demonstrators. We felt that the Army was using the Paratroopers—a group trained for battle, not crowd control—specifically to bring an end to all civil rights marches. They behaved extremely aggressively towards the peaceful protesters. They were very rough and using rubber bullets.

The following week, a march was planned for Derry. As we planned for the 30th January march, our intention was to have a number of small parades, drawn from different areas of the city, feeding into the main demonstration. Meetings were held in various parts of the city to organize the routes that would feed into a main demonstration, ending at Guildhall Square. The Guildhall in Derry is the seat of power of the local council—the local corporation—but at that time, symbolically, it was the political heartland of the city.

Invitations to speak at the rally had gone out to Lord Fenner Brockway, 91-year-old member of the British House of Lords, who had a lifetime of campaigning for human rights and civil rights in various parts of the world; Reverend Terrence McCaughey, Presbyterian chaplain at Trinity College, Dublin who was also a personal friend of mine; Bernadette Devlin, the youngest ever Westminster MP, elected at age 23, who by that time was already enjoying an international reputation; Rory McShane, the chairman of NICRA; and me.

The treatment of marchers by the PARAs at Magilligan and discussions with the police led us to believe that it could be dangerous to have feeder parades coming from various parts of the city. It was felt that perhaps there would be counter demonstrations capable of inflaming the situation and so we abandoned the idea of having the feeder marches and decided to have one main march starting at Bishop's Field and taking the route via William Street to the Guildhall Square. We informed the police or our decision.

During that week, I met with the IRA and made clear that if there was any possibility of the IRA engaging the Army with gunfire I would use my influence as a leader in the civil rights movement to call off the demonstration. The IRA listened intently and told me that they would come back to me shortly.

Martin McGuinness, in a statement to the Saville Inquiry, has accepted the figures, which I have been on record as saying that in Derry in 1972 there couldn't have been any more than thirty to thrity-five members of the IRA and they had very little weaponry. I have never spoken to McGuinness about Bloody Sunday but it is interesting that his assessment of the strengths is similar to mine.

The leadership of the IRA in Derry at that time was getting substantial criticism from the leadership in Dublin about their lack of real activity. I believe that their lack of real activity emanated from the fact that they had very little support on the ground amongst the general populace despite the fact that internment had been operating for quite some time. The campaign against internment was led by people who were committed to non-violence and the general population of the city was of that frame of mind.

The second thing that McGuinness has accepted is that there was very little weaponry. Meaning the Derry IRA lacked hardware. I believe the reason for that was the IRA didn't have enough money coming in to properly equip their various units.

The leadership of the IRA in the city was scared of the general antipathy toward the IRA so it wasn't a terribly effective paramilitary. It didn't have a great deal of support as a political organization either. Ill-equipped, lacking in purpose, lacking in hardware, lacking in manpower, lacking in general support of the population, condemnation of the activities they were involved in, and widespread support of the expressions of condemnation, the Derry IRA wasn't making any headlines. The anti-internment campaign was spearheaded by people committed to non-violence who made their views known. The consensus of the population at that time was, we are opposed to internment and we are opposed to pursuing violence.

After internment was introduced in 1971, the people of the Bogside erected barricades on the perimeter and refused access to the police and the Army. Approach by forces at any of the twenty-nine barricades was met with stone throwing and harassment. They thus created the first effective no-go area. They took the stance of full resistance to the Army and police forces in an attempt to make certain no further people from that area would be scooped by the Army, taken to Magilligan, and interned without trial.

In 1971 the Citizens Defense Committee (CDC) was created. As anyone approaching the barricades could be subject to harassment, the CDC issued permits to people delivering essential goods and services. Leaders of the CDC, Sean Keenan, Michael Canavan, and Paddy "Bogside" Doherty, insured safe passage for milkmen, bread men, postmen, social security payments, etc. The CDC also dealt with petty criminality and potential petty criminality operating in the area.

The no-go area was a source of great concern to the unionist government and indeed to the British Government because here was a place, ostensibly part of the United Kingdom, where the writ of the Army, police, and government did not run.

This open defiance to the British Government should be seen in the context that it was: Open defiance and protest to internment without trial. Something which struck at the heart of the whole nationalist community.

DERRY

Ivan and I walk. We. Us. Friends. Traveling companions. Given the impact to Ivan's life, I should know more about Bloody Sunday. It's time. We stand near Bishop's Field in Creggan and begin our routine.

I pull the digital recorder from my bag, attach the pen microphone and place it in Ivan's breast pocket. I place the microphone pen to the inside of his working pen. Just in case. Then I tell him, I'm listening. Tell me again why you had to march that Sunday. Geez, wasn't it cold? It's cold in Derry in July. It's cold today.

I stamp my feet, rub my hands, and tighten my scarf. How do you go around in a suit jacket like that all the time? I know you have a coat. It's in the back of your car. It's just never on you. Anyway, hadn't the civil rights demands had been met? One man one vote, equal opportunity for jobs, education, and housing? I reach over and rub Ivan's arms. He takes my hand and we walk.

Well my dear, many of the civil rights demands had been met. One man one vote had been conceded, an end to electoral gerrymandering had been achieved, the Derry City Corporation — the old unionist corporation — had been shelved and replaced by a commission. Legislation in relation to discrimination in employment and a points system with regard to the fair allocation of houses had been invoked. But one civil rights demand was still outstanding: internment without trial.

Our bright sunny spring day is a stark contrast to the rainy day thirteen coffins lined the church to our left. Saint Mary's, Creggan, filled with mourners was a stark contrast to the jovial crowd that filed past her on the 30th of January 1972.

It was a carnival atmosphere as the crowd gathered. Marches had become a culture and these people turned up because it was a day's outing. There had been a lull in the marches. We had taken the pursuit of civil rights off the streets and into Parliament. A lorry was placed at the head, followed by the twenty thousand marchers, some of whom were singing the civil rights song 'We Shall Overcome.' This was the anthem that had been used by the Northern Ireland civil rights movement from 1968. The atmosphere on the march that day was extremely good. I can remember the songs.

You've got to remember that Derry is a city where its women worked. In those days its men were largely unemployed. There wasn't any employment. The women worked in the shirt industry and before I became an member of Parliament I was an executive in the shirt industry. If you look at the fingers which a Derry girl has and many years ago I used to remember them round my neck, it's a long time since they've been there. Derry girls have long slender fingers and this is derived from the shirt industry because we've had a shirt industry in this city for over 250 years. So the atmosphere was a carnival atmosphere of men, women, and children.

Ivan and I walk down the New Road. Technically the street name is Eastway but no one in Derry calls it that and if you ask someone to show you where Eastway is they will look at you like you have two heads. Ask for the New Road and all is well.

I've always liked holding hands. I've always held hands with friends. It is nice holding hands with you.

I like holding hands with you too Ivan.

When John and I were elected to Stormont, our intention was to take the civil rights struggle off the streets and into Parliament. But on the ninth of August nineteen and seventy-one, the largest and deadliest internment raids swept through Derry and Belfast. Internment meant being awakened before dawn to the din of garbage can lids being banged on the streets. Internment meant that none of the men in a Catholic household were safe. They could be removed at any time without warning or justification and held indefinitely. By the New Year internment raids had swept more than nine hundred Derry men from their homes and families.

Reports of illegal interrogation techniques began to surface including stories of sensory deprivation and beatings, a diet of bread and water, and being kept spread-eagle against a wall for up to sixteen hours at a stretch, always hooded and denied sleep while the roar of a jet engine drown out the sound of everything else. They were beaten when they fell, then dragged before Special Branch officers for questioning before being sent back to the wall again. These interrogation techniques were developed based on the experiences of British soldiers who had been taken prisoner in the Korean War.

I wonder if the British soldiers captured in Korea would say they were subjected to inhuman and degrading treatment, or, if they would say they were tortured?

Must you always provide color commentary? Ending internment through diplomatic and political channels was unsuccessful. We decided, therefore, that it was necessary to bring international attention to the issue of internment. The civil rights demonstration was our outlet.

As you know we marched from Bishop's Field, down past St. Eugene's and on to Rossville Street. There were young men who stopped to throw stones at the Army at Barrier 14 but most of the marchers followed the lorry which would be used as a platform for the speeches. I had just stepped up on the bed of the lorry to join the other speechmakers when up to my right, I noticed—positioned on the Derry walls I could see soldiers. I knew that some of them were snipers and from their elevated position were capable of firing down on our platform. In the distance I could see soldiers charging into the Bogside accompanied by Saracen trucks. Then, for the first time in my life, I saw lead skipping on the road.

Hysteria and fear had taken over. Bullets were flying all around us. The snipers on the walls were firing down and the

Paratroopers were firing straight at us. People were scurrying in all directions. I noticed ahead of me a man. A young man who had been at every civil rights demonstration. I spoke to him before this march moved off.

Jim Wray and his father were almost fanatical converts to the whole philosophy of non-violence. We had taught Jim: sit down in front of the Army Saracens. Non-violence is the way to highlight our cause. Refuse to be drawn into violence. Let the violence be used against us. That was the philosophy of Gandhi in India with the British. That was the philosophy of Martin Luther King, Jr. in America.

I caught sight of Jim sitting on the ground near the Rossville Street barricade. A one-man sit-in. He had something on his head. A woolen hat. I remember him sitting there, this student of non-violence, this believer in non-violence. He was carrying out the plan. Sit down. Let them bring the violence upon you and the world will see it. Later, as Jim fled approaching soldiers, he was shot.

Then, as Jim lay wounded, a soldier picked through the bodies laying in the grass. One PARA appeared to be wearing a different coloured jacket to the other Paratroopers. Although the jacket was green, its colour and markings seemed to stand out more than the jackets that the other Paratroopers were wearing. He was holding his rifle down by his hip with the muzzle down toward the ground, as if patrolling.

He made no move to search Willie McKinney or Joe Mahon dying and injured nearby. Effectively he walked in a direct line toward Jim Wray. He did not try and search Jim or look for a weapon of any kind. He saw Jim's shoulders move and realised he was still alive. The soldier then pointed the rifle at Jim's back and fired two shots at point blank range.

BANG!
BANG!
Jim Wray's coat moved twice and he was dead.

I had also spoken with William McKinney. Willie worked as a compositor for Derry Journal and had a hobby with photography. When I spoke with him he had two cameras around his neck. He told me about the pictures he hoped to take. Willie was twenty-six years old. The eldest of ten children. He was shot while running for cover with his hands over his head. A woman who saw him just before he was shot said he looked absolutely terrified.

Dr McClean was with Willie for the last. He went over to him and Willie said, "Doctor am I going to get better?"

Dr McClean says, "I told that fella a wee white lie, I said, 'The ambulance is coming now and they'll take you to Altnagelvin and you'll be all right.' It's wile lonely when you're dying, so I held his hand until he died."

"When I was a young man I bought my clothes from Austin's, the largest shop in the Diamond. It has been established for one hundred fifty years. I used to buy clothes in the men's department of that shop from a man called Johnny Johnson. Johnny was a man who always attired himself in smart suits. He was 62. He wore a hat. He was the second man shot that day. Johnny and Damien (Bubbles) Donaghy were shot about fifteen minutes before the heavy firing began.

It has been speculated that they were shot in an effort to draw fire from the IRA. As there were no IRA guns in the Bogside that day no gunfire was returned. As with much of Bloody Sunday why Bubbles and Johnnie were shot in a waste yard away from the march will probably never be known.

But there is one particular memory which is burned into my mind and it probably will be forever and that is of a man named

Barney McGuigan. I was his boss in the shirt industry. I knew him very well and I also knew his brother Chuck who was a country and western singer. I was very heavily pinned down with the gunfire and I was crawling toward the high flats. Barney was calling to me and he was trying to alert me to the fact that someone was seriously wounded right beside him.

I remember him waving a white cloth or a white hankie and as I called him. As I was shouting to him. As he was shouting back to me. I saw him shot down dead.

The summer before Barney died a friend of his asked him could he make a headstone for this fella's mother who had died? This particular family couldn't afford a headstone at the time and so Barney made the headstone in his back yard and he and his sons took it down and placed it at the woman's grave. As a result, Barney was inundated with people who wanted a stone. Before he died, Barney made nine in all. The nine headstones stand in the City Cemetery today.

If Barney had stayed by the phone box he likely would have survived Bloody Sunday. But he heard Paddy Doherty crying for help so he took a handkerchief and waved it over is head saying, 'They won't shoot me. I've got to go help this man.' Then he stepped out to go to Paddy's side.

I have never been able to face Barney's family. His widow. His six children. Barney was going to help Paddy Doherty, a father of six as well. A stranger to Barney. Paddy was crying out, witnesses have said, crying that he did not want to die alone. It was a senseless loss of life.

In the midst of this terrible hysteria, I was carrying a great feeling of personal guilt. I helped to bring those people onto the street. The march started off in a carnival atmosphere. People sang songs. I walked down in front of the lorry for a short period with

John Bearman of the BBC. It was a jovial, happy, strong march of men, women, and children. Now people were dead. I didn't know exactly how many. Ten? Twelve? In the end there were thirteen names. We were faced with telling the families. I don't think I can ever forget the way some of those people cried.

In John Hume's house that night I received tidbits of information about the large number of people who had been arrested in an arrest operation that ran parallel to the murder of innocent civilians. I learned that many people, including priests, had been badly abused. The bad news. This horrible day. Seemed to go on and on.

Then, the most devastating thing of all happened. As people watched the television news reports, the moment came that sealed Northern Ireland's fate for the next 30 years. The British Government told the world that those shot dead were nail bombers and gunmen. I later learned that the main instrument for the promulgation of that propaganda was the British Consulate in New York. They poured out the lie to the international community.

In the following forty-eight hours, the entirety of Derry stepped out to wake our dead. Thousands of people moved from house to house offering solace to as many families as they could reach. On Tuesday, caskets containing the bodies of the men and boys murdered by the British Paratroopers were delivered to St. Mary's Chapel streaming down from Creggan and up from the Bogside all through the evening.

Conducted by the Cardinal, the funerals were attended by the great and the good. I decided I had to walk to the funerals because I wanted to walk part of the route. The route which had been followed on Sunday by those people who were asking the British Government for the same rights as the people of Cardiff, London, Glasgow, and Birmingham. And as I walked to the church the

Cardinal's car passed by. He was comfortable and safe in the backseat.

When I got to the church the official cars of the Irish government ministers were arriving. Cabinet members and politicians. I couldn't help thinking all of these great people weren't with us on the streets on Sunday when the blood of innocent people was spilled by a regiment of the British Army sent in to do a job. Sent in to end the embarrassment of the Unionists and the British Government.

Not many of them, the great and the good, I felt fully appreciated what had happened in our city that day. Because those of us who believed in non-violence, those who followed it passionately, realized only too well that the IRA were the greatest victors. People were now saying to me, fuck your non-violence Cooper. Fuck your Martin Luther King, Jr. There is only one way to deal with this now.

I have carried a tremendous guilt since that day. I had a hand in putting those people on the street and they were gunned down in cold blood.

ONE END

I traveled. I neglected my children. My family. My work responsibilities. I worked my ass off. I paid people when I was not getting paid. I told my children, 'Shhhh.....just a minute, I'm writing' hundreds of times. Missing out on two years of their young lives. I gave the Bloody Sunday families and the book all of me. But the day came that I simply ran out of money.

It's over. Still I am plagued with questions: "What could I have done differently? How could I have better helped the project be a success? Was the timing bad? Everyone is so exhausted from the Inquiry. Maybe it was the timing?" I wished all the families could share in what I thought was such an enriching and positive experience. I am angry and frustrated, yes. But more so, wondering: "If only....What if....How could I have...."

I wish they knew how much I came to love them all. How much I treasured every minute I sat on the living room floor at the feet of Mrs. McKinney; dining late into the night with the Gerard McKinney clan, listening to Uncle Louis' stories and joining his boisterous laugh; how I was giddy with the simple fact that I knew a short-cut to the McDaid's house; my feeling of gratitude to Lee and Hazel from Ivan's office who were there for me everyday through thick and thin never judging, always available, endlessly kind; Leo Carlin's insistence that I eat every day and his family's open embrace; how Kathleen Gilmour's smile and always ready offer of a cigarette made me feel welcome; Gerry Duddy's gruff exterior that was belied with his tenderness for his family and his engulfing bear hug; his wife Ann's fry; the Nash family supper table where we hashed things out and especially Padraig who brought me chocolate; Maura Young who let me off the hook when I was human and walked me around Derry that first week making sure I had my bearings; Mary Doherty's kind smile and gentle spirit; Tony Doherty's leap of faith; the twinkle in Margaret Wray's eyes that must remind people of her mother; Karen Carlin nee Doherty's raw honesty; the Kelly family devotion to their mother; John Duddy's wink, smile, and coffee-talk; and of course Ivan who got me into this mess. In spite of all the problems I wish we had more time. Carpe diem. You may not be granted one more moment to sit on hills and watch the sun set.

HOME

They are remodeling Terminal 1 of Heathrow. The Gate to Belfast is still dodgy but now it's Gate 2 not 12 and it is a whole contained section on its own. It is still the only place to smoke in Terminal 1. It is comforting to know that some things are sacred.

I had to stop traveling to Derry but I kept my promise. Though I was exhausted and close to bankruptcy, I saw it through and the book was published.

THE BOGSIDE

Ivan and I sit in the lobby of the tower hotel. Ivan prepares to board a bus filled with geriatric tourists. Ivan sees me frantically texting and enquires as to the status of a friend arriving from Cork.

Where is he?

In Donegal, being chased by the cops.

What does that mean?

His last text said he was hiding on a beach, evading the police.

Does the guy know Donegal roads?

I'm not saying he knows anything.

The bus is going to be back at five. So you're going.

Two hours with geezers. Geez, Ivan. Here she comes.

"Oh Ivan! How wonderful of you to do this. We are all so looking forward to your talk."

Ivan gestures toward me. *She's coming along. She is writing a book about the families of those who died on Bloody Sunday.*

"Ahhh, OK.....so that's not a Derry accent."

Right, Jennifer, on the bus.

This is where learning to drink whiskey in Ireland pays off. I consume what's left in my glass with no ill effects—like it's water—and head for the loo. By the time I get on the bus they are looking for me. The head geezer sings out, "Here's the blonde you're looking for!" and I sing back, 'I'm the blonde he's looking for!' I put on my best face, but Ivan upstages me asking the bus driver, *What do you think?* To which the driver replies, "She'll just do, ya know?" They get a big belly laugh out of that. I stick the pen microphone in Ivan's breast pocket and take my place next to an aging Canadian.

The head geezer announces, "OK ladies and gentlemen, I'd like to introduce you to Ivan Cooper. To any of you who are Irish or anyone who knows anything of the history here, he's certainly a well-known person. Yesterday we saw the film Bloody Sunday as a group so thank you so much for doing this for us Ivan. We much appreciate you who had the real experience of what this was about so please say hello to Ivan Cooper and the lady in the middle of the bus who is writing a book and I am sure Ivan will tell us what that's about."

Thank you. First, to put it in complete perspective, I am a contradiction in Northern Ireland in relation to politics because although this city is a predominantly Catholic city and the civil rights movement, of which I was a part, was a predominantly Catholic cause, I am afraid I am Church of Ireland. I'm a Protestant. I became involved in this area down here which you see which is called the Bogside. I have been going to that area since I was twelve years of age and I befriended some people in this area who are still my friends to this day. I became very much involved in the struggle for civil rights. The housing conditions which you see today bear no relation to the housing conditions which existed in nineteen and sixty-eight. In nineteen and forty-five the Americans had a camp just outside this city and when they vacated that camp people started to live there. I can recollect in nineteen and sixty-eight there was a forty-four percent mortality rate in that camp for children under the age of seven. People were living in desperate conditions and when I think that it is only a matter of thirty-five years ago it's hard to imagine the conditions in which people lived.

Can I just tell you, before I start to do the tour, can I just tell you that I have a special nostalgia for Toronto because my father went there in nineteen and twenty-seven with the intention of taking all of us there to seek a new life. Unfortunately my mother took septicemia and he had to come back. I was there last November and every time I go there I have a lump in my throat because I can remember the stories which my father told of him going out on a liner to go to Canada to seek a new life. You may know Eaton's, a famous store in Toronto. That store was founded by a family who lived not far from where I was brought up just outside this city. So we have a very special affection for and a very special connection with Toronto.

So we'll go on this little journey. As you probably have seen our city is a walled city. The siege we had here was the longest siege in European history. It lasted from the eighteenth of December sixteen and eighty-eight to the twelfth of August sixteen and eighty-nine. The siege of Derry has very special significance to Protestantism. When I was a young man being brought up these walls had a very symbolic effect to Protestantism. Nowadays these walls belong to all of us. Catholic and Protestant. The walls themselves have had an effect in shaping our political history in Northern Ireland our modern day political history.

This is the Bogside we're going down into now. Unfortunately over the last thirty five years it has seen some very tragic events. Many people lost their lives not far from where we are now. In particular I think of Bloody Sunday. I'm glad to hear that some of you have seen the film. As you probably know the role of Ivan Cooper, the role of my person was taken by a man called Jimmy Nesbitt and I believe that he played it with great sensitivity and great courage.

When I look at the housing conditions that exist in this city today, my mind goes back to the housing conditions which prevailed thirty-five years ago. A very high rate of tuberculosis. Very high rates of all types of illness and disease which shortened people's lives. People were living here in hovels. The conditions they were living in were not much better than those for animals. The other important thing to remember is that thirty-five years ago, people in this area did not have the universal franchise. In other words they couldn't vote in local governmental elections to shape the future of the city.

Unionism and Protestantism had a system of controlling this city called gerrymandering. Gerrymandering meant that two-thirds of this city, which was nationalist, only elected eight members to the local corporation and the one-third unionist and Protestant population elected twelve members to the corporation.

That was a permanent feature and they achieved that by two things. First of all they achieved it by failing to build houses. It was a deliberate policy not to build houses. Secondly they achieved it by maintaining a policy which meant that if a father and mother lived in a house with five children over the age of twenty-one only the mother and father had a vote. So in other words they disenfranchised a large number of people. They also maintained their power by the use of something called the Special Powers Act and if you had an interest in Irish history or Irish music what was very likely to happen to you is you would be interned without trial under something called the Special Powers Act. We had discrimination in employment. We had discrimination in housing. The overwhelming bulk of this discrimination was used against the Catholic community. Against the nationalist community.

When I came to the Bogside at twelve years of age I was appalled by the housing conditions which I had seen. I was appalled by the fact that many young men who were the same age as me stood less of a chance of getting employment even though their capacity and education was even greater than mine. Because of my Protestant background I would have been able in those days to obtain employment in a position of status much easier than any Catholic young man of my age. Out of that was born the civil rights movement.

The civil rights movement in this city was not led only by people from the Catholic community. I was chairman of the civil rights movement in Derry. The vice chairman was at that time a man called John Hume. John Hume went on to become a Westminster Member of Parliament. He went on to become a winner of the Nobel Peace Prize and he lives in these houses which you see just ahead of us. John is still a European Member of Parliament and he is still a Westminster Member of Parliament.

There is a political party in Northern Ireland called the SDLP and the SDLP was founded by a man called Paddy O'Hanlon, John Hume, and Ivan Cooper who's speaking to you now. The three of us founded what is now the second largest political party in Northern Ireland. All of my political career I was committed to non-violence. That was my stand in nineteen and sixty-eight and that is how I feel today.

I have looked at the world and whenever you reach the age of almost sixty you tend to look at the world in a wider vision. When I look at the world the more I look at it the more I believe that the only way to solve any problem is by peaceful means and by attempts at reconciliation. We are now approaching the Creggan Estates. My principal reason for asking the driver to be kind enough to take us to the Creggan Estates is this is where the Bloody Sunday march started off in nineteen and seventy-two.

All of the civil rights reforms had been achieved within a period of three or four months after our march on the fifth of October in nineteen and sixty-eight. The march on the fifth of October nineteen and sixty-eight was held on the waterside in Derry. We were to march to the cityside. The police banned that march and when we went ahead with it the police battened us.

But the wider world saw that we were people demonstrating peacefully. We were told by the British Government that we were part of the United Kingdom and we were demanding the same rights as the people of Manchester or Birmingham or Glasgow or London or Cardiff. When the wider world saw us on television being treated in such a brutal way there was a massive amount of outrage and arising from that there were further marches which meant that all of the civil rights demands were conceded within a period of 3-4 months.

The Derry Corporation was kicked out and a commission was put in place and that commission set about to building much of the housing in the Bogside and that housing revolutionized housing conditions. This is the Creggan Estates and as you can see the housing is of a very good standard. There was one civil rights *demand which remained outstanding in nineteen and seventy-two and that was the use of the Special Powers Act. The Special Powers Act gave power to the government of Northern Ireland to intern people without trial. In nineteen and seventy-one once again the unionist government decided to intern people without trial and we decided to hold a civil rights march on the last Sunday of January nineteen and seventy-two.*

The thing that you've got to remember is that in nineteen and seventy-two I had then been elected a Member of Parliament. We had attempted within Parliament to obtain an end to the Special Powers Act legislation which meant that people were interned without trial for having an interest in Irish music or Irish culture or anything of that nature anything which unionism described as alien.

To the right we've just come back from Bishop's field. This is where the march started on the last Sunday of January nineteen and seventy-two. It was our intention to go to the Guildhall Square in Derry—that's the city hall—hold the demonstration there, and disperse. On the thirtieth of January nineteen and seventy-two our twenty thousand people came down past the Cathedral and entered this street which is ahead of us and which is called William Street preceded by the lorry. Ahead of us we could see that the Army had cordoned off the bottom part of the street. They had erected barriers which prevented us from being able to gain access to the Guildhall. You can see the Guildhall ahead of us here which is a replica of the Guildhall of London. We could see that we could not get down the full route and so we took the decision to bring the lorry to the right. Right into the Bogside.

It was our intention that the crowd of twenty thousand would follow us and there were stewards positioned just here to wheel the crowd into the Bogside. We would make speeches about the use of internment without trial and the use of the Special Powers Act. The Army barrier was situated down ahead of us where you see the news agents. We decided not to have a confrontation but to head over to Free Derry Corner which is ahead of us now. So, the platform was situated immediately in front of that wall. There were four speakers that day: Bernadette Devlin who was the youngest ever Westminster MP, Lord Fenner Brockway of the British House of Commons, the Reverend Terrance McCauley who was a Presbyterian minister from Dublin, and Ivan Cooper.

I had just started to speak whenever I heard bullets being fired. I believed it was rubber bullets being fired. Fired from this direction down here that we've just come up. And I remember, I said to Bernadette Devlin, I paused when I head the thumping of what I interpreted was rubber bullets, and I said to her, 'Rubber bullets' and she said to me, "It's lead, Coops."

For the very first time in my life, I looked on the ground and I could see lead skipping on the ground. It's a remarkable quick quirk of the mind, but as I saw that led skipping on the road, my mind went back to my boyhood days. At the bottom of some of the fields near my home was the Fahan River where my brother and I and our friends frequently skimmed stones. The tactic was to try to get a stone to skip six times. That indicated a great skim. As I watched those lead bullets skipping off the road, near our platform at Free Derry Corner, I couldn't help thinking of the skimming days near the Faghan River. But then very quickly I was conscious of the crowd. Hysteria and fear had taken over. Bullets were flying all around us. The snipers on the walls were firing down and the Paratroopers ahead of us were firing straight at us.

It was like hailstones there was so much of it. My father had served in the British Forces during the war. My Protestant family had a tradition of respect for the British Army. Even though I was involved in civil rights encounters I couldn't believe that any regiment would open fire where there were twenty thousand men, women, and children.

In a period of sixteen minutes thirteen people had been shot dead. A short time later Johnny Johnston, who used to work in a clothes shop where I used to buy clothes, died as well. So fourteen people died from gunshot wounds on Bloody Sunday.

Those of you who have seen the film will know that Bloody Sunday had a devastating effect in this city. Because by far the greatest sin of all was that that night the British Consulate in New York put out the message that those who had lost their lives were all either carrying weapons and firing them or throwing nail bombs. Those of us who had been here that day knew that that was a lie. Those of us who were committed to non-violence knew the Army had not been fired on by our march nor had there been any petrol bombs or nail bombs thrown. They pumped out their propaganda and we buried our dead.

Two days after Bloody Sunday residents of Dublin burned the British Embassy to the ground. It is my view that Bloody Sunday was the greatest watershed in recent Irish history. First of all it created a chasm between Dublin and London that took years to repair. It created a breach between Catholic and Protestant which we are still reaping the rewards of today.

Then it was the turn of the unionist government to poison and lie. They told the Protestant population of Northern Ireland that the civil rights leaders were enemies of the state. They were all Republicans. That NICRA was a front for the IRA, determined to overthrow the unionist government and force people into a united Ireland. The smears, the propaganda, the lies, poisoned the Protestant people into believing the murders on Bloody Sunday were justified.

But more important still, from a situation in which very few people in those days supported the IRA and where they had very few weapons, it breathed into the lungs of militant and armed Republicanism a large degree of public support because of the outrage. In my view, as a result of Bloody Sunday, we've had to live with thirty years of violence in which the IRA carried out very dastardly deeds including the murders of many innocent people.

The outrage over Bloody Sunday throughout the world was so great the British Government decided to hold a Tribunal of Inquiry. Headed by the Lord Chief Justice of England and Wales, Lord Widgery, he held that whilst some firing by the Army bordered on the reckless, a number of those who died that day had either been throwing nail bombs or firing weapons. I come from a stubborn race of people. They call them Irish. Those of us that were there that day knew that was a lie. But more significantly it was a whitewash. In other words, a Lord Chief Justice got into bed with the lies perpetrated by the Consulate.

So the relatives of those who died on Bloody Sunday held a campaign which went on for many years demanding a second enquiry. For the first time ever in British judicial history, a second inquiry was convened. It is called the Saville Inquiry. I don't know what the outcome of that inquiry will be but I can tell you a couple of extremely significant things. The lawyer who represents the Queen's Counsel on the very first day stood up and said that the ministry and government accepted that none of those shot that day were carrying a weapon or throwing a nail bomb.

After all these years. After all the propaganda. After all the whitewash. He said that on the first day of the Inquiry. There are people in this community who criticize the vast amount of money which has been devoted to the holding of this inquiry and it is significant. There are other people who point out that the IRA carried out some terrible deeds in this land. That is true. They did. But Bloody Sunday was perpetrated by the forces of the Crown. It was perpetrated by those who should be upholding law. Who should be serving all of us. Who should be protecting all of us and that is a significant difference.

And so we don't know what the outcome of the Inquiry is going to be. What are we after? A judicial declaration of innocence. Now, the young lady who is sitting in the bus who is a friend of mine, Jennifer Faus, who comes from Chicago, has been here I think about thirty times and she's writing a book and she's concentrating her book on the young men who died. And I must tell you that it has been an illuminating experience for me. To read some of the things which she has managed to research and find out. Because those who died were young men.

In nineteen and sixty-eight this area had housing which was so very very bad. It's almost indescribable in today's terms. Secondly, we had forty-four percent of our men out of work. Thirdly, we were denied rights. We were denied the right to vote. To influence. Fourthly, we had a Special Powers Act which was destined to crush anything Irish. Fifthly, we had discrimination in employment and housing based on a person's religious beliefs. And lastly we had discrimination in housing because housing meant that people were given votes.

What of the future? I am optimistic about the future. We have two right traditions in this community. One is the Protestant tradition which is a rich hard working tradition and the other is our Catholic, Celtic tradition. We have got to work together. We have got to build reconciliation to build a future.

I'm hopeful. I'm hoping that we can translate the tragedy of the past into real and meaningful reconciliation which we can share with others in the future. All of us. All of us have a great deal to *give each other and its my hope we can do that. It is not an idle aspiration. I have been very privileged to have been part of this civil rights campaign coming from my background—my Protestant background. I've also been privileged to know people in this city who even though they endured great poverty have a spirit of reconciliation in their hearts. Thank you.*

Ivan and I disembark. The geezers get out to take photos by the Bloody Sunday memorial. Ivan poses, talks to some passers-by, and then calls out, *Come on Jennifer! Let's get you a drink.*

Jennifer & Ivan

Derry, 2002

LIFE STORIES OF THE BLOODY SUNDAY VICTIMS

Jennifer Faus

Foreword

On the third Saturday in January 1972, the North Derry Civil Rights Organisation held a protest march to Magilligan Internment Camp in Magilligan, Co. Derry. The march was to protest against the Special Powers Act, which enabled the Unionist Government in Northern Ireland to intern thousands without trial. In August 1971, internment without trial was used exclusively against the Catholic community. A number of those interned were no longer active members of the IRA. Many were selected because of their commitment to Irish history, the Irish language or Irish culture. In many instances, internees had been subjected to horrendous acts of brutality on the part of the Royal Ulster Constabulary, which was the police force.

One of the basic demands of the civil rights movement was an end to internment without trial. Other issues, which were to mobilise thousands of people in Northern Ireland in 1968 and 1969, included 'one man, one vote'; an end to electoral gerrymandering; and an end to religious discrimination, both in the construction and allocation of social housing and in public and private employment. The Civil Rights Movement had a strong commitment to non-violence.

John Hume, Paddy O'Hanlon and I, all civil rights leaders who had taken our seats in parliament until internment without trial was used in August 1971, were at that march to Magilligan Internment Camp. There the marchers were confronted by the Parachute Regiment, which was new to the Derry area. The regiment enthusiastically dished out harsh treatment to the marchers. Eight days later the regiment was used by the British Government at a civil rights march in Derry, where they killed fourteen unarmed marchers, and severely injured fourteen more. That day is now known as Bloody Sunday.

This tragedy was followed by a disgraceful whitewash inquiry, set up by the British Government, under the Lord Chief Justice of England and Wales, Lord Widgery—an inquiry which was subsequently proved to be seriously flawed. As the result of constant pressure from the families of those who died, and in an unprecedented move in British constitutional and legal history, another inquiry was convened. This one is headed by Lord Saville and is known as the Saville Inquiry, the outcome of which is still awaited.

I met Jennifer Faus, a Chicago attorney, five years ago as part of a group of divinity postgraduate students from the USA to whom I was giving a talk on the civil rights movement and Bloody Sunday. The daughter of ordained parents and the single mother of three children, she was deeply moved by the events of Bloody Sunday and showed a special interest in those who had died on that day. Consequently she decided to write this book. A book which conveys a very touching insight into the personalities who were taken from us on Bloody Sunday.

The events of that day were a watershed in terms of Irish contemporary history. Jennifer Faus, in this book, has personalised our loss. Her personal sacrifices to achieve the writing of this book have been enormous. Her commitment to the relatives of those who died has been unflinching.

- Ivan Cooper, 2007

Background to Bloody Sunday

On 30 January 1972, the British Army deployed the 1st Parachute Regiment to conduct an arrest operation in Derry. But these were not arrest-operation type soldiers.

They are firstly, all volunteers and are then toughened by hard physical training. As a result they have that infectious optimism and that offensive eagerness which comes from physical well-being. They have jumped from the skies and by doing so have conquered fear.

Their duty lies in the van of battle: They are proud of their honour and have never failed in any task. They have the highest standards in all things, whether it be skills in battle or smartness in execution of all peacetime duties. They have shown themselves to be as tenacious and determined in defence as they are courageous in attack. They are in fact, men apart.

Training is hard but it is really the easy bit; you can always give up in training - you can't give up in the bush. Recruit training in the Parachute Regiment is arguably the toughest and most professional in the world today. All instructors at the training establishments are amongst the best officers and non-commissioned officers from the Regiment. Training is hard, but it must be remembered that it is preparation for service in the finest Regiment in the British Army. It is achievable. However, you don't have to be superman to complete this training. All you need is guts and determination, and the desire to be a Paratrooper.[1]

In the words of Byron Lewis, a paratrooper attached as radioman with anti-tank platoon on Bloody Sunday:

Recruits for paratroop training are selected volunteers and in my case of the fifty-six men who comprised the platoon at the start of training, fifteen of the original number marched out. Fifteen

---

[1] The Parachute Regiment, www.parachute-regiment.co.uk.

men all considerably stockier than six months earlier, able to run ten miles before breakfast without giving it a second thought. As with all human beings petty dislikes and ordinary friendships existed, but there was something more, an unspoken bond of pride, togetherness and professionalism.

This encompassed us all to the extent that it was what our lives were all about. Any group of men who have suffered humiliations and privations together, who have sweated and frozen together, but have always found that little bit extra to keep pushing on when others have fallen by the wayside, after weeks of seemingly interminable months of this finally to finish to reach the other side of the hill and have your efforts recognised in the symbolic form of a pair of "wings" and the coveted "red beret" will know what I mean.[2]

On 24 August 1968, Northern Irish Nationalists marched from Coalisland to Dungannon and although police prevented the group from entering the town, the marchers succeeded in setting the Northern Ireland civil rights movement into motion. Northern Ireland's civil rights movement was rooted in decades of outrage against Unionist bigotry levied against Catholics, tracing back to the Government of Ireland Act of 1920 that segregated Antrim, Armagh, Derry, Down, Fermanagh, and Tyrone County from the south's Dáil Éireann. The Stormont Parliament, Northern Ireland's ruling body, served the Protestant Unionist majority almost exclusively, while gerrymandering denied the Catholic majority a voice in their government.

---

[2] Statement of Byron Lewis, Soldier 027, Widgery Tribunal, 1972.

In conjunction with peaceful protests including marches and sit-ins, the Northern Ireland Civil Rights Association (NICRA) set forth six clear demands:
- One-man, one-vote in local elections
- Removal of gerrymandered boundaries
- Anti-discrimination laws
- Fair allocation of public housing
- Repeal of the Special Powers Act
- Disbandment of the B Specials[3]

Northern Ireland Catholics had endured brutal treatment by members of the police force for decades and as the civil rights movement gained momentum, protestors encountered increasingly heavy-handed opposition from the Royal Ulster Constabulary (RUC) and other Unionist bodies. Violent acts, coinciding with the movement, were perpetrated by both sides. The civil rights movement progressed as follows:

5 October 1968: RUC injures approximately 100 protestors marching along Duke Street.

6-7 October: Derry's first petrol bombs thrown.

9 October: Students of Queen's University, Belfast march against RUC brutality in Derry. Students form the People's Democracy organisation.

9 October: Derry Citizens Action Committee (DCAC) is formed. Ivan Cooper (Protestant) serves as Chair and John Hume (Catholic) as Vice Chair.

19 October: 5000 people attend DCAC sit-down protest in Guildhall Square. William McKinney is photographed sitting in the middle of the crowd.

---

[3] An auxiliary police force, the B Specials were a part-time Protestant militia that had been used occasionally since the founding of the state.

16 November: 15,000 people re-enact the October 5th March. Minor clashes with Loyalists do not deter the demonstrators.
22 November: Housing and local government reforms are enacted. Northern Ireland's prime minister makes an appeal for peace.
23 November: Stormont announces the abolition of the (Unionist) Derry Corporation and the appointment of a special commission to replace it. NICRA and DCAC follow with a self-imposed ban on marches.
1-4 January 1969: Forty members of The People's Democracy march from Belfast to Derry. Despite Loyalist deterrence, the body grows to about 500. The RUC stands by while Loyalists attack the group.
4 January: The RUC breaks windows and assaults residents of the Bogside. Nationalists paint 'You Are Now Entering Free Derry' on the gable end of a small house off Rossville Street, form protectionist forces, and build barricades.
19 April: Samuel Devenny is beaten by the RUC.
July: Derry Citizens Defence Association (DCDA) is formed to protect Bogside.
17 July: Sammy Devenny dies. 20,000 people attend his funeral, which is filmed by William McKinney.
10 August: The DCDA asks the Apprentice Boys to rethink marching along Bogside, but they refuse. Republican, Nationalist, and Labour leaders vow to defend the Bogside against Loyalist and RUC incursion. Women and children evacuate vulnerable areas, including Paddy Doherty's wife Eileen and their children who move from Hamilton Street, an incursion point, to Creggan Heights.
12 August: Apprentice Boys march along the edge of Bogside. Rioting breaks out. Three hours into the rioting the RUC breach the barricades and charge from Little James

Street and Waterloo Place towards Rossville Street, the heart of the Bogside.

During 72 hours of constant battle, Britain uses CS gas in its own jurisdiction for the first time in history firing 1091 canisters and 14 grenades of gas into the Bogside. Citizens treat nearly 1000 injuries in make-shift casualty units. All able-bodied men are called to fight. The violence prompts over 500 women and children to flee over the border into Ireland.

Irish Taosiseach Jack Lynch requests a UN Peacekeeping force. Lynch sends Irish Army Troops to the border to set up field hospitals. At 4:00 p.m. on 14 August, the British Army marches on Waterloo Place bringing The Battle of the Bogside to an end.

Initially, the Army and the Catholic population live in peace. Catholic women bring soldiers tea and buns on china and offer warm drinks at night. Soon, however, these citizens regard the Army as yet another instrument of oppressive British rule.

6 February 1971: The first British soldier of the conflict dies in Belfast.

8 July 1971: The army shoots and kills two young Catholic men, Seamus Cusack and Desmond Beatty. Official inquiry into their deaths is denied.

9 August 1971: British Soldiers launch operation Demetrius.[4]

By 1971, nearly all of the civil rights demands had been met. One man, one vote had been conceded, an end to electoral gerrymandering had been achieved, the Derry City Corporation (the old Unionist corporation) had been shelved

---

[4] Marching On. Exhibition Catalogue of Gasyard Wall Feile 2003. Opening Statement of Queen's Council Christopher Clarke to the Bloody Sunday Inquiry, 27 March 2000.

and replaced by a commission. Legislation in relation to discrimination in employment, and a point system with regard to the fair allocation of houses had been enacted. One demand was still outstanding: imprisonment without due process.

Internment was levied exclusively against the Catholic population in the 1930s, '40s, '50s, and '60s. The official line of the government during those decades was that internment was used to curb IRA violence. Many people were interned, however, who had no connection with armed uprising. People who had an interest in Irish music and Irish culture were likely to be interned. People who decided, because of their interest in the Irish language, to write their names in Irish, to be addressed in Irish, to speak the Irish language, were also lifted and interned.

Despite warnings against using interment from John Hume and other politicians, in 1971 internment was again used to arrest and detain persons in the Catholic community. Elderly people and people with long-lapsed connections with the IRA comprised a large number of those imprisoned at Magilligan Camp in County Derry.

On 9 August 1971, the largest and deadliest internment raids swept through Derry and Belfast. As police and military forces swept through communities arresting Catholic men, women banged garbage can lids on the streets. The raids often began before dawn and those who were not roused from their beds by the hands of soldiers were warned of the imminent threat by the clanging of garbage can lids.

Internment meant that no man in a Catholic household was safe. They could be removed at any time, without warning or justification, and held indefinitely. By the new year, internment raids had swept more than 900 Derry men from their homes and families.

Reports of illegal interrogation techniques began to surface including stories of sensory deprivation and beatings, a diet of bread and water, and being kept 'spread-eagle against a wall for up to sixteen hours at a stretch, always hooded and denied sleep while the roar of a jet engine drowned out the sound of everything else. The men were beaten when they fell, then dragged before Special Branch officers for questioning before being sent back to the wall again.'[5]

Such interrogation techniques were based on the experiences of British Soldiers who had been taken prisoner in the Korean War[6] and their use against interned Irishmen resulted in "the United Kingdom being found guilty of inhuman and degrading treatment by the European Court of Human Rights."[7]

Ending internment through diplomatic and political channels was unsuccessful. Stormont would not budge on the issue. Cases at law were unsuccessful as the soldiers, granted broad powers of arrest, detention, and stop and search,[8] effectively operated above the law. It was felt that the only way to get to a resolution was to bring international attention to the problem. If other countries saw what the British government was doing, certainly, Britain would have to end the practice of internment. Historically, international

---

[5] Holland, Jack. Hope Against History: The Course of Conflict in Northern Ireland (Hodder & Stoughton: London, 1999), 41.
[6] Carver, (Field Marshall, Lord). Britain's Army in the Twentieth Century (Macmillan: London, 1999).
[7] Walsh, Dermot. Bloody Sunday and the Rule of Law in Northern Ireland (Gill & Macmillan: Dublin, 2000), 40.
[8] The Special Powers Act conferred police powers on British soldiers.

media outlets came to Derry to cover civil-rights marches. Therefore, it was decided that a non-violent civil rights demonstration—a peace march—would be their platform.

Johnny Johnston

Johnny was a big man. He dressed well. How could a soldier at a distance from here to that house up there have missed him? Paratroopers who are trained, you know? How could they have mistaken him?
- John Duddy

To be the oldest victim shot on Bloody Sunday is a dubious honour. To be the only one not to die on 30 January, but five months after the fact. To be the post script on every memorial, "and John Johnston (59) who died later as a result of his injuries." It might have been better to end with an unadorned grave in the city cemetery, unknown, forgotten. Indeed, if Johnny Johnston had taken one step differently on Bloody Sunday, if he had not gone to the aid of another, anonymity would likely have been the result.

Had Johnny lived, he would have passed through his life like most of us—ordinary and forgotten. Johnny's life was unremarkable. He sold clothing, married late, never had children, drank, played cards, golfed. Likewise, most of us move though the world quiet and ordinary. But Johnny strayed from the pack and did an extraordinary thing.

With the exception of his brother-in-law John Duddy, Johnny Johnston's family and friends are long dead. Johnny's father died tragically. While stepping onto the ferry that travelled from the Guildhall to the Waterside, he lost his footing, plunged into the river, and was drowned. No one remembers when Johnny's mother passed away or the circumstances of her death.

His brother-in-law knew only one of Johnny's siblings. Johnny kept no diary or journal. There are no surviving photos of his childhood. In 1946, at thirty-three years of age, he met, fell in love with, and married Margaret Duddy. Johnny's life is largely an enigma.

But the puzzle of his life increases in complexity when we add the puzzle of his death. How does an old man, not participating in the march end up shot, 200 yards away and a full twenty minutes before the paratroopers opened fire on the crowd? Johnny and Damien Donaghey were standing on open ground. The shooters wounded Johnny and Damien only in the legs and arms. The shooters were just across the street, a distance of less than fifty yards. Why didn't they fire fatal wounds when they had ample opportunity?

***

On the last Sunday in January 1972, a bright, pleasant, crisp day, men, women, and children assembled in Bishop's Field at the top of Creggan Heights. It was a carnival atmosphere as the crowd gathered. A lorry was placed at the head, followed by the marchers, some of whom were singing the civil rights song *We Shall Overcome*. The march mirrored the civil rights marches of the southern United States, and Martin Luther King Jr and Gandhi were the leaders, and provided the strategy on which the activists in Derry modeled their own behavior and campaign.

This march, the previous marches, and the entire civil rights movement from 1968 in Northern Ireland had been demanding the same rights as the people of London, Cardiff, Glasgow, and Birmingham. They were telling the British Government that if they were part of the United Kingdom, then they wanted precisely the same rights as the people of London, Cardiff, Glasgow, and Birmingham, where they enjoyed due process, legal representation, and the right to trial by jury. Only after a trial and conviction in London, Cardiff, Glasgow, and Birmingham, was a person incarcerated. None of the men at Magilligan had been charged with a crime, none had been allowed to contact a solicitor, and none had been afforded a trial.

After observing the morning deployment of a heavy body of troops on William Street, now known as Barrier 14, the march leaders decided there was no way the march was going to be permitted to proceed to the Guildhall. Chief Superintendent Lagan of the RUC advised the march leaders that the army would not permit the march to proceed to the Guildhall Square. With this information, the leadership decided to change the route. At the apex of William and Rossville Streets, instead of turning left toward the Square, the lorry would turn to the right and drive along Rossville Street to Free Derry Corner where the meeting would be held.

Lagan was advised of the decision to change the route and he conveyed this information to the army. The IRA informed the march leaders they would stand down that day and that no operations would take place on Sunday 30 January 1972.[9] The leaders departed Bishop's Field confident that the march would proceed safely.

At the apex of Rossville and William streets, the march, led by the lorry, went to the right, followed by most of the marchers, singing civil rights songs, chatting, holding banners and signs, enjoying their afternoon. However, a group of young men, intent at throwing stones at the army, went down to Barrier 14.

After a bit of rioting—stone and bottle throwing, CS gas deployment, water canon soaking, and many verbal exchanges between the army and this small contingent of marchers—they went their respective ways, the army back to patrolling Barricade 14 and the marchers toward Free Derry Corner for the speeches.

On 30 January Johnny Johnston woke, dressed, had his breakfast, read the paper, and left the house to go sit with a friend. On the way, Johnny ducked gunfire to go to the aid

---

[9] Interview with Ivan Cooper.

of Damien Donaghey who had been shot by British soldiers. The time was 15:45. Just over twenty minutes before the paratroopers stormed Rossville Street. In that moment Johnny became one of the keys to unlocking the Army's claim that they came under attack, only returning fire on gunmen, nail-bombers, and petrol bombers. In the moment he was shot, Johnny's fate was sealed, he would not go quietly, ordinary, forgotten.

At the other end of the march, Barney McGuigan was shot at 16:20 as he went to the aid of Paddy Doherty. Johnny and Barney were fifty-nine and forty-one years respectively; neither set out to participate in the march that day; both were 'old men' and would have been considered working men, family men, not brick-throwing young hooligans. But they weren't the only ones.

The twenty-eight people killed and wounded on Bloody Sunday were primarily young people. Eighteen of them were under thirty; of those, twelve were between the ages of fifteen and twenty. Six of the twenty-eight were between the ages of thirty-eight and fifty-nine.

Alex Nash (51) was shot going the aid of his son William who lie murdered at the rubble barricade. Alex's hands were raised over his head when he was shot. Patrick Campbell (51) was shot as he sought shelter at Joseph's Place. Daniel McGowan (38) was shot as he helped the wounded Patrick Campbell to safety. Paddy O'Donnell (41) was shot when he threw himself down to protect Winifred O'Brien when the shooting began.

British Information Services in New York stated the British army *only fired only at identified targets;* they reported that the army *only fired at attacking gunmen and bombers.* At the Saville Inquiry, Queen's Counsel, Mr Glasgow described a disciplined force as one that would unquestionably follow orders. Any breech of orders would be a matter of disciplinary investigation.[10] It follows then that if the paratroopers were a disciplined force, they would have followed orders without question and if they had breeched orders, they would have been subject to a disciplinary investigation. For his actions on Bloody Sunday, their commander was decorated by the Queen. How then, can we come to any other conclusion than that they were acting under orders to kill?

If the British Army had stayed within the framework and shot only the young men and boys, they might have gotten away with it. It is no secret that young men regularly engaged the army in stone throwing and rioting. It is known in Belfast young boys were luring soldiers into areas where IRA snipers lay in wait. In the latter half of 1971 the tension between the army and the Irish citizens was escalating.

It would have been easy to lay the blame on the riotous hooligans. Plenty of footage shows them throwing bottles, rocks, bricks, anything they could put their hands on at Barrier 14 the day of the march and nearly any other day after the army came in and the Bogside declared its independence. But the soldiers killed two old men and shot and wounded four others. Can it be true that Britain's best trained soldiers mistake tall, aging, balding men with a bit of a paunch for riotous teenagers?

And so, this ordinary man, Johnny Johnston, whose claims to fame were a mean hand of Whist and a penchant for whiskey takes a stroll on a Sunday afternoon to sit with a

---

[10] The Bloody Sunday Inquiry Transcript of Proceedings 132: 13-16, 25: 133:1 (Monday, 24 November 2003, Day 400).

friend and unravels the British Army. Is the ordinary hero sitting next to you in the coffee shop? If the bomb blasted would he carry you to safety? Would he stay with you so you wouldn't have to die alone? Would he step into the line of fire to offer you comfort and ultimately give his life? If so, would you want people to know his name? Would you want people to know something about him and his very ordinary life?

***

The E. Duddy Bar was in the original Bogside. Everything west of the walls from Strand Road to the flyover is the Bogside these days. But then, Bogside Estate was a short stretch along the Lecky Road.

The bar on Bogside Street stood for five generations before progress intervened. Margaret was Eileen (E.) Duddy's sister. Johnny was the patron. At thirty-three, for the first time in his life, he was smitten. They met, fell in love, and were married, and for us, that's when Johnny's life begins.

Until he was married, Johnny worked as a salesman for McDevitts Drapery Business. Good at his job, it seemed no one got out of the shop without buying something. Upon moving from the Waterside to the Bogside side after his marriage to Margaret, he opened his own Drapery (clothing) shop in the drawing room of the house attached to the bar. Delivering clothes and collecting payments weekly, his vans went into the country offering fashions to folks who could not get into the city.

Work, play, and home were all contained within the building: the bar and shop at street level and the five bedroom house above. Situating his business next to the bar may not have been the best idea. Johnny enjoyed a drink and after a few years, he closed his shop and went to work for Hassons on Ferryquay Street down the town.

Margaret worked in Bryce and Weston's shirt factory and minded the house. Her sisters, Eileen and Lily, shared the house with Margaret and Johnny. Eileen ran the bar and Lily worked in the shirt factories. Johnny wasn't Margaret's first love, but it was her first marriage. Her first fiancé died of cancer before their wedding day. Margaret and Johnny didn't waste any time: they were married, skipped having children, and went right to enjoying their life together.

On a Sunday afternoon they could be found in the house playing Whist. A game of four players, two teams, it was won by counting cards, memorising what was played, and getting the most tricks. Johnny and Margaret also travelled as much as they could. Cobh in County Cork was a favourite destination as were Donegal and Galway.

In 1968, redevelopment, which had started up the hill in Creggan Heights, reached the old Bogside. The E. Duddy Bar, home, and nearby houses, all built by Margaret's ancestors, were razed. Eileen, Lily, Johnny, and Margaret bought a house at 50 Marlborough Street with the small compensation the city paid for the taking of their home, livelihood, and land.

Johnny felt the civil rights campaign should be supported but only attended a meeting or two. The extent of Johnny's physical activity was a round of golf. His trophies still line the shelves at 50 Marlborough Street. He couldn't be bothered with marching, stone throwing, or rioting. Unless he could have been riding along in his car, Johnny wouldn't be attending any marches or rallies. Johnny thought the civil rights movement ought to be supported, so long as he didn't have to put himself out to do it. He made a token effort, but a round of golf was the extent to which Johnny would walk.

However, on 30 January 1972, Johnny walked. He couldn't drive on account of the march. Johnny left the house and fell in with the march on Marlborough Terrace and on to William Street. He was on his way to sit with a man who lived near the meeting site. The man was a recluse and Johnny thought he might be nervous with all the activity. Johnny didn't get far. Mid-way down William Street, as he crossed a patch of waste ground, Johnny stopped to help Damien and was shot.

When John Duddy arrived at Altnagelvin Hospital, Johnny was sitting with the sleeve of his shirt and the leg of his trousers cut off. He was injured in his right leg, left shoulder, and back of his right hand. John thought it was odd that a man who panicked when he cut his finger at the house, would be sitting up calmly talking after having been shot twice and rushed to casualty. But this was only the start of Johnny's strange behaviour.

He was the never was the same after that day. When he was shot he fell and hit his head. The injury caused a growth that put pressure on his brain. Johnny's mind started to wander. Once a good driver, he now ran off the road. Once the best salesman at Hassons, he turned his customers away. Instead of talking his customers into things, he talked them out of them. Once able to count cards and memorise four hands at Whist, he forgot things. He was confused.

Diagnosed with a subdural haematoma caused by the fall on Bloody Sunday, Johnny endured six months of headaches, confusion, epileptic fits, loss of speech, numbness in his arms, depression, and incontinence. In mid-May, he was sent to Royal Victoria Hospital in Belfast for an operation. His doctor noted that during his pre-surgical exam, Johnny was unable to give his history because of "a drowsiness from which he can be roused but he is totally disoriented. His level of consciousness seems to fluctuate."[11]

On 23 May, his doctor performed a right frontal lobectomy and removed part of the tumour. On 6 June 1972, Johnny's doctor described his situation as hopeless and transferred him to Altnagelvin in Derry. Johnny died on 16 June 1972. His wife followed him exactly fifteen months later.

In the days and weeks after Bloody Sunday, the media reported the paratroopers were engaged in a gun battle with the IRA. They couldn't have gotten it more wrong. When the British Army shoots Johnny Johnston (59), Barney McGuigan (41), Alex Nash (51), Patrick Campbell (51),

---

[11] Medical Record of John Johnston. Royal Victoria Hospital, Belfast, May 1972.

Daniel McGowan (38), and Paddy O'Donnell (41), how can they stand by their accusations?

Johnny was a big man. He dressed well. He was mostly bald. He wouldn't have been described as youthful. So how could a highly trained soldier with a clear view from less than fifty yards have mistaken him for anything or anyone else? Why did they shoot Johnny?

John Duddy has a theory. A theory that is overwhelmingly supported by the citizens of the Bogside, Creggan, and Creggan Heights and brought to light in the Irish Government's Assessment. It is this: the shots were fired in an effort to draw IRA into the area and incite a gun-battle.

Why the soldiers chose to shoot Donaghey and Johnston remains a mystery. Don Mullan agrees that many believe these early shots, fired by support company of 1 PARA and hitting Donaghey and Johnston, "were aimed at drawing the IRA units down into the Bogside...the IRA reaction did not materialise…When the PARAs moved into Rossville Street twenty minutes later, the fusillade of bombs and bullets they later claimed they encountered simply did not occur."[12]

It is clear that the Army approached the situation anticipating trouble. General Ford wrote a memo just prior to Bloody Sunday, which reads, in part:

I visited Londonderry on Friday 7th January with ACC (Ops) and held discussions with Commander and Brigade, Commanding Officer the City Battalion (22 Lt AD Regt), and the Police Divisional Commander.

In the last two weeks there has been the usual daily yobbo activity in the William Street area and this has been combined with bombers making sorties into Great James Street and the Waterloo Place area. Neither foot nor mounted patrols now operate beyond the bend in William Street to the West of Waterloo Place as a regular feature of life. They claim that all foot patrols are put at risk from snipers in the Rossville Flats area.

In addition the vast majority of the people in the shopping area not only give no help to our patrols but, if they saw a youth with a very small bag which might contain a bomb, they would be likely to shield the youth's movements from the view of our patrols. We now have 52 men patrolling in this very small area constantly.

The IS (Intelligence Services) situation in Londonderry is one of armed gunmen dominating the Creggan and Bogside backed and protected by the vast majority of the population in these two areas, and of bombers and gunmen making occasional sorties out of these hard core areas to cause incidents, mainly in the shopping areas of the Strand, William Street, and Great James Street.

---

[12] *Bloody Sunday and the Report of the Widgery Tribunal: The Irish Government's Assessment of the New Material*, para. 146, 79 quoting Don Mullan, Eyewitness Bloody Sunday, The Truth, (1997) p. 86.

The Londonderry situation is further complicated by one additional ingredient. This is the Derry Young Hooligans (DYH). Gangs of tough, teen-aged youths, permanently unemployed, have developed sophisticated tactics of brick and stone throwing; destruction and arson.

The weapons at our disposal – CS gas and baton rounds – are ineffective. I am coming to the conclusion that the minimum force necessary to achieve a restoration of law and order is to shoot selected ring leaders amongst the DYH, after clear warnings have been issued. I believe we would be justified in using 7.62mm but in view of the devastating effects of this weapon and the danger of rounds killing more than the person aimed at, I believe we must consider issuing rifles adapted to fire PV.22 inch ammunition to sufficient members of the unit dealing with this problem, to enable ring leaders to be engaged with this less lethal ammunition.[13]

We have also to face the possibility of a NICRA march from the Creggan to the Guildhall Square at 1400 hours on Sunday 16th January 1972 (sic). This would be followed by a rally which will be addressed by Members of Parliament and leading members of NICRA. It is the opinion of the senior commanders in Londonderry, that if the march takes place, however good the intentions of NICRA may be, the DYH backed up by the gunmen will undoubtedly take over control at an early stage.[14]

A letter from Frank Lagan to the *Irish News* confirms that the army had been informed of the march leaders' intention to avoid confrontation with the army:

On Sunday 30 January 1972 a member of the NICRA[15] informed me that the march route had been changed in that the

---

[13] The Bloody Sunday victims were shot with 7.62mm (high-velocity) rounds.
[14] Letter titled 'The Situation in Londonderry as of 7th January 1972 from General Ford to GOC.'
[15] Northern Ireland Civil Rights Association.

marchers would now go along William Street, turn right into Rossville Street and not come into contact with the Army blockade. I saw Brigadier MacLellan at his office at 2pm on that date. He was with General Ford. I advised these Officers of the message I had received from the NICRA member.[16]

But the army had been briefed. On 29 January, nine pages of restricted information[17] were distributed to twenty-five companies deployed in Derry for the march. This document shows the British Army believed it took 1000 baton rounds, 1000 CS containers, 400 CS grenades, 200 pairs of handcuffs, and hundreds of soldiers to monitor a peaceful civil rights march. Coincidently, the briefing, made public through the Saville Inquiry, does not include the briefing that 1 PARA received.

Johnny Johnston was a victim of that briefing and the actions of the soldiers who followed it. He became a victim when he set out that day simply to be a friend. His death stands as silent testimony to what happens when armed soldiers decide to use helpless targets to provoke violence. It has taken thirty years, but the British cover-up has failed. No better evidence can be found than the death of Johnny Johnston—anonymous hero.

---

[16] Letter of 26 January 1998 from Frank Lagan to the *Irish News*.
[17] Confirmatory Notes to Oral Orders given by Co 1 R Anglican at Ebrington at 291000 Z, Jan 1972.

Jim Wray

My mother used to say,
'Jim, you don't fall in love—you fall in love with love.
You fall in love with the idea of love.'
- Margaret Wray

There's a certain blessing in dying young. And that is, you never grow old. If you are lucky, and die young enough, you are never disappointed in love. No one has ever truly wronged you. You have hope for the future. You still believe you can do anything. You are fit. You haven't had the time or experiences that make you bitter, calloused, cynical, or indifferent. Because Jim never got the opportunity to grow old and become jaded, he not only left this world with joy, excitement, hope, and passion in his heart, he left those who knew him with those rays of light as well.

When Jim turned seventeen he began going to dances. It was his first foray into looking for love. He attended an all-boys school so his first real smell, taste, and feel of girls came late. But his nights out gave his young sister Margaret an early glimpse into the teenage world.

Starry-eyed Margaret served coffee and tea to Jim and his friends after the dances at the weekends. She sat quietly listening to the stories the boys told about whom they'd met out in the town that night, whom they fancied, and whom they didn't. Jim knew Margaret fancied one of the lads, but he just smiled and let her be.

Jim would come in from work and say, 'I'm taking a walk down to so-and-so's house tonight. Do you want to take a walk?' Well that was just like an offer to go out. I felt wonderful walking out with him because he was a handsome strap of a fella. I'd be in school and people would say, 'Is that your brother? He's beautiful!' I was so proud.

Girls in the Wray house weren't to be let out until they were 18, but after two years of hearing all the details, 15 year old Margaret was desperate to go to a dance. Jim intervened with her father volunteering to take her to the dance, stay outside, collect her, and bring her home. After some negotiation, her father relented and let Jim escort Margaret. The dance turned out to be the least exciting part of the evening.

'We came out of the dance, he met up with his friends, and the whole lot of us walked home. So then my girlfriends in school the next day were envious of me because it wasn't just my brother who walked me home!'

But Jim's kindness and generosity didn't stop there. It is almost as if Jim's love of the idea of love infused everything he touched, and everyone he knew, but that didn't mean it was appreciated—especially by Margaret's friends! If Mary talked to a boy at a dance, Jim would go over and say, 'Are you all right Mary? You having any problems?' The boy would take one look at the six-foot man staring down at him and go the other way! Which was fine if she didn't like the bloke, but if she liked him, it was, 'I hate you Jim Wray! I really do!'

'I hate you, Jim Wray!' was a refrain echoed by Margaret's friends throughout their teen-age years. Jim lifted Mary and twirled her around every time he saw her in town in a short skirt. He scared them when they watched Dracula and Frankenstein on Saturday nights. He reminded them to be home on time and generally looked out for their well being whether they liked it or not.

On 24 July 1971, Jim gave Margaret away. Her father said he didn't raise his daughters to give away, so Jim walked her down the aisle. As the family sat down to the wedding meal, news came to the house that young Damian Harkin had been killed. Damian had been crushed by an Army lorry, just outside in the car park.

Not typically one to riot, Jim nonetheless joined his brothers, all wearing their hired wedding suits, as they took out after the lorry. Photographs of Jim and Liam on top of the Saracen in the hired suits dubbed them the best dressed rioters in Derry. It wasn't for the sake of rioting that Jim stood on that Saracen; it was for the sake of young Damian that Jim made a stand. Damian had just gone to run a message for his mum in his own street and the army rammed him up against a wall. It was a painful and tragic injustice.

'We couldn't just go on with the wedding could we? Just sit there and say "Naw, I'm about passive resistance." It was only times like that, that Jim went out to riot,' said Margaret. Otherwise Jim was a strong believer in gaining civil rights through peaceful means.

For example, Margaret was harassed daily by the soldiers on the walls as she went to and from work. They had a great view of her from on high and weren't shy with their opinions. It bothered Margaret but Jim bolstered her, 'Well!

Aren't you good looking! Let them see that our Derrygirls are gorgeous.'

At the same time, Jim worked the channels to do what he could to stop the harassment. He went to their father and said, 'The soldiers are shouting things at Margaret and other women that are not appropriate.' As a member of a liaison group between the army and the community, Mr Wray could get word to the officer to get his men to behave.

Reasoning it was better for the soldiers to keep their opinions quiet than for word to get to the fellas from the Bog who would not take kindly to their women getting harassed, Jim saw a situation and tried to diffuse it. He wanted to avoid confrontation and settle things peacefully when he could. Jim Wray was a man who respected authority.

Jim's respect began at home. Jim's actions on one occasion solidified this for Margaret who remembers:

One day Jim, he must have been 19, came in for his lunch. My father was standing at one end of the fireplace, Jim was at the other, my mother was putting out the lunch, and I was futtering around. The conversation turned to a riot in the town that day. Jim turned around and said, 'The bastards!' My father got up and slapped him across the face. We weren't allowed to use bad language. I held my breath. Jim was taller than my father at that time and had he put his hand on my father, he would have dropped over. I thought, 'Oh God what's going to happen?'

Jim turned around and said, 'I'm sorry Daddy. I'm sorry Mammy. I'm sorry Margaret. I shouldn't have used that language.' I could not believe it. Any other fella of that age would have walked out of the house and said, 'I'm not coming back.' But it was my father's home, and Jim knew the rules. He broke one, took his punishment, and then apologised. Jim respected my father and my father's views.

But nowhere are Jim's beliefs more vividly expressed than in the photos of him on Bloody Sunday, conducting his own sit-down protest in the middle of the Barrier 14 riot. As the rioters pegged stones and the Army spewed purple dye, Jim sat on the pavement in his dark cap, making his statement. He had said on more than one occasion, 'If we sit down, they won't run over us. Just sit down.'

Jim's love affair with the idea of love was clear, too. At twenty-two years of age, he'd been engaged three times. Engaged to an Israeli girl when he died, everyone thought this one would stick. She was beautiful, kind, and gentle. His family saw that she and Jim were very happy when they were together. They were waiting for permission from the church when Jim was killed.

To marry a Jew, but still remain a Catholic meant Jim would have to receive special dispensation from the church. So Jim and Miriam went to the local clergy and made their application. Then, at the beginning of January, 1972, Miriam went home to Israel to break the news to her parents that she wanted to marry a Christian. She asked Jim to go with her but he declined. 'Naw, I'm not going there for them to shoot me!'

Funny how things turn out. Jim didn't think he had anything to fear in Derry. He joked about getting shot in Israel. Instead, he was murdered in Glenfada Park. Witnessed by Joe Mahon who lay wounded next to dying Willie McKinney and not 15 feet from Jim. In his statement to Saville, Joe said:

As I lay on my side my face was looking toward the North and I saw a PARA walking toward the body of Jim Wray. This was the same PARA I had seen [earlier] shooting from the hip. This PARA appeared to be wearing a different coloured jacket to the other

Paratroopers that I had seen that day. Although the jacket was green, its colour and markings seemed to stand out more than the jackets that the other Paratroopers were wearing. He was holding his rifle down by his hip with the muzzle down toward the ground, as if patrolling.

He made no move to search Willie McKinney or me and effectively he walked in a direct line toward Jim Wray. He did not try and search Jim Wray or look for a weapon of any kind. He saw Jim Wray's shoulders move and realised he was still alive. The soldier then pointed the rifle at Jim Wray's back and fired two shots into his back at point blank range. I could see Jim Wray's coat move twice.[18]

Jim's brother Liam and their uncle went to the morgue at Altnagelvin. Picking through the bodies, having to step over bodies lying on the floor, they found Jim on a trolley against the wall. He was cold. His eyes were open. Liam tried to close them. Jim's mother howled horrible shattering screams that haunted the neighbourhood. It seemed to her family from that moment on, she never came back to herself. For nearly a year, she, Mrs Kelly, and Mrs Nash could usually be found in the City Cemetery or in the kitchen talking about their sons.

Mrs Wray died two years after Bloody Sunday, Mrs Nash seven years, and Mrs Kelly emerged from her grief in 1977 with no memory of the previous five years.

For Mrs Wray's family, the last two years she lived was time spent never letting Jim die. It was Jim morning, noon, and night. She spoke to anyone who would listen, telling them how Jim was murdered, how the British military and media smeared his name saying he was a gunman, that her

---

[18] Statement of Joe Mahon to Saville Inquiry, 17 September 1999.

Jim would not take anybody's life! When she learned Jim was first injured and then murdered while lying on the ground, she was desperate to have answers to unanswerable questions, 'Between the first shot and the second shot, was he aware? Was he alive? Did he feel the pain? Did he pray? Did he think of me?' She tormented herself and everyone around her.

Margaret said, 'We tried to bring her out of it. But she just wouldn't come back to us. We tried to get her to embrace her other sons. She said, "I love them, but what am I going to do without Jim? Jim's getting married. I have Jim's wedding money up the stairs. I have Jim's this and Jim's that." It was endless.'

Mrs Wray had not one moment's peace from the time she learned of Jim's death until the moment of her own death. The woman from whom Jim inherited his love of life, his love of love, sobbed endlessly. Angry and bitter, she raged at the world that took her Jim. She couldn't grieve and let him go and be the mother her other children needed and wanted.

But as much as she couldn't let go, the Army wouldn't let her grieve. They raided the house relentlessly. They swept Jim's room time and time again. Mrs Wray insisted the house be spotless before anyone went to bed at night. 'They will not say our Jim came from a dirty house. Jim loved this house and when they come in here they will know what type of lad he was and they'll understand that they murdered a decent fella.'

Her health deteriorated. She didn't care about herself. She carried a great hatred against England and the British Army. Her family tried and tried to help, but they could not reach her. The children were devastated watching their mother deteriorate. But she slipped away from them, and they were forced to go on without her.

Twenty-five years after her mother's death, Margaret organised a memorial Mass. At the evening meal, the siblings started to talk. Margaret shared memories of her mother,

Our mother was always a very happy person. She loved being at home. On a good summer night she came into the street with us. If we were skipping, she skipped along with us. She showed us how to play hopscotch and how to play ball. When she was in the house doing her work, she sang. Even today, when I hear certain songs, I think, 'Me mammy used to sing that!'

Our mother had great strength of character. She was the stability, the mainstay of our house, from greeting us at lunchtime to the minute we opened the front door always knowing what we were getting for dinner, she was in middle of it all. Mother never went out because there was no need to - everybody came into our home. It never emptied. No matter what time of day or night, some cousin or some aunt or some uncle or some neighbour was sitting in the house talking to my mother as she worked, getting her advice or counsel.

Our mother was happiest with her children around her. She loved us wildly. She wanted us around so much we were never put to bed. We just fell asleep on the couch or the floor, and then our father or Jim picked us up and took us up to bed. Whenever anyone gave her a hard time about it, saying, 'Your children need a proper bedtime.' She always replied, 'I know where my children are tonight. Do you know where yours are?'

When she finished, Margaret's youngest brother, John, said, 'The woman you described and my mammy are two different people. You were talking about a woman that sang songs and laughed and skipped and played hopscotch and football. I remember a woman who was always crying and sad.'

Margaret realised the soldier did more than murder Jim and take her mother away. He denied her young siblings a wonderful mother and brother. A mother and brother they never knew. Margaret has lovely memories, memories denied her younger brothers and sisters.

Jim didn't live long enough to be sullied by life. His idealism was never taken away from him. His passion was never denied him. He never had a bad back or a plump gut. Life never got a chance to corrupt or batter him about. He was just a good guy.

Jim's personal possessions on the day he died were a packet of cigarettes, 10p, and rosary beads. He didn't need money to enjoy himself. A walk out the road, a yarn with the lads, lifting a few jars on the Saturday night. That was Jim. Happy. In love with love. In love with life.

Gerald McKinney

*'Everyone makes choices. We choose to love and to forgive.
That is the legacy that was passed to us from our parents.'*
- Regina McKinney

The McKinney family story is complex. The beginning is the story of Willie McKinney. He buried two wives and seven children. His third wife was twenty years his junior. Protestant blood runs through the clan. In grand patriarchal style, he was a clever man; a pragmatist. A business owner. One of few Catholics to own a shirt factory in Derry. He lived into his 90s.

Next is the story of Gerry McKinney, James Gerald McKinney to be exact. William McKinney's third son. He was a suave devil-may-care fella who skated through life and maintained a charming and cheerful disposition despite losing his beloved younger brother. Fred, Willie's fifth son, was killed in a car accident on his 23rd birthday.

Gerry was in the first generation of educated working Derry men, and he took full advantage. An engineer, Gerry inherited his father's cleverness and ran several businesses including a roller rink, a TV shop, an electrical business, and an engineering firm. Gerry married Ita O'Kane on 20 April 1960. He and Ita had seven children and were expecting their eighth when Gerry was murdered by British Paratroopers. Gerry was thirty-four years of age. James Gerald was born eight days after his father's death.

After his death, Gerry's wife Ita struggled to raise her children while grieving her murdered husband. She spends the first sixteen years calling her son Gerry, 'Baby' because she can't bring herself to call him by his father's name.

Ita succeeds in raising her children to carry on their father's legacy—even though they were young when he died. All eight children share their father's traits, beliefs, and each has a piece of his personality. On 18 August 1999, Gerry is killed in a car accident on the Tobermore to Magherafelt Road. His wife is pregnant with their first child.

On 18 July 2003 Gerry and Ita's second daughter, Regina, loses her husband to cancer while she is pregnant with their first child.

In August, 2003 James Gerald is born to Ita and Gerry's first son, Kevin, and his wife, Siobhan. He is the image of his grandfather.

***

When I started this project, I hoped readers would find someone with whom they identified. To me, if each reader could connect with at least one story told in the book, then I could say the book was a success. Though I discovered that many of the families were similar to my own, Gerald McKinney's family reminded me time and time again of my father's family. There were five boys in my dad's family: Jay, Bob, Glen, Hen, and Jerry. There were six McKinney boys: Louis, Laurence, Gerry, Denis, Fred, and Willie.

After it nipped Gerry in the backside, the McKinney brothers locked the dog in and lit the kennel on fire. Their Da released the dog, it shot out, and never returned. After it nipped Jerry in the backside, the Faus brothers lured the boar into the truck and drove it to market. The boar was not liberated by the Faus brothers' da.

The McKinney brothers painted the neighbour's dog green, white, and gold for the 12th of July. The Faus brothers sold a horse (trained to respond to whistles) to the neighbouring farm and then hid over the hill and whistled when the farmer tried to work the horse in the field.

The McKinney brothers broke into their own home when their da locked them out to teach them a lesson. The Faus brothers blew a fifty gallon milk bucket into the sky with a stick of dynamite they 'found.'

The McKinney brothers dug a hole in the garden in which to bury their nemesis neighbours, the Huey's. The Faus brothers tricked their nemesis neighbours, the Stauffer's, into sledding down a hill onto a not-so-frozen swamp.

Their brothers would have you believe it was Laurence and Gerry of the McKinney clan and Bob and Glen of the Faus clan who were the instigators of it all. 'The two of 'em together, they were terrible,' was the complaint common to both families. I imagine, however, where five or six boys are gathered, trouble is not far behind.

Given the activities of the boys, confession became part of the McKinney household routine, and Willie had a way of easing it out of them. Willie and Margaret had a knack for knowing everything their sons were about, and there just wasn't any wriggling out of it. Under the skilled examination of their father, confession typically resulted.

Over a bowl of porridge, for example, Willie might innocently ask his son, 'How did it go today?'

'Oh aye, good.'

'And the soap boxes were working OK?'

'Aye.'

'Had you a wee bit of bother there?'

'Nope.'

'I thought the wheels came off it.'

'Naw I fixed them.'

'Had you no bother at all?'

'No, but Archie had.'

'Oh. Did the wheels come off his?'

'Naw, he has a sore foot 'cause I hit him with the hammer.'

It didn't stop when the boys grew up and became young men. My father, Bob Faus, and Gerry McKinney shared the same smooth style: a cool confidence. When I think of my dad and Gerry, James Dean, Frank Sinatra, and Dean Martin come to mind—the cool guys—nothing rattled them.

When he came of age but still lived at home, Gerry stayed out until four in the morning and didn't apologise. Instead, in the morning, he sat at the table reading the paper.

'Where were you till half-four in the morning?' His da demanded.

Gerry shook the paper and read on.

'I'm speaking to you. Where were you until half-four in the morning?'

Gerry let the paper down. 'I was out enjoying myself.'

'You were up to no good.'

Gerry lifted the paper back up and went on reading.

'You were out till half-four in the morning last night. What time are you planning to come in tonight?'

'Probably half-four tomorrow morning.'

Is a person born with that kind of confidence or it is part of how he was raised? Gerry's parents were unique for their time in that Margaret was twenty years younger than her husband. Also, there was no physical chastising in the house. Instead, it was psychological motivation. 'It wasn't very nice what you did' or 'I don't think you should be proud of that' were phrases often spoken by Willie and Margaret McKinney who also double-teamed their sons.

Willie would go down the stairs to meet his late-coming sons while Margaret stayed up stairs and hollered down, 'Are they drunk? They better not be drunk! Are you taking care of this?' Willie shooed his sons up to bed, telling them they better hurry, they didn't want what their mother would dish out if she got to them. Of course, she never did. As the boys got older, their capacity for trouble expanded and their parents' strategy became more complex.

One of Willie's favourite games was the obstacle course. The boys only drank from eight till half-ten when the pubs closed, but they stayed out 'sobering up' till the wee hours of the morning before sneaking in the house. Arriving home to find the gate locked, Fred said to Louis, 'Come on, I'll give you a lift up.' Gerry and Fred boosted Louis to the top of the fence, from where he whispered down, 'Jesus, Fred, Da's hooked a chain to the post and strung it across the garden and the car's parked underneath me!'

Gerry whispers up, 'Fall in on the roof of the car.' Louis falls. He crawls off the car and lets Gerry and Fred in the gate. By now every dog in the neighbourhood is barking. They rest against the garden wall waiting for the light in their father's room but none appears.

Now it's Fred's turn. He raises the kitchen window and puts one leg through. He steps into the sink, does a contortionist move, and he's in. The sink's filled with water so he is wet up to his knees, but he opens the door for Gerry and Louis and they are in. They pause. No noise comes from the rooms upstairs. Gerry looks at Louis and Fred, 'Let's sit for a wee while and see.' They sit on the kitchen floor smoking, quietly chatting, and laughing about the night's craic. Twenty minutes pass. 'Let's try the door to the living room,' Louis suggests.

'Jesus, it's locked.' Fred turns to Gerry and Louis, 'Screw this!' The door breaks open with one swift kick. The room is dark, save for the red glow of their father's pipe, 'Ah, so youse have finally come home!'

I don't know where Margaret and Willie found their sense of humour, especially in the face of so much tragedy, but maybe they enjoyed every day together because they knew the next wasn't promised.

Fixing dinner in the kitchen one evening, Margaret asked her husband, 'What's that racket out the back?'

'A goat.'

'A goat?'

'Aye, Margaret, it's a goat.'

'And just what are we doing with a goat?'

'Fresh milk, darlin'. Fresh milk.'

The next day the goat was let out. Margaret didn't know it was security given for the loan of a fiver, which at the time was a tidy sum for them to loan. From then on, whenever Margaret said, 'That milkman never came this morning! Louis, would you go to the shop for a bottle?' Willie responded, 'If you hadn't let the goat out, you would have plenty of milk!'

Parental advice in the McKinney house always came with a story. One lesson from Willie to his sons went like this: 'If somebody asks you for money, just give it to them.'

'No, I don't believe that one, da,' the son replied.

'Aye, it's true. But! Give them as little as possible.'

'I don't understand the logic in that.'

'It's very simple. If they ask you for a lot of money and you give them a lot of money you'll have to go try and get that back again and that is very difficult. But, if you lend them a little money and they don't pay you back, you can live without it. Either way, they won't come back and ask you for anything again.' Willie rested his case.

'Well Jesus, Da, that's a terrific plan so if I meet ten people on the Strand Road tomorrow morning …'

'You're exaggerating son. You'll only meet one at a time.'

Not only did Willie and Margaret subscribe to a somewhat different parenting philosophy from their peers, they showed affection in front of their children! Louis remembers his mother telling him she loved his father saying, 'Oh my, he's a fine man.' Louis was shocked. Parents just didn't share stuff like that with their children. They loved each other! Imagine!

Even with six boys, there were occasional subtle, quiet moments in the McKinney house. Louis recalls springtime Sunday evenings when his father played the piano in the sitting room, his mother hummed along in the kitchen, and Michael O'Hehir commentated Gaelic football on the radio. The smell of apple cakes and the occasional order, 'Get your feet off the mantle!' came from the kitchen to the boys as they lounged listening to the matches.

The boys in a rare moment of silence: listening to football, 'Green Glens of Antrim' coming out of the sitting room, their mother singing, and a golden glow of sunshine casting shadows through the amber front-door glass 'is one of the nicest family memories I have,' Louis recalls. 'Back then, I never thought it would come to this, sitting here telling you about my murdered brother. I look at my life now and think, "I'm lucky. I've had a good run."'

Maybe it was the constant bustle of raising her own five boys and three stepchildren that made it go so fast, but to their mother it seemed no time at all before Margaret's boys were dating and then married. Friday night was chaos. Five boys. One bathroom. Endless quarrels. Louis preferred getting punched up on the way into the bath than on the way out. He figured if you got punched going in you could clean yourself up. Cleverly, Gerry slipped in while the others argued. He sang as he washed and showered in a voice that rivaled mating cats and bad fan-belts. Gerry emerged with wavy hair, checked shirt, and 'smelling like a rose' as his brothers enjoyed pointing out. Gerry didn't mind the ribbing once he met Ita.

Ita O'Kane was a real doll, a catch, and after five short years of dating, she finally said yes, she'd marry him. Patience wasn't Gerry's virtue but Ita was worth it. She had blonde hair, a great figure, and whether it was her hand in his, her head on his shoulder, his arms around her waist, or their giddiness at seeing one another, she fit him and he fit her. 'Here ya go doll,' Gerry tossed his empty teacup to Ita.

In Gerry and Ita's five years of dating, he brought her cigarettes and chocolate every time they went to the pictures. In eleven years of marriage he never stopped bringing her cigarettes and chocolate. And in eleven years of marriage, Ita caught every teacup.

When Gerry met Ita, he was absolutely certain she was the one. However, Louis found anxiety blocked his true feelings for Frances. On more than one occasion Gerry approached the grieving Louis and asked, 'What's wrong?'

'Nothing.'

'Do you want to talk about it?'

'Aye. But I'd need to trust the person.'

'Did you talk to Fred?'

'No.'

'Well, that's a good start.'

'What happened, Louis? You finish with your woman?'

'Aye, Gerry, we're through.'

'What did you do?'

'Nothing. We just fell out.'

'Well, Louis, if I were you, I'd be on that phone and talk to her and sort it out.'

'I'm not doing that. It wasn't my fault.'

'Oh, so you will lie there and break your heart hurting, but you won't apologise. Hmm. Where is she going tonight?'

'Jesus Gerry, I don't know.'

'How do you know she's not sitting at home doing the same thing as you? Jump in the car. I'll take you over.'

'I'm not going.'

But Louis went. Gerry gave him a lift to Frances' house, and then Louis had to think of a plausible excuse for being there, which was usually something like, 'I just thought I'd come see what's the craic with you.' Frances was a forgiving woman and offered the olive branch, 'We're just going to the pictures. You wanna come along?' It's amazing Louis ever managed it, but he eventually asked her to marry him. However, it took Gerry to get him to the altar.

On his wedding day, Louis paced the floor muttering to himself, wringing his hands, and was just plain miserable looking when Gerry took him by the shoulders, looked him in the eye and said, 'Are you sure?' Louis replied, 'I don't know! Do I love her? Does she love me? I don't know!' Gerry said, 'Well, this is important. You've got to be sure! I've got a fast car out there. There's still time to get out. I'll take you away if you want to go.' It wasn't gentle but Gerry pushed the right button. Louis was forced to decide: Yes. He was sure. He pulled himself together, stood proudly, and married Frances. Forty-two years later he is still sure.

Gerry's first business was the Ritz. He'd met Ita at a dance there and when the owner wanted to retire, Gerry couldn't bear to see it close so he took it over. Dance halls were a dime a dozen, so he invested in skates and opened it as a roller rink. Gerry always saw the bigger possibilities in life.

One customer, an Englishman, had a beard and always came on his own. He drank the god-awful camp-coffee that cost 7 pence a bottle but made £2,50 in coffee; it was that thick. He skated round the rink at a slow, steady cadence. Night after night Gerry chatted him up. 'Jeff said to put a ring around the floor.' The next morning Gerry had a boy painting a ring around the floor. 'Jeff said to practice changing from right foot to left foot on the ring.' Gerry skated around the ring from right foot to left. 'Jeff said to get a partner.' Marie Kelly became Gerry's roller-dancing partner. Next, a sailor started skating around the ring and then another and then a few civilians and pretty soon Sunday nights were filled with roller-dancing enthusiasts.

The boys weren't out of the house long when Fred died. Fred's death was the first time Gerry's brothers saw Gerry slow down. The man who played cards for the fun of cheating at them, who never drove his car under ninety miles an hour, worked a full time job, ran several businesses on the side, and had just married and started a family slowed down. Gerry visited his mother every night and attended chapel with her. He was devoted to her until his own death nine years later. After a year of visiting her every day she insisted he get on with his own life. He was alive, he had a family to raise, and she expected him to do it well.

Lawrence and Denis were away, so after Fred's death, Louis and Gerry became nearly inseparable. It was a natural, easy relationship. Gerry concocted the business-promoting schemes and Louis carried them out. One night at the rink, Gerry turned to Louis, 'It's a cold night isn't it.'

'Aye, it's cold.'

'See them soldiers standing out there?'

'Aye, Gerry, I see 'em.'

'I was thinking about bringing them in for a cup of coffee.'

'Jesus Gerry, if your customers see them in here, they will leave.'

'We are warm and dry. They are cold and wet. Give them a nice cup of coffee and stand them in the corner.'

Louis went out but quickly returned, 'Gerry, the cops are there as well.'

'Bring them in, too.'

Louis went out again and approached the soldiers and police, 'Hello boys! Would ya like a wee cup of coffee?' They followed him in and Gerry told Louis, 'Go up there now and tell the girl to make the men coffee.' Louis rolled his eyes at Gerry but told the girl working the refreshment counter, 'See the guys in the corner? Give them coffee, Gerry said it's alright. And throw in some buns, too.' The girl replied, 'There's gonna be trouble.' But Louis was now on to the scheme, 'Naw, there'll be no trouble now, cause they're in!'

During Lent the dance halls were closed on Sunday nights. For a full six weeks there was no dancing on Sundays. Gerry saw not only a religious holiday but an opportunity to make money. It was easy to turn the roller-rink back into a dance hall once a week. But Louis saw trouble. Their mother attended Mass every morning and prayed the Stations of the Cross every evening. She might not approve of dancing on Sunday nights especially as it violated the wishes of the Church. Louis also thought, however, if they were opening on Sunday night, they should advertise, but Gerry said word of mouth would be enough. Nonetheless, on the Saturday before Lent, Gerry turned up in a van with a loudspeaker on top and pressed Louis into action.

'What are we doing?'

'You said we should advertise.'

'Jesus, Gerry, you said word of mouth!'

'It'll be words from yer mouth. Just say, "During Lent all dance halls are closed except the Ritz Ballroom run by Gerry McKinney!"'

The first Sunday they had 900 people at a half-crown a piece. When Gerry brought the money box into the house at the end of the week their mother was thrilled. Their father was wondering about the bumper crowd.

'You're marvellous! How did you get that?' he said.

'You only have seventy pairs of skates. You run it three nights a week and your normal takings is £45.'

'Well, we decided to open on Sunday for waltzes and foxtrots, you know, to keep people off the streets.'

'Really? Who's the band?' their mother inquired.

'Gay McIntyre Allstars', was the reply.

Gerry's parents were sure the priest would be coming down on him and there would be public outcry and then the police would get involved. It was sure to be a terrible mess. But for the next five Sundays, they packed the place. Gerry never had any trouble with the police. He'd been inviting them in out of the cold all winter for free coffee and buns.

Televisions were the next business target and once again Louis was part of the show. By this time, he was giving Gerry advice, which didn't mean Gerry took it.

'Gerry, that's the wrong place.'

'Why? What's wrong with it?'

'It's at the back of a women's shop. You have no shop windows. You can't sell TVs without displaying them in the window.'

'I'm not selling it that way, Louis. When we go round on debt collection, we can tell them to call up to the shop.'

'No man is going to walk through a woman's shop!'

'Louis, when they are walking in here, they are looking at the models. Besides, Derry women work. They'll be buying TVs too.'

The location of the shop proved no barrier to the sale of the TVs but Louis and Gerry had adventures trying to collect the payments. Once one-third the price was paid, by law they couldn't re-possess the set, so there was little incentive for folks to pay more than one-third. Week after week Louis heard the same refrain, 'I can't pay you this week'. Back out to the truck he'd report, 'She has no money.' The brains of the operation, Gerry would reply, 'That's alright. Jump in.'

Louis was the brawn and if persuading was to be done, he was your man. But, he was clever as well. At one house especially deep in arrears, Louis heard once again, 'I can't pay you this week.'

'Well, that's interesting. Gerry had to pay for it when he bought it. You bought it from Gerry, now it's your turn to pay for it.'

'Well,' the man dressed in a white suit replied, 'I can't pay you this week. Besides, this TV is rubbish; we shouldn't be paying for it.'

'What's wrong with it?'

'It's always flickering and blinking.'

'You want another one? We'll bring the new one in the morning. Would that be alright? Will you pay me then?'

'Aye, we'll pay you then.' Louis unplugged the set, took it in his arms and headed for the truck.

'Gerry! Open that door!'

'What are you doing?'

'It's a chance of a lifetime. They haven't paid us in three months. I am taking the TV. They told me to bring back another one in the morning. I'm not bringing them back a new one in the morning. They never paid us!'

'God almighty, Louis, that was a terrible bad thing you done.'

'Nah, Gerry, not terrible bad; terrible clever.'

Even with the slow-payers and no-payers, Gerry's TV shop in Derry was a success. So successful in fact, he decided to open a shop in Strabane, a town near Derry. He hired a young man just out of school to run the shop. The guy planned to become a priest and was in-between secondary school and seminary. Louis argued against leaving a stranger in charge of the shop. But Gerry had faith, and for goodness sake, the guy was going to be a priest, 'who's more trustworthy than that?'

Louis argued back, 'He's gonna give everything away.'

'You're awfully cynical,' Gerry retorted, 'You'll see, he'll be a good guy.'

Gerry was right, the first week sales were good. The second week sales were good. The man sold TV's, sewing machines, portable radios. The guy was doing terrific. In the first month, sales reached an unheard of £1000.

Out on their Friday collections, Louis worried the payments from Strabane were slow. He and Gerry finished their rounds in Derry early and headed over to ensure that week's payments had been collected. Louis knocked on the first door:

'Are you Mrs Doherty?'

'Aye.'

'I'm here to collect your payment.'

'Payment for what?'

'The TV.'

'Aye. That's the Doherty over there.' And the next door:

'Are you Mrs Doherty?'

'Aye.'

'I'm here to collect your payment.'

'Payment for what?'

'The TV.'

'Aye. That's the Doherty over there.' And the door after that:

'Are you Mrs Doherty?'

'Aye.'

'I'm here to collect your payment.'

'Payment for what?'

'The TV.'

'Aye. That's the Doherty over there.' When he finally got back to the truck he told Gerry, 'There's ten Doherty's on this street. Your man has down Doherty with no addresses.'

'He sold a thousand pound of merchandise. We've got to collect.'

'But Gerry, there's no addresses. What are we going to do?'

'I don't think there's a whole lot we can do. That's a terrible thing that guy done.'

'Aye, and he wanted to be a priest.'

'Aye, he's still going on to become a priest.'

'I told you he would give things away,' Louis reminded him.

'Aye. Put it down to bad experience. We'll go on.'

On they went. Gerry worked in Antrim, Strabane, Belfast, England, wherever he could get work that would teach him and further his skills. He trained in electronics, engineering, drafting and architecture. The sophistication of his businesses increased. Louis found his own line of work and although the brothers had families to raise and their work-lives were diverging, they met every Sunday morning to talk, 'I reckon I'm in this here because of you.' Gerry said to Louis about his work in engineering.

'Don't blame this on me,' Louis shot back.

'You told me to do what I'm good at,' Gerry said.

The two talked about wives, and children, and bills, but mostly Gerry talked about the future, about his plans and grilled Louis, asking him what he thought. Louis often said to his brother, 'Why are you asking me? I don't bloody know much.' But he was honoured to be asked. Gerry was educated and exceedingly bright but he wanted to know what Louis thought, even if he didn't know anything about engineering. Louis' opinion mattered to Gerry and every week Gerry asked.

At thirty-four years of age, Gerry didn't get to fully develop his skills as a father and husband. In the early years, he travelled a lot for work. Driving to Belfast, an hour and a half each way with long and varied work hours made a daily commute impossible. In those days, Derry men had to go where the work was. A young husband and father, Gerry was away working for much of his children's early years, but he was fully present with his children when he was home.

Gerry's children took centre stage. He took his children along on errands. He involved them. He gave them wee treats like a late night of football-watching with Kevin, or chocolate tea-cakes for toddler Mairead who was then covered head to toe in chocolate. Mornings, when he was home, Gerry let Ita sleep and carrying a basket and tray to his children's rooms, waking them with tea and buns. He was strict with bedtimes and routine. His children knew what to expect. He was generous with love, affection, and praise and the home their children remember was one of respect, love, affection, and fairness.

Surviving her husband's death is a testament to Ita McKinney's strength and also, a testament to her character. She raised eight children with no money, and they all turned out grand. Her husband was murdered in the street and she kept her family together. She lost her sole support and the love of her life at the hands of another and she forgave. She taught her children to choose love and forgiveness over hate and revenge. In the words of her daughter Regina:

At the end of the day it all comes down to choice. I choose to let what has been done to affect me positively. I choose to want to make my daddy proud. I choose to be who I am with the circumstances I've been dealt. I choose not to go down the road that he was accused of. I choose to go down the road of forgiveness. I choose not to let my family down. Not to choose these things, to me, would dishonour my father's memory. I wouldn't wish on anybody what was done on us. When a person is killed, the person who killed him isn't hurting him—he is hurting that person's wife, children, parents, and friends.

Kevin was eleven years old when his father was murdered; Aileen, ten; Regina, nine; Tracy, eight; Martine, six; Fred, five; Mairead was eighteen months and then there was Gerry junior—born eight days after his father's death.

At eleven years of age, Kevin was just starting to develop a relationship with his father. They shared an interest in cars, sport, mechanics and engineering, an active lifestyle, curiosity, and a thirst for knowledge. On the morning of January 30th, Kevin stood with his father in front of the hearth. Their backs against the warmth, Gerry's hands on Kevin's shoulders. Gerry had a new copy of 'Men Behind the Wire' and was playing it over and over again, singing the words to the song. Kevin can still feel the strength and pride he felt with his father's hands on his shoulders.

When Gerry joined the march that day, he was marching for civil rights. He wanted his children to have the same rights as Protestant children. He wanted the wives of Derry men to rest well at night, not fearing their husbands would be abducted and interned. Gerry was shot while he and others attempted to take cover, fleeing from Glenfada into Abbey Park. His brother-in-law, John O'Kane, witnessed his murder:

He walked forward onto the cobblestones and across them at a right angle, which led him on to the second of the three shallow steps. He was watching the alleyway all the time. As he approached the steps he turned his head to the left and put his hands in the air saying, "no, no, don't shoot." A shot rang out and he fell across the steps. He landed on his back and I remember him saying, "Jesus, Jesus," and blessing himself. The bullet had passed through his body, in one side and out of the other, from left to right; into the left chest under his armpit and out of his right chest under his armpit. He landed on his back. I remember seeing his coat moving as the bullet went through.[19]

After his father's death, Kevin was pressed into the role of man of the house, but at eleven years old wasn't ready for the role. Nonetheless, he kept watch over his mother (whether she liked it or not!), learned to keep the house, pay bills, and mind his siblings. He wrapped his arms around Regina when she missed her daddy and needed to feel the protective warmth of a man's arms. He encouraged the young Gerry to take his first steps. He rebelled as a teen—fought with his mother and struggled to find his identity. He accidentally killed a wee lad who dashed out in front of his car and lives with the sorrow and pain that he is responsible for the loss of another parent's son as he and his wife raise their own precious children.

He walked each of his sisters down the aisle. He carried his brother's coffin and walked beside his sister when she buried her husband. He calls into his mother since Gerry's death in 1999, just as his father called into his mother when her Fred was killed in 1963. He is a kind and generous soul, and he and his wife have a house filled with love, respect, affection, and fairness.

Kevin and his father were only twenty-three years apart. By the time Kevin was twenty, they'd have been near enough like brothers had Gerry lived. I think about my own

---

[19] Statement of John O'Kane to Saville Inquiry, 12 May 1999.

son, just twenty years younger than me and how much I enjoy him. I would hate to miss the rest of our life together. There is so much yet to do. Kevin wishes his father had lived long enough for the two of them to lift a few pints together, listen to Kevin's concerns, give advice, and especially, to meet his grandchildren.

In August 2003, Kevin's wife gave birth to the third James Gerald McKinney. Perhaps in twenty years my son and I can return to Derry so we can all raise a glass to the first Gerry McKinney. For remembering him not only reminds us of a tragic injustice, it also testifies to the strength and character of a Derry family whose lives personify a legacy never to be forgotten.

John Young

> *I'd rather be the mother of a murdered son,*
> *than the mother of a murderer.*
> *-Lily Young*

The air was unusually dry for a late January day in Derry. John woke at half-seven and put on his new suit and the white shirt his mother had just bought from Graham Hunter's. The dark blue suit with a fine pinstripe looked sharp, professional. Specially made, John had designed the single breasted, three button suit with a narrow revere and a raised vent in the back. Not the style of the day; this was cutting edge. He always wanted to look his best, especially if girls were about, and with John Young, girls were always about.

As I put the final touches on me look for the day—graduation ring on me right ring-finger, garnet ring on me left ring-finger, watch face-up on the thumb side of me left wrist, and me tie-pin, I could see it all coming together. I looked good. Business would be good today. Men in buying jumpers to keep out the Derry wind would be easily convinced that they should have a new button-down to match. Women picking up hemmed trousers would buy fresh socks or a new belt fer their men. I was doing well at the shop. It was January 1972, that meant the 1971 Salesman of the Year would be awarded soon and I was in the running. Good looking, well dressed, I was going to be a very successful man.

According to John's diary, girls appeared wherever he went. His closest mates played in a band. That this may have contributed to the girls appearing phenomenon isn't revealed in the small green notebook he kept. The ticks next to the list of girls at the back of the school diary swiped from his sister remain unexplained as well. John seemed to be developing a reputation among his friends for two-timing, but this discord may have stemmed from the fact that John's girlfriend in England was a Protestant. John was unconcerned about this detail. His response to his critics: *She likes me. What do I care what church she goes to?!*

Protestant or Catholic didn't bother me, but I was to be eighteen in May and that's just when life begins. I want to enjoy life, not settle down and have a family. I want to move up at the shop, buy a car, make a name for meself. As me mammy always says, 'If you have a job, the world is your oyster.' A final look in the mirror — the hair — perfect.

John had been offered a promotion: a training position in England. He planned to take it. He'd confided in Maura but telling his mother would be a different story. In 1972 Derry was very much a small town. People knew each other's business and weren't reticent in voicing an opinion even in the queue at the shop, 'Don't waste your money on that, I bought one last week and it fell apart.'

Except to find work when none was to be had, people stayed in Derry generation on generation. Men went to England and Scotland to find work. They didn't go for promotions in jobs they already had. John's father, Tommy, worked for the same company forty-eight years and never received a bonus, promotion, or recognition for a job well done.

John's generation was the first generation of Catholic Derry men to find meaningful, rewarding work. They were the first Catholic Derry men to have the opportunity to pursue higher education. John had no intention of being left behind. But John was his mother's son and Derry mothers don't sit well with anyone taking away their sons—even for better jobs and opportunities—so John was putting off telling his mother until it was absolutely necessary.

John Young came from hard working parents. For ten years, Tommy and Lily walked six miles a day, from Springtown to the city centre and back, for work. His parents set a good example for their children and, like his siblings, John not only enjoyed his work but took it seriously. Jobs and money were hard to come by in Derry, and John understood the power and freedom they offered.

John Temple's was one floor, but up-scale. Derry was filled with shirt factories but the shirts in Temple's were imported from England. They carried off-the-rack attire but encouraged special order. John was always well dressed, and he understood the importance of having a suit made to fit. John didn't set out to be a clothier, the headmaster at St. Joe's had told him about the opening, but there was no better job for him. John's father Tommy was a seed man. His brother Leo was a coal man. John was a clothes man and that suited him.

I hadn't been at work long that Saturday when me ma come in the door. Gosh she was smiling. 'John, you got out the door before I got a chance te see you in your new suit. Let me look at you. You look so handsome.' Then she touched me face. She just looked at me and touched me face—in front of everyone at the shop. Nobody moved. People stared. It started te get uncomfortable. I looked down at her and smiled. 'Go on now Lily. I'll see you at dinner.'

Imagine me mammy turning up at work like that! What was she thinking? It wouldn't be like her to turn up like that. She worked off Butcher Street on Magazine, just across the Diamond and around the corner, but she didn't turn up at me job, just like I wouldn'ta turned up at hers.

At the time, it seemed like an odd occurrence. But, at the time, nobody knew John would be murdered the next day. John's mother, through this act, was granted the gift of remembering her son in that moment—tall, handsome, smiling, alive—her John.

Until now, most people have known two things about John Young: that he is one of the fourteen murdered by

British Paratroopers on Bloody Sunday; and the lies the British government told about him. You'd think John was an important person for the British to go to so much trouble to smear his name. The truth is John was just a seventeen-year-old lad who went to a peace march to have a bit of craic with his friends. John wasn't carrying a weapon or throwing a nail-bomb. He pegged a couple of stones at Barrier 14 but when they turned on the water cannon his vanity about his clothes and hair drove him out.

It's been more than thirty years since John was murdered. He would be fifty this year (29 May 2004) if he'd lived. The stalwart dedication of the families of the killed and wounded in an effort to clear their names has produced two major motion films and a dozen books detailing witness statements and evidence that clearly demonstrate all the victims were unarmed and innocent of any serious wrongdoing on Bloody Sunday. The Bloody Sunday Inquiry, begun in 1998, brought the startling bare-faced lies of the soldiers into the public domain. Nonetheless, many people still accept, rather than question what the British government told them: that the men and women murdered and wounded on Bloody Sunday got what they deserved; that John Young was a criminal; a Derry Young Hooligan.

It is difficult for people to believe the government would tell outright lies. Jokes about politicians' honesty aside, when the government makes a judgment, people want to believe it is true, or at least partially true. After all, if John Young was innocent, you or your son might be murdered on any given Sunday. It's not easy to believe the British government would sanction and then lie about cold-blooded murder in the streets, but that's what they did. So why did they murder John? It would give his family a world of peace to know the answer to that.

Bloody Sunday not only ended and destroyed the lives of twenty-eight men and women, it scarred an entire city.

Visit the Bogside today and ask about Bloody Sunday. You'll find the horror and pain are still palpable, but it is likely that the person you talk to will graciously show you the sites, tell you what they witnessed, and hope you will share what you learned.

In 1972 crisis counselling was not available for the 20,000 people who ran for their lives, and the families were told that their sons, daughters, husbands, wives, and parents were responsible for their own deaths and injuries. These innocent civilians were painted as terrorists by a propaganda machine so strong it reached around the world before the final body was delivered to the morgue. John Young was one of twenty-eight killed and wounded by British Soldiers on Bloody Sunday. This is his story.

On Christmas eve, 1948 the Young family arrived at Springtown Camp. They moved in with one chair and twins on the way. Derry's housing shortage goes back long before John was born. Like many places around the world, suffrage was not universal in Northern Ireland. The rule was not one person, one vote, but one house, one vote. Therefore, ten adults could be living in the same house and still be allotted only one vote. This resulted in two typical governmental activities: first, they didn't build houses and second, the few that were built were crammed in one area so the Catholic population would occupy the fewest constituencies. So, even though a few anti-Unionist candidates managed to get elected to Parliament, their ability to effect substantive change was limited.

For such political reasons people had moved from the Bogside to Springtown Camp. John's mammy, Lily, moved her family to Springtown for smaller reasons. 'Smaller' meaning she was living with another family in a two bedroom house. Lily was living in a 10 x 10 room with a bed, a fireplace, no running water, an outside toilet, a husband and two boys, Patrick and Leo. When she discovered she was pregnant with their third and fourth, she took action.

John's father, Tommy, wasn't crazy about moving three miles out of town, but Lily was determined. Moving with one chair on Christmas Eve, Lily received the best Christmas gift a woman could wish for—a home of her own.

The US Army Base, Springtown Camp, was a promised land of corrugated tin huts awaiting the cramped Catholic families of Derry. As soon as the Americans left, those living three, four, and five families to a house began a steady migration down the Strand, up Buncrana Road, and out to squat the huts in Springtown. The abandoned U.S. Army Base was the first taste of home-ownership for hundreds of Derry families and this contributed its own chemistry to the catalyst of the Derry civil rights movement to come.

When the Young family first moved to Springtown, they had a hut without water. Leo fetched water from the community well. Lily soon discovered the officer's huts and the family moved again. She was thrilled. Lily's home was three bedrooms, living room, indoor toilet, and kitchen. She was ready for the twins. To Lily's heartbreak, one of her babies was still-born and the other lived just six weeks. Grateful for her job, she returned to the shirt factory and worked away her sorrow.

Life continued at a practical pace for the Young family. Leo walked across the field everyday, taking his shoes and socks off to wade through the stream that cut through Springtown on his way to school. Lily didn't discourage the practice. At least his feet got washed everyday. When Maura came along and grew big enough to go to school, Leo carried her across the stream. This was not because Leo was benevolent, it was because Maura insisted.

Tommy worked for Thompson's Seed Shop. He was lucky to have a job. Few Catholic Derry men were able to find steady work. Tommy's duties included stocking and mixing seed and servicing farm implements. Every day, Monday through Friday, Tommy rose at five to walk the three miles to work. There were no buses from Springtown and when putting bread on the table and keeping children in shoes was a challenge, a car was a luxury few Catholic families could afford. Lily was happy in her corrugated tin-hut so Tommy faithfully completed the journey each day.

Tommy started working in the back of the store hauling and stocking seed when he was 14. He wore dungarees and a flat cap. His brother, John, worked at the front of the store and wore a suit. Neither of them was ever promoted. They worked at the jobs for which they had been hired, and that was that. If a Protestant came to work at the shop, he would be given a better position and better pay than Tommy or John. Neither brother ever earned more than £8 a week. Tommy took retirement at sixty-two because he had developed chronic asthma from the seed dust. His full retirement pay for 48 years of work was £360.

A man called Senator Barnhill was the managing director of the store and a Unionist member of the establishment. Senator Barnhill was 6'3" and stocky. He covered his bald head with a wide brimmed hat, wore a perpetual grin, and travelled on the public bus. Given that he was murdered in 1971 by the Official IRA, he probably wasn't fooling anyone.

Tommy never bothered with politics. He was employed. He had to earn money to put dinner on the table and clothes on his children. There were so few jobs for men in Derry at the time that you took what you could get and didn't complain. Working for Senator Barnhill must have been miserable, though, because for a while everyone in the house suffered, even the dog. The dog would know on the

Friday night that Tommy was different, because he would say to the dog during the week, 'Up and we'll go for a walk.' But on a Friday night no walk. The silent treatment. Tommy would take a drink on a Friday, and he'd brood until Sunday noon. Then he'd gather his children and the dog and walk through the oak trees and hawthorn bushes down to the Springtown Bridge and watch the train traveling from Derry to Buncrana.

Lily worked first in Wilkinson's and then Graham Hunter's shirt factories. For one hundred years, approximately 1874-1974, some of the best shirts in the world came from Derry and the shirt factories in Derry employed the women who wanted jobs, which, at 20,000 workers, meant nearly all of them. Lily could sew a shirt from start to finish and when John got older, she always bought his shirts to match his suits.

Lily loved her work. She, too, walked the six mile return between Derry and Springtown. She left her children with a neighbour and went to work. She loved going to town everyday, working with the women. On bank holidays the shirt factory girls would organise buses to Donegal or Portrush for a day's outing, dining, and dancing. The friendships she made at the shirt factories and her love of the work would later sustain her as she grieved her murdered son.

Springtown was hard living. The child mortality rate stood at forty-two percent. Domestic violence ran rampant. Leo and his friends would often listen at different huts, when people had been at the drink. As objects smashed against tin walls and alighted through windows, they knew there was trouble inside. The boys hung around to hear the craic, but also silently witnessed murder and attendant lawlessness that was kept quiet and put off to rumour.

The Young's experienced their fair share of hardship at Springtown as well. They had more space and a sink with running water, but there was no electricity or heat. There was no washing-up tub and when Leo was older and came home from delivering coal he stood in his underpants as his mother dumped a bucket of water over him and scrubbed him down. The cold of that experience is not something one ever forgets—but that wasn't the only cold. Leo used to say, 'Ye put more clothes on ye going to bed than what ye did when ye're up.'

Tommy's mood at the weekend was damaging and hurt Lily more than she could express. Springtown was hard, but before long joy would come into the house. On 29 May 1954 John was born: 10 pounds, 11 ounces, and the apple of his mammy's eye. From that day, things would be better.

The only thing I remember about Springtown wasn't about the camp but bein' in hospital for appendicitis. I was a wee wain of three and a half and I remember me mammy hidin' and peeking through the winda. Helen would be sittin' wit me and I'd say, 'There's me ma! I can see the feather in her hat!' She always wore a hat and pearls. She was a very refined, respectable woman and I slagged her, but I loved her more than anything.

Two years later the Young family was allotted a house in Creggan Estates. John and Maura discovered electricity at 120 Westway. With a button at the top and the bottom of the steps, they ran up and down the stairs switching the lights on and off. John's was the back room at the top of the stairs, the smallest room in the house, just big enough for his bed, wardrobe, chest of drawers, and for a while, his father.

Patrick and his wife moved into the house so Tommy

bunked in with John, and Lily with Maura. With lino floor and no heat upstairs they still 'put more clothes on ye going to bed than what ye did when ye're up,' so even though John had to share, Tommy added extra warmth to the room for a while.

John had the job of cutting the wee patch of grass and was always sent out to be cutting when a new baby came into the world. In 1963, with three children in tow, Patrick and his wife moved to Shantallow and John finally had his own room, which was the envy of all his friends.

Up in Creggan Maura and I also discovered that Patrick and Leo weren't our only siblings. We had two older sisters as well. Elish and Helen lived at 28 North Street with me mammy's two aunts because there was no room at 32 North for them. Helen and Elish woulda had to walk too far to get to school from Springtown and, they had a choice, so they stayed on in Rosemount wit the two aunts. When Maura was born Helen got taken out of school to help her mammy but Maura and I never knew she was the sister. Maura was thrilled. Didn't make no matter to me. S'long as I got me own room, what did I care how many sisters there were.

Tommy cleaned his shoes every night. He said they kept longer that way. On Saturday nights he took on the boys' shoes as well. He lined them up by the door for the boys to slip on as they left for Mass. John's family gave him endless grief about his feet and shoes. His dad used to say, 'Take a look at them shoes, take a good look at them shoes ...' John's response was, 'They're not looking at the shoes, they're looking at me face. This is what they're looking at, from here up.'

I dunno why I walked the soles off my shoes, they just come off. I once walked to a dance and me feet was bloody from the condition of me shoes. I danced the night away. Did me family take pity on me? No, they give me grief. Me feet were me own business. Maura would say I was a dirty bugger where my feet were concerned, but what was she doin looking at my feet? She said I'd buy three suits for one pair of shoes but why have two? They'd both be black and nobody would know they were different. If I wore the same suit everyday, the girls would definitely notice, but nobody ever said, is that the same pair of black shoes you wore yesterday?

The time to buy new shoes in Derry would have been right before or after retreat. With all the walking done during that week, you were either buying a pair to break-in or something to replace what you ruined with all the walking. The May retreat meant that for week you had to be at 6 a.m. Mass, then home for breakfast, then down the town to work, then home for dinner, then back to work, then home for tea, and then back to chapel from seven till nine. Derry women said they did two weeks of retreat every year, for having to get the men up and see that they went.

At the end of the retreat all of the men wear suits with flowers. You hold onte your flower and give it to your special girlfriend. You know, your number one girl. Sometimes you give it to just the right girl, but that's probably only if you're engaged or married. 'Cause if you're single, like me, there's always someone gonna be upset.

John was well liked in school by his peers and teachers alike. A good student academically, school also provided the essential social training necessary for later in life. In the midst of John's secondary schooling, a distraught Lily approached Helen:

'I don't know what to do … this will kill your father.'
'Mammy what is it?'
'Oh it's terrible. I didn't raise my son to do this to me.'
'Mother, what's the matter?'

'Our John has dirty books upstairs.'
'Are you sure?'
'Aye.'
'Well, let me see the book.'
'Let you see it?'
'It's alright mammy I'm married, I have a family, let me see the book.'
'I don't know what the world's coming to …'

Lily showed Helen the book. It was John's biology textbook. Lily responded, 'A school book! Are you kidding? I'll be down to that headmaster in the morning!' Lily was forty-three years old when John was born and by the time he reached secondary school, her hair was white. Just as the family gave John grief about his feet, he slagged his mother about her white hair, 'Now ma don't you be coming to school. They'll think you're my granny 'cause you have white hair.'

Ach, she acted sore about that, but she could never be mad at me. I was her John. If she was talking about Helen or Maura, it was 'our Helen, our Maura' but if she was talking about me, it was always, 'My John.

We was like that, just like any family I s'pose, we'd get mad and huff off, but never for long, and in my case, never far. Once when I was a wee lad, Helen was watching me and (she says) I said something sarcastic so she thumped me. So I said, 'I'm leavin' this house!' But then I had a realisation and changed my mind and said, 'You don't live here. You go.' Helen stood her ground and told me, 'I'm not goin.' You can go.' So I got me school bag and left. I sat across from the house in the green so she could think about what she done and how much she would miss me. I sat for a long time. Well, least till I got hungry for me dinner.

If John had a falling out with his mother, instead of grounding him, she'd hide his record player. He always found it, played his records, and then put it back where she had it hidden. John spent his money on suits and records. Like just about every other Catholic family in Derry at that time, they didn't have money for anything extra. John quickly learned the power of money and from an early age devised ways to get it. He worked for it and schemed for it, but he got it nonetheless.

I helped collect the coal money, for one. I could walk inte 40 houses in Creggan. Open the door, walk in, lift the coal money, and walk out again. And everybody would say, 'God who was that came in?' and someone in the house would say, 'It's probably just John Young liftin' the coal money.' I used to collect one side o the street, and the man who owned the coal lorry would lift the other. I learnt which houses the pretty girls lived in, and I'd be like, 'Rest yer feet, I'll get this street.'

John had a biscuit tin all felted on the inside. On the outside he wrote 'Save John Young Fund.' And when Patrick, Helen, and Leo were up on Sunday, John brought out the box and fined them a shilling for every bad word. Helen was his best customer. He loved to see her coming. She was a guaranteed jackpot. When Helen came in he'd just set the box on her knee.

Me mammy used to say, 'Food on yer table, clothes on yer back, and ye're grand.' But I wanted more. The money in that box was gonna save me. It was money for me car. I got the job, got the suits, got the girls, my next conquest? The car.

John managed to save some money but there were important expenses he had to keep up with like suits, records, and girls. So he took advantage of every opportunity. Helen supplied the record player and chess board: gifts to her favourite brother. John 'roadied' for Roddy's band and got in free to all the dances they played. Lily got a discount at the shirt factory so she bought the shirts for his suits. 'See, everything worked out. How could it not? I was me. John Young. Life was good.'

Every Thursday and Saturday me and Maura would go down to Helen's to watch the colour TV. Me and Helen was trekkies and didn't miss a Thursday night. But on Saturdays Helen would sometimes be out on her civil rights marches and then I hadda watch what Maura picked. Don't know why exactly Helen kept goin' to them marches. She started goin' 'cause she wanted a house to get outta that 10 x 10 back room she and her husband and three girls were livin' in. Anyway, she'd got a house and she had a colour TV, so why she was out still marchin' and not home relaxin' was beyond me.

Maura and John never expressed any interest in the marches. They had it good. They lived in a big house with their own rooms. They had jobs and therefore some disposable income. They had not experienced sectarian violence and generally lived quiet, happy teenage lives. They also worked on Saturdays when the marches were held.

I could see them marchers going right past the shop. Out marchin' in the rain and the cold. That didn't appeal to me. Gettin' off with the girls, makin' money, going to England, gettin' a car. I had my priorities.

The January 1972 march was the first Derry civil rights march ever held on a Sunday. Many people worked on a Saturday, but Sunday was a day of rest and relaxation. You went to Mass, cooked your dinner, visited with family and friends. Therefore, this particular march drew whole families and groups of friends, many of whom had never attended a civil rights march. Patrick, Leo, Helen, Maura, and John all departed from 120 Westway. Helen and Patrick went to support civil rights; John & Maura went for the craic; Leo went along to keep an eye on John.

How could I miss this march? Every girl in Derry and a whole lot from Belfast were out. I wore my grey trousers, striped shirt, grey jumper, the bomber jacket that my number one Derry girl ordered from America, and a hat. It was dry but I'd be out all the afternoon and I didn't like it rainin' on me and messin' up me hair. Me friend Joe slagged me bout dressin' up for a march but I knew he'd regret not looking good. Most of the girls I seen were still in their Sunday dresses. The craic was good. It would be a good day.

It turned out to be a tragic day. John became a well-dressed corpse, an incidental martyr whom the government and public press degraded and ridiculed. John Young was well named as he was too young to die and too innocent to be defamed. John's headstone stands quietly in the city cemetery but he is not at rest. John's presence is strong in Derry, and thirty-one years later the people who loved him continue to walk the soles off their shoes to clear his name, so some day he may truly rest in peace.

Hugh Gilmour

If mischief was around it would find Hugh Gilmour.

Hugh was the baby of the house. The youngest of nine, small and wiry, his family called him the German, in honour of his flat head. Keeping track of Hugh was no easy task and two brothers, Bernard and Floyd, were assigned to look after him. Every day Bernard and Floyd were sent: 'Get Hugh. Bring Hugh in. Go see where Hugh is. If he's in a safe place, well, that's OK, stay there.'

Hugh Gilmour was born at 16 Springtown Camp, 1954. The entire Gilmour family lived together in Springtown. The four girls, Olive, Doreen, Sara, and Brigid in one bedroom; the boys, Tony, Bernard, and Floyd in the other, packed like sardines. Hugh, being the baby, stayed with his parents Henry and Kathleen. 'They must a thought we'd smother him, or choke him, or maybe we'da been that hungry sometimes we'd probably eat him,' said Bernard, 'Keep him away, they'll probably eat him.'

Hugh was perhaps the nuttiest member of his family, but being the youngest earned him a coveted place in the household pecking order. According to his brothers and sisters, Hugh's position meant he got more than they ever did. Not that the family had much but, while his seven brothers and sisters went to school without shoes, Hugh always had them. While the rest of the siblings regularly beat the hell outta each other, nobody was allowed to touch Hugh. He wasn't to be hit. 'He's too small.' If the brothers touched the German, his mother and sisters rallied to his defense. Fortunately, it never became an issue. Hugh was his mother's world and his mother was Hugh's. Kathleen was the love in Hugh's life.

The other children were sensible enough to watch themselves. The German went head-long into everything. So Kathleen employed them, Olive, Tony, Doreen, Bernard,

Floyd, Sarah, and Brigid, one after the other, to watch after Hugh. Bernard and Floyd, on German-patrol before leaving for Scotland, were sent in to respond to a letter from the primary school headmaster that Hugh was not attending all his classes. Their orders were to, 'go on over to that school, into the classroom, and make sure he stays in class.' Bernard and Floyd went to the headmaster who said, 'Hugh's not here, he doesn't come to school here.'

'Aye, he does.'

'No, Hugh comes in here for his dinner, and goes back out again.'

'Would ye not keep him in?'

'Stay there and watch. Watch for him coming in. He'll be in at noon.'

Bernard and Floyd watched and waited. They didn't see him come in.

'Well I don't know what happened today, I see him every other day.'

Hugh was smart, he knew Bernard and Floyd were there. He had managed to evade his captors. Bernard and Floyd left the front door and went down to the canteen and sure enough, there was the German, eating his dinner. Bernard and Floyd stood guard in the corridor to escort Hugh to class. His class came through, but no Hugh. The German had escaped over the roof of the canteen with the help of a builder's scaffolding. Later at home, Bernard led the interrogation.

'We were in your school today.'

'Aye I seen ye.'

'Where did ye go?'

'I went inte me class.'

'Ye jumped over the roof and down.'

'Aye, I was down sittin' wi' big Gerry the caretaker.'

'Naw ye weren't, ye sneaked off and ye went somewhere else.'

Reconnaissance and interrogation complete, Bernard and Floyd went back to the headmaster who said, 'He does that every day, he comes in here for his lunch and goes again, that's the only reason I wrote a letter to your mother, to make sure he doesn't get into bother.'

'Why ye not stop him?'

'You try and stop him. If you can get over the roof as quick as that wee boy there … there he is now. Look! Try and stop him.'

'I will, aye.'

Hugh was up the top of the scaffold and back down again, like a monkey. All muscle and mischief, there was no stopping Hugh Gilmour. He enjoyed his school dinner uninterupted from then on.

Hugh's brothers left home to find work at early ages. By the time Hugh reached the proper beatin'-up age or had enough meat on him to make a decent meal, Tony, the oldest son, left home. He went to England at sixteen and joined the Royal Air Force. As soon as Bernard and Floyd were relieved of duty—patrolling the streets for the German—they went to pick spuds in Scotland. Unfortunately, finding Hugh would take on tragic significance before any member of the family was prepared for it.

The family moved from Springtown in 1960 to a small street in the Bogside called Pilot's Row. Hugh lost no time making friends. These friendships were forged by freedom and geography. As soon as all of his six year-old self stepped out the front door, Hugh's closest friends became Gerry Doherty, Jim Duffy, Jack McDonald, and Andy McCauley.

Hugh was christened 'Gilly,' and although fate would intervene from time to time, the bond of these friends was unbreakable for the next ten years.

If ever there were a gaggle of ruffians roaming the streets, it was Hugh and his friends. Closed on Sunday, the docks provided plenty of opportunity for exploring and futtering about. The day might start with a walk from the top of the docks to the bottom. The dumpster behind Hunters bakery provided day-old pastries for the lads and leftover dough for their fishing lines. As they meandered along the docks the boys took turns telling stories, posing questions, 'What if you went down here in the river and found a dead body …' as they walked to the slaughter houses where pig entrails were flushed into the river.

Present at the right time, the moment of the flush, you could catch a mullet—the rat of the sea. Mullets would eat anything, and they feasted on pig entrails. With string lifted from building sites, the boys constructed lines, attached the dough lifted from Hunter's bins, and bobbed it on the surface of the water. When the mullet took the dough and went down, they hooked it, reeled it in, and chopped it up to use for bait to fish for flukes and eel.

Walking two miles to get a piece of dough to catch a mullet to cut up to fish for flukes made perfect sense to the boys because you could eat a fluke, a flat fish like a plaice. Once you knew what a mullet ate, nobody could eat it, but you could eat the flukes so that was the goal. There was an old crane at that part of the river, and the boys spent more time swinging on its hook than they did fishing. So they weren't great fishermen, but they liked to think they were.

In spite of their antics, Hugh and his friends were gentlemen. They pulled a lot of stunts among each other but remained polite and respectful to their elders. When it was time for Hugh to come in for his dinner or bed, his father whistled—a sharp twittering whistle. Hugh would whistle back and home he'd go quick as a flash. He would never turn a bad word to his parents.

The boys often spent an evening listening to the yarns of an old night watchman who sat in a hut like a sentry box with a brazier full of coke, the cheapest form of heating fuel. The 'old' watchman was forty years old or so, but the boys thought he was ancient. So they gathered around the hut, erected for the watchman to guard a hole in the road or some other pressing duty, in the sulfurous smoke of the coke, listening to yarns of the man's exploits about England and other exotic destinations.

The boys pumped away at him, 'go on tell us again about ...' and he spun yarns long into the evening just to keep them there and help kill the time. The boys listened intently —any excuse to stay out another moment longer—hoping their parents would forget the time. But true to form, Hugh's dad sent out the timely call. The sharp-twittering whistle piercing the night air sent the boys home to get a clip on the ear for smelling of sulphur.

A five man Derry clean-up crew, the boys would do anything to earn a couple of shillings. They plundered derelict houses looking for lead, copper wire, scrap iron, and wood, anything that could be turned into money. During one of these forays they uncovered a German life-raft complete with insignia. They had visions of floating down the river, but when they tried to blow it up it was full of holes. They'd sell what they could to the scrap man for a couple of shillings which they turned over for sweets or saved until they had enough for a day's hire of bikes to ride to the seaside at Buncrana.

In another scheme to earn money, the boys collected old wood from houses set for demolition and unused wooden pallets from all over town. They sat in the back yard and broke and chopped it up and made bundles of sticks to sell. They were always on the hunt for bits of elastic to bind the bundles. Cutting up old bicycle tubes was one solution and on this particular day, Hugh lifted some tubes hanging in his father's shed, 'These old things'll work, Right?' Hugh's father came in that evening and said to Bernard, 'I was going te ride down te Buncrana, but somebody's stole me tyres. Broke inte the wee shed down there and cut me tyres up and off the bike.' Hugh sat staring sideways at Bernard, sheepish grin attached to his face, nodding.

Summertime was the go-carting season, a time when everyone in the district made a go-cart to race down the Derry walls. A go-cart was a complicated piece of machinery for a ten year-old to construct. First, they had to find the wheels: large ones for the back; small ones for the front. These were found by knocking on doors and asking for old prams. Then the body had to be constructed out of wood. The boys had no access to drills so the hole attaching the front axle had to be burned through the wood using a hot poker. This took time and patience—something the boys had in abundance. Their efforts paid off when racing season began. Some guys were better than others at building carts; especially those who had access to paint. This process was repeated in the winter, without wheels of course, during sleigh-making season.

Collecting wood, tyres, and anything that would burn was a year-round activity in preparation for the annual

August 15 bonfire. With the fire roaring, they would sit at the end of the street telling ghost stories, trying to scare the pants off each other, seeing who could come up with the best story. Sneaking into the cinema by using a coat hanger to open the fire-exit door and then crawling on hands and knees to find a seat; stealing apples from orchards; and experimenting with smoking by cutting unfiltered fags in half was the extent of the young lads' lawless behaviour.

'Daring' only began to describe Gilly in his early teenage years. One of his more popular stunts was scaling the multi-story flats where he lived. Hugh would place his back against a column which supported the catwalks crossing between each block of the flats. The column was two feet from the main wall. From this position Hugh inched his way up from floor to floor, pausing at about ninety feet to brush his hands dramatically and wave to his friends below who were petrified at this spectacle.

Gilly also discovered riding inside the lifts was optional. Instead, they could ride on top. Going up required a properly timed dive to disembark without being crushed. When crossing Craigavon Bridge, linking the Cityside and Waterside, the average person chose the footpath. Not Gilly, he chose to walk on the four-inch parapet on the railings. Coming in covered in dirt and grease at the end of each day his mother would say, 'What were you up to?'

'Nothin', Ma.'

While swimming in the Faughan River one day, Gilly's friend Andy was pulled under by the current. John Duffy, fishing nearby, went into the river but the boy was caught up on some wire rubbish that had been discarded into the river. Andy could not be brought up in time. Hugh and his mates went silent as church-mice. They didn't go home crying. They didn't reveal their secret to their parents. None of the boys spoke a word. Their families found out about the tragedy when the police showed up at their homes to question the boys the next day.

Not telling about the death of his friend was part of Hugh's world. He and his mates did daring stunts all around town, but no one ever told. Telling that Andy drowned would have been like tattling. The lads' were loyal. They never ratted each other out. They weren't calloused; Hugh and his mates suffered the loss of their friend. It was a sad time for them, their families could see it. But the lads lived by a code and they would never tell.

Andy's father had received a commendation for rescuing a sailor who fell from his ship into the river Foyle. It was ironic at Andy's wake that the award his father earned for rescuing a drowning man hung near the coffin of his drowned son. In Andy's death was a helplessness far too many Derry families would experience in the years to come.

On 5 October 1968, Gerry and Hugh went down to the Templemore School football pitch for a game and no one showed up. So they spent an hour running around after frogs—just chasing frogs around the field trying to catch them. Tired of frog-chasing, they wandered down to the bottom of the pitch, which took them out onto the Buncrana Road where they could catch the bus back to town. They headed into town but the bus was diverted up along the back of the quay which was unusual.

The driver drove across the double-decker bridge and dropped them off at HMS Sea Eagle, a British Naval Base. They couldn't figure out why the bus hadn't stopped at the Guildhall but instead had taken them all the way over to the Waterside. Nonetheless, they didn't ask any questions; they just walked back toward town. They didn't know there had been a baton charge up Duke Street through a civil rights march and that people were all beat up.

As they walked home they came across discarded placards, wet streets that had been hosed with water, police tenders, and cops in riot gear. The hassle they got crossing the bridge into town was hotter than usual but they really didn't think much of it. They were just two kids, oblivious. Hugh and Gerry crossed the Diamond and turned down Butcher Street to find a full-blown riot: people kicking in windows of shops, stones hurled at the police, and just as they reached the gate, the RUC made another a baton charge.

As the boys fled, Hugh down the bank of the flats and Gerry down Faughan Street, Bang! Gerry's head opened up —split open by a rock. He couldn't tell who had thrown the rock and he didn't care; he just couldn't believe it! An hour before he was chasing frogs in a field and now his head was split open in a riot. And so, at the end of the day, Gerry and Hugh found themselves throwing stones at the police. They didn't know exactly why they were throwing stones or why exactly the police were there; they just did what everybody else was doing. Sporadic rioting continued throughout the year culminating in the Battle of the Bogside, which took place in August of 1969. During those three days, men occupied the roof of the Rossville Flats as a vantage point. Gerry and Hugh were given the assignment of delivering a box of apples to the roof of the flats. Arriving with the apples, Hugh was ready to join the lads preparing petrol bombs. Gerry was not as impressed, 'What the fuck are youse doing up ere? The cops are way down there.'

'Stay up here,' Hugh tells him, 'Cause when they come in, ya got a good shot at the cops.' Gerry sat up there for a while but boredom set in and he was away. Later that day a journalist snapped a photo of Hugh on the roof, at the ready.

After three days and nights of rioting, the British Army was deployed onto the streets forming a buffer zone between the rioters and the police. As a result of that riot and the distrust the police created by their actions over the previous year, the Bogside residents built barricades around their area forming Free Derry. Here the writ of the British government did not run.

Hugh's family had moved to the flats in 1965. By the end of 1969 the boys began to drift apart. They left school, got work, and developed different interests. Go-cart building and frog catching gave way to girls, jobs, and cars. Though they lived just steps away from each other, they lived in different neighbourhoods. They made new friends and fell out of touch. The friendships closed and faded away as fate, geography, and politics intervened. But the memories of a wonderful carefree childhood endured.

Aptly named the Gilly-mobile, one of Hugh's greatest loves in life was his car. While the origin of the car is unknown, whether someone gave it to him or he paid £20, the fact it was Hugh's second love was clear. As a child he loved and adored his mother. As a teen he loved and adored his mother and his car.

Throughout the last half of 1971, Hugh and his friends, Christy Tucker and Thomas Barr, would put five or six shillings together for petrol, and drive the old Austin 40 all over creation. 'Bern, we're doing 38 mph!' That car wouldn't do 10 mph, and barely reached 30 down a hill. With no brakes in the car, Hugh's friends had to leap out of the car on the way down the hill to stop it. (All those years of go-cart racing experience were paying off!)

The lads painted a white stripe along a curb of the car park and lettered 'GILLY'S CAR PARK, LIVERPOOL' in black. That of course is where they always pushed the car. That was home base. Nobody else was allowed to park there, so Hugh's family always knew when he was out. From their window in the flats they watched the lads racing off in the car and pushing it back again.

Every day, here would come Hugh and the lads, pushing it back to base. Another few shillings, another gallon of petrol, and they were driving all around town. When she ran out of petrol, push her back again. They'd have three miles to home but they'd still push her all the way. They never would abandon the wee A-40. After Hugh was murdered, his family looked down one day to see the car was burning. A sad sight, because that car was a great joy in his life.

Hugh and his friends continued their turns at throwing stones. First at the RUC and later the British Army, but pretty much everybody in the Bogside took a turn throwing stones or bottles at one time or another. The game with the soldiers was just too enticing for most to resist; teenagers, mothers, small children, the elderly. Nobody ever thought some boys would come across the Irish Sea, shoot Gilly, then go back to their barracks and congratulate each other.

Hugh wasn't an IRA man or a terrorist. He was a wee lad of seventeen. His mother scrubbed his back for him at the end of the day. Hugh would come in from his work as a tyre fitter, stand at the sink, and she would wash his back, 'scratch me back now mammy, down another wee bit, aye wash there mammy' but as soon as somebody came in, he was embarrassed. If Bernard came in and said, 'Are ye washin' him again?' The German replied, 'She is not, shutup!'

Hugh was his mother's son. She didn't sleep until he was in at night. She sent Bernard or Floyd after him if it were past eleven. Hugh rested his head on her knee as they talked. She went to his room and watched him sleep. Hugh and his mother shared a deep and steadfast love for one another.

One day at work a big tyre fell and broke Hugh's toes. He wouldn't go to hospital. He walked to work with the foot inside his mother's slipper. He walked to work in the house shoe and put his boot on when he got to work. Even though he was a mammy's boy, Hugh wasn't the type to ask for help. His mother would say, 'Go on and help him up.'

'Naw I'm alright. I'm grand.'

He climbed trees, stole apples out of orchards, drove his car around with friends ready to employ the brakes, smoke flying out of the end of it, lads coughing up shillings for the petrol. They threw stones at the army, rode the top of the lifts, walked the railings, plenty of things, crazy things, but nothing bad. Hugh and his friends had respect for their elders, they saluted the priest in the street, kept their misfortune quiet, took their oil, and kept their friends' secrets. Hugh was mischievous, 'Bern, we're doing 38 mph!' and oh, that smile—that was Gilly.

30 January 1972 brought another civil rights march. Since the first Derry march on 5 October 1968, the peace march had been a powerful way to attract media attention to civil rights issues in Northern Ireland. Some were peaceful, some ended in riots and injury. Still, none of the 20,000 marchers on this Sunday expected mayhem and murder.

Before he left for the march, Hugh gave his mother a half a crown for her birthday. He said to her, 'That's fer yer birthday.' He wasn't a huggy boy. He kissed her and said, 'There, that's all ye're gettin,' cocked his head, smiled, and away he went.

In 1972, the British Army stated that Free Derry was an IRA haven. The reality was that at that time the Derry IRA was a small force seriously out-manned and out-gunned by the British Army. Derry men had been romanced, drawn-in by the peaceful-protest ideals and schemes. Nobody wanted to go to war; they just wanted their children to have the same rights as their Protestant peers. And while they marched in protest, threw stones at the army, and eventually shut down the Bogside to British incursion, they were not queuing to join the IRA.

Even so, somehow those army boys coming over got it into their heads there was some force to fear and on 30 January 1972, they murdered unarmed civil rights demonstrators in the streets. If Hugh had joined the IRA and been shot, his family would have been devastated, but they would have been proud of him for fighting for his people. That wasn't the reality. Hugh was a civilian murdered in the street, and from that his family never fully recovered. The Paras shot Hugh as he and others fled for their lives and then went back to their barracks to celebrate.

That Sunday evening Bernard was sent out for the last time to find the German. Everybody thought Hugh was wounded. At Altnagelvin Hospital Bernard said to a couple of boys, 'Did ye see Hugh?'

'He's over there. He's wounded. Been shot in the arm.' Sorting through the wounded in wards eight and nine, Bernard and Olive were unable to find Hugh. Rumours circulated that some of the wounded had been taken to Letterkenny but these turned out to be false hopes of people desperate to find sons, brothers, and husbands alive. Bernard and Olive made their way to the morgue, identified Hugh, and went home to face their mother.

They went home with the news, 'Hugh's not wounded. He's dead.' Kathleen sat in denial until Hugh's body was brought home. His beautiful face at peace, his appearance, neat and tidy in his coffin, belied his last moments of pandemonium and terror: people screaming, bullets flying, CS gas in the air, being advanced upon by black-faced soldiers trained to kill, lying in the arms of young marcher Geraldine Richmond crying, 'Mammy! Get me Mammy!'

After the funeral; after Hugh's coffin was lowered into the ground; after the cold sound of dirt hitting polished wood faded away; his family was left with a gaping wound. Gilly had been murdered.

There was no more searching for the missing German; no more jokes; no more games. There was no more back to scrub; hair to tussle; not one darling boy to watch while he slept. There was nothing to do but pass his room; go up to his bed; look at his clothes hanging in the closet still holding his form, waiting to be pulled out for another day at Northern Ireland Tyre. No broken toes to fill a slipper. No mischievous grin. No one left to push the wee A-40 into Gilly's Car Park. Kathleen would never again receive a half-crown for her birthday or a wink and a smile.

'I wonder why they shot Hugh?' Kathleen asked. 'Why not shoot the man in front of him or beside him? Why him? There were thousands there. How'd they happen to pick him out? What was that boy thinking when he shot Hugh? Ah – he probably feels bad fer it now, ye know.'

'Why did it kill him?' Bernard wondered. 'Why didn't the bullet just pass though him and wound him? He'd a wile bad run when ye think o' it. It was bad luck that they shot him, and worse luck that he died from it, ye know.'

Bernard, no more than twenty yards away, couldn't hear his brother crying for his mother. He didn't know that Hugh was dying. 'Mammy, go an' get me Mammy.' They were just around the corner. They could see his feet. They didn't know he was dying. From her window Kathleen could see him but she didn't know it was him. She could see his feet on the ground, but she didn't know it was Hugh. The image plagued her. How could she not know? Isn't a mother supposed to know? Isn't a mother supposed to feel it when her child is crying out for her?

After Hugh's death, Kathleen was annoyed she had so few photographs of him. First communion, confirmation, retreats, friends, she had only memories, no photos. It wasn't unusual. When you're happy to have bread and your children go without shoes, a camera isn't at the top of your wish list. Besides, no mother ever plans for her child to die. She doesn't record things so she can remember them in the event of her son's death. Mothers die before their sons. That's the proper course of life.

Kathleen loved talking about Hugh up to the day she died. If anyone talked about Hugh, she loved it. But the television footage haunted Kathleen. There were the Paras entering the Bogside, 'Hugh's still alive. There look, in the crowd, is that Hugh there?' Bernard would respond, 'Naw that's not him. Naw, he's away down in the flats somewhere.' But whenever that bit of the footage was played she insisted. 'Hugh's still alive there, look.'

Hugh's family desperately wanted to stop time. If they could just step into that moment, go into the picture, and move Hugh from that place. If Bernard could just move time back twenty seconds when Hugh ran past him at the door, he could shout at him to come in. All Hugh needed to hear was his father's sharp twittering whistle and quick as a flash, he'd be home.

Gerald Donaghey

By the time she was twenty-four Mary Donaghey had buried her father, mother, and brother. If burying three family members was not enough burden to bear, of all the Bloody Sunday families she's had the toughest job clearing her brother's name. So difficult, she was initially kept at arms length by other families because they believed Gerald's case tainted the others. Gerald was no angel. First, he was a teenage boy. Teenage boys, even the good ones, are rarely described as angels. Gerald was a member of Fianna Eireann. His buddy Gearóid O'hEara was the leader of that pack. Gerald ducked jail for a time and went on 'holiday' in the Free State. He probably pegged stones at soldiers. Not an angel. So what. That doesn't make him guilty of carrying nail bombs on Bloody Sunday.

Nail bombs are awkward buggers. Constructing one is not a difficult task but it is messy and it is impossible to build one without getting gelignite all over your hands and the bomb itself. Therefore, even if he didn't build the bombs, his hands, jeans, and jacket would have been contaminated when he shoved the bombs in his pockets. The tests for explosives residue on Gerald's hands were inconclusive as 'Dr Martin did not regard the results of the tests on Donaghey as positive but Professor Simpson did.'[20]

A nail-bomb is a fairly simple recipe:
1. Gelignite – four to six inches per bomb
2. Corrugated cardboard
3. Nails – preferably the 16-penny size
4. Fuse – typically in 5-6 second lengths
5. Detonators

---

[20] The Widgery Report, 1972, para. 84.

6. Electrical Tape
7. Red-tipped Matches

Cut the gelignite into the desired length. Slide the nails in alternating directions into the cardboard. Wrap the nail-lined cardboard around the gelignite. Secure with tape (wrap completely, leaving top exposed). Make a small hole or well in the top of the gelignite about half-way down the interior. Place one end of the fuse inside the detonator and crimp detonator to secure fuse. Cut fuse at a 45 degree angle to expose gunpowder. Tape several matches to the end of the fuse. Put fuse, detonator end first, into the well. Secure fuse with tape. If you can do all that without contaminating yourself, the bomb, and everything around you—you are a better bomb-builder than I. Finally, try shoving the thing in jeans you wore in the '70s and running down the street. Good luck.

Gerald was shot by Soldier G as he fled from the soldiers opening fire in Rossville Flats. The crowd ran across Rossville Street, along the south end of Glenfada Park North, between the buildings and into Abbey Park; soldiers firing and people falling all along the way. By the time Gerald went down, bodies had dropped all around him: Patrick O'Donnell, Joseph Mahon, Joseph Friel, Michael Quinn, and Danny Gillespie lay wounded. Jim Wray, William McKinney, and Gerald McKinney were dead or dying. In fact, the bullet that blew the 5 cm hole in his stomach, may have passed through Gerry McKinney before hitting Gerald.

There are too many unanswered questions to convict Gerald Donaghey of carrying nail bombs on Bloody Sunday. The first point that confounds is the nail-bombs don't turn up in anyone's testimony until he arrives at Coy HQ. Denis

McFeely, Raymond Rogan, Mrs Rogan, Leo Young, and Dr Swords tended Gerald at the scene. None of them saw nail-bombs and Denis admits if he had seen nail bombs in Gerald's pockets, he would have removed them himself. Raymond Rogan brought Gerald into his house where his wife and five children were. He loaded Gerald into his car. Had he no care for the safety of his family or himself? Leo Young held Gerald in the back of Rogan's car. Did they just throw caution to the wind and decide to drive to hospital with four nail bombs in the car?

Six soldiers testified they were present when the car was stopped on Barrack Street, that Gerald was examined to determine he was dead and that the car, with Gerald still inside, was then taken to Coy HQ. None of their statements mention nail-bombs. Why didn't they call for an ambulance? Were the soldiers qualified to certify death? Why did they take the car to HQ and not to the hospital or morgue? What was their motive? If Gerald did have nail-bombs shoved in his pockets, wasn't the commanding officer putting his men in danger when he ordered them to drive the car to HQ?

Then there's the testimony of Dr Martin. His notes indicate that the bullet passed through the lower left front pocket of the jacket, leaving a ragged hole. An apparently undamaged nail bomb had been recovered from this pocket and yet nothing in the notes suggests that Dr Martin considered there was a possible conflict of evidence needing to be resolved.

However, Dr Hall, an explosives expert at DIFS, recalls that he placed the nail bomb taken from the lower left pocket into that pocket in order to determine whether or not a bullet could have passed through the pocket without striking the nail bomb. Dr Hall concluded it could only have occurred if the nail bomb had been placed deep into the pocket, but not if the bomb were half out of the pocket.[21]

These tests do not appear to have been documented nor does it appear that notes were made of any discussions between Dr Martin and Dr Hall on the matter. Neither Dr Martin nor Dr Hall dealt with the issue in their reports or testimony to Widgery. Also, the explosives residue only turned up in two pockets. It is claimed there was a nail bomb in each of four pockets. According to the investigation:

Item (1) consisted of a blue denim jacket. Both side pockets had been recently cut open and a nitrate ester consistent with nitroglycerine was detected on the inside surface of the right pocket. Both breast pockets were intact and, no explosive residues were detected. Item (2) consisted of a blue woolen sweater. No explosives residues were detected on its surface. Item (3) consisted of a blue shirt. No explosives residues were detected on its surface. Item (4) consisted of a white handkerchief. No explosive residues were detected on its surface. Items (5) and (7) consisted of under clothes and were not examined for explosives. Item (6) consisted of a pair of blue denim jeans. The left side pocket had been recently cut open but no explosive residues were detected in any of the other three pockets or on the outside surface. Item (8) consisted of a pair of black leather boots. No explosive residues were detected on their surface.

Nor was any explosives residue found on Gerald's hands. How does a person handle four nail-bombs and not get any explosives residue on him? It is practically impossible – if Gerald did not make the bombs, and even if the bombs sat for months before use, once he picked them up, his hands

---

[21] Statement of Dr Hall to Inquiry, para 48.

would have been tainted. How do you shove four nail-bombs in your pockets without touching any of your clothes? He was a boy. He likely wiped his hands on his jacket or shirt. Yet there was no explosives residue.

According to Professor Dermot Walsh:

Very strong circumstantial evidence suggests that the bombs were not present until just before they were found on him. One of the bombs in his jacket was so tightly squeezed into the pocket that it had to be cut out. Moreover, his jeans were tightly fitted with pockets opening to the front. Any bombs in these pockets would have been clearly visible. Indeed, when the first one was spotted it was actually sticking out of the top of his pocket. Nevertheless, they were not spotted by Dr Swords, who examined him shortly after he was shot. It was worth noting here that Dr Swords actually searched his pockets for identification. They were also not spotted by the Army medical officer who examined the body twice, actually opening the front of the trousers in the process. There was also compelling evidence that the position of the body had been moved on the seat after the medical officers last examination and the time when the bombs were discovered. Finally, there was ample opportunity for the bombs to have been planted after the body had been examined by the medical officer and before the bombs were found. All in all, the case for concluding that the bombs were planted seems more credible than the reverse.[22]

The nature of the entry wound led Dr Swords to believe that if Gerald had been taken immediately to hospital, he could have survived. But he didn't make it to hospital. The car was stopped and taken to the Army medical post on Craigavon Bridge (Coy HQ). Entering through the stomach,

---

[22] Professor Dermot Walsh LLB, PhD, The Bloody Sunday Tribunal of Inquiry: A Resounding Defeat for Truth, Justice, and the Rule of Law, 51 (November 1999).

the bullet lacerated his aorta and inferior vena cava. It passed through his intestines and lodged in his back. From his injuries Gerald bled to death: five pints of blood slowly leaking into his stomach as he lay in the back of Raymond Rogan's Cortina.

The pain and loss Gerald's family suffered after his murder have never left. The lies about Gerald's life, of IRA men, of nail-bombs, and of his court conviction have been told hundreds of times over by the British Government and public press. Mary Donaghey has earned the right to tell her brother's life story: the way she remembers it.

Three devastating losses. One remarkable woman.

Gerald Donaghey

The photo of Gerald as a beautiful blue-eyed, blond curly-haired baby in his blue fur coat and white boots has been lost to the years but the love of the Donaghey family and their memories of a quiet boy who captured his family's heart live on.

Scampering down the red-lino stairs through the long hall, past the living room, and out to play skipping on the street was a favourite treat. But more often, Gerald's route was over the red, black, blue, green, and white squared lino of the scullery and out to the back garden for games with neighbourhood pals. Keeping her children close to the apron, Rebecca created a children's play paradise of soft green grass, free from plantings or flowers.

Whether they came for sweets or games is a closely guarded secret, but as the neighbourhood filled with the aroma of Rebecca's apple cakes, pies, and scones, her backyard filled with children. Gerald's father filled the house with music, playing piano and guitar while the children sang along. At the weekend the house was filled with adults. Women knitting and chatting and men playing cards were happy as well to find trays filled with cakes and pies.

As soon as Patrick was born, Rebecca left her job at the shirt factory to be home. Rebecca adored her children and thus was not the disciplinarian in the house. Never able to stay cross with them for long, the children were often called from their rooms for a treat. Rebecca preferred talking with her children to thumping them when they got out of order, and sang to them in her sweet soft voice when they were hurt, scared, or sick. Small gifts were left for the children whenever she could arrange them: a pram for Mary's doll, a tin of sweets, a ball for her boys.

Charles showered affection on his children as well and rose every morning to make their breakfast and chat before they left for school or work. On Friday, Charles stopped for a stout at Duffy's on Rossville Street, and then headed home with fish and chips. Patrick, Mary, and Gerald watched expectantly from the front window for his tall, lean figure to come ambling up the hill. They were frequently discouraged when Charles kept one hand behind his back. Did he have the dinner, or didn't he? Charles enjoyed seeing their distressed faces turn to joy when he produced the hidden treasure.

Family life was sweet for the Donaghey's. One time, it was too sweet. One afternoon Mary came home from school to a strange but familiar scent. It wafted down the street, getting stronger and stronger as she approached and entered the house. While she'd never smelled it in quite such a concentrated form, it reminded her of Manhattan, the perfume she'd saved for weeks to buy. As she climbed the stairs there at the landing stood the culprit: six-year old Gerald happily spraying the final contents of the coveted bottle. Mary took out after Gerald but Rebecca intervened, telling Mary she could always get another perfume but this was her brother and there was no replacement for him. Rebecca didn't hit her children, and she wasn't going to allow them to thump each other.

When Gerald was eight years old, his mother started keeping him home from school from time to time. Rebecca hid Gerald in the wardrobe until Charles left for work. As soon as he was gone, she and Gerald would play games, bake, and sing songs. Rebecca and Gerald enjoyed their stolen time together until the day Charles forgot his lunch. Rebecca and Gerald were found-out and their intrigues together came to an immediate end. Perhaps Rebecca sensed something and just wanted every moment with her son, as Rebecca soon learned she had cancer. A swollen thyroid gland, then lump in the neck proved to be throat cancer.

Returned to school, Gerald worked hard, did his home work, and was considered by his teachers to be a very smart boy. His brother completed secondary school and left for seminary to become a priest. Life continued happily for the Donaghey's for the next four years. Family holidays to Buncrana, walks on a Sunday at Holywell Hill, grand Christmas celebrations, wonderful cakes for birthdays, and always a house filled with friends, songs, and laughter. It was good. And then, it was over.

The Donaghey's happy life would be forever altered in 1965. On the tenth of December Charles fell while changing a light bulb at the Post Office. Attended by Dr Sullivan Jr, at hospital, Charles was sent home to rest in his bed. Alarmed at his rapidly deteriorating condition, Rebecca phoned Dr Crawdey on Saturday morning who came out and immediately phoned the ambulance. Charles had been bleeding internally. At hospital, Charles implored Mary to care for her mother and brothers. Mary authorised emergency surgery when police arrived with release papers that night.

Sunday morning Charles sat up in his bed at hospital. He said, 'Me da was in te talk te me the day. He was sitting at the end of me bed this morning.'

'Well, he's a bit delirious,' Mary thought, 'but he's up and talking.' She felt this was good news; a sign he was recovering. He fell from his hospital bed that night and on Tuesday, 14 December, Charles died.

Rebecca lost all heart longing for her husband and the cancer took her four weeks later. Rebecca died on 13 January 1966.

Attending seminary in Spain, Patrick didn't receive the news of his father's death until after Charles was buried. When Rebecca's doctor broke the news that Rebecca was also soon to die, someone suggested to Father Daly that he write to the seminary Patrick attended. Fr Daly obliged, and Patrick came home.

The cancer in her throat had taken Rebecca's lovely melodious voice and at the end she motioned for Patrick and Mary to take care of Gerald. Essentially orphaned, the post office took up a negligence case against the hospital on behalf of Patrick, Mary, and Gerald. The case was settled out of court for less than it took to feed the family for a year.

Mary, nineteen years old, confused and devastated over the loss of her parents, refused to let her family be further torn apart. Gerald was scared. He was convinced that without parents he and his siblings would be separated. He desperately missed his mother. She was his champion, confidant, and first true love. Patrick returned to Spain and Mary kept what was left of her family intact. A smaller family yes, but filled with love and a friendship that would deepen, grow, and blossom.

In the years Mary nurtured him, Gerald grew from a quiet boy into a confident young man. He liked football, music, dancing at the Stardust, and was very congenial. At home he was good natured and quiet. He and Mary would often spend an evening talking about their home and lives, watching TV, or Gerald's favourite activity: going early to his bed for a long night's sleep. This suited Mary. Knowing her teenage charge was safely in his bed left her free to be courted by John Doherty, a handsome young man with a good job.

Gerald was a very caring person. When Mary was sick, he would stay with her, and care for her, just as she would for him. For a time there was no one else. Even though extended family lived near-by, poverty touched every life in the Bogside and relatives had little to give.

Mary and Gerald relied and depended on each other, and built a new life together. Visiting Patrick in Portrush (taking time off from seminary to help the family finances) buoyed them and fostered their feeling of family.

1969, the houses on Wellington Street were slated for demolition. Assisted by an uncle, Mary searched for a new home and chose one at Meehan Square. Maisonette 27-A. Mary and Gerald mourned the loss of their family home, but looked forward to a new beginning, a new chapter in their lives. Six flights up, a trash chute, large living room with floor to ceiling windows, heat on the first floor, two bedrooms and a bathroom up, Mary covered the walls in blue paper with a white frieze. She adored her lovely maisonette. Her first home on her own. Just the right size for Mary and Gerald, with enough space if she and John Doherty decided to marry.

Mary worked for Birmingham Sound Reproducers, a company that produced record changers and in Derry employed upwards of 5,000 workers. At the stroke of a pen, the company's owner, Dr MacDonald, closed the doors and moved the operation to Scotland.

Without severance pay and a teenage boy to feed, Mary promptly went to work in the shirt factories. Gerald started college at Strand Tech but soon decided that working would be better for him and for Mary who had struggled to keep food on the table and him in school. He went to work for Carlin's Brewery loading the delivery lorry.

Life was hard. For the first four years after their parents' death, enough money for potatoes and bread was all it took to keep Mary and Gerald happy. In 1970, John Doherty joined the household. His presence relieved the loneliness Mary felt. She now had someone to help her make decisions. She'd spent four years often not knowing where to turn. Jackie joined Gerald in filling the void in Mary's heart left by her parents' deaths and contributed another income to the household.

As Mary's life grew and changed, Gerald was beginning to gain independence. His job at Carlin's supplied him with money, confidence, and a growing social life. Just as his father had done with Rebecca, Gerald faithfully turned over his wages to Mary who managed the family finances. In reality, Mary let him keep whatever he wanted or needed and put the rest away for his future.

A stroll into town one spring afternoon changed Gerald's life. Laughing and joking as they walked along, Gerald and his friends looked forward to checking out the girls who would be promenading around the Diamond on the Sunday afternoon. The group of lads ambling into town was crossing the Diamond when two police cars screeched to a halt. The police got out and pointed to Gerald and his friends Gearóid (O'hEara), Eddie, and Charlie. They said, 'You are under arrest for riotous behaviour!' The police claimed that the lads had just attacked an RUC car at the bottom of Fahan Street. They had walked up Fahan, but they didn't see or do anything on their journey including vandalise an RUC vehicle. Only an idiot would vandalise an RUC car so close to the Diamond, which was a haven for the police.

Unbeknownst to them, there had been a bit of a skirmish down Fahan Street, but they were not too worried about the police. They figured it would get sorted out. They would have been complete fools to vandalise a police car and then, as a group, continue casually strolling up the street, through the gate, and into the Diamond. They figured the police would realise this and conclude they could not be the culprits.

At Strand Road Barracks, Charlie ended up being thrown out. He was significantly younger than the other boys and his clear distress (crying like a baby) motivated the police to dismiss him. One by one a series of policemen came in to formally identify Gerald, O'hEara, and Eddie, 'Yes, that's definitely the man I saw attacking the car.' O'hEara requested a solicitor and for them to ring his parents which they eventually did. Soon enough, family friend and MP, John Hume arrived.

John informed the boys that the RUC was about to charge them with riotous behaviour, which carried a mandatory sentence of six months. Regardless of the boys' true activities, several policemen signed statements saying they could positively ID them as the people who were at the front of the crowd. Two or three policemen against the lads' word meant they had slim chance of reprieve, but John negotiated and postponed their trial a week.

Their families paid their bail and the lads got out. After a bit of time thinking over their options, go to prison or go on the run , they decided to take off over the border. It seemed a good idea at the time. They fancied the idea of being desperadoes on the lam.

They gathered a few contacts, names and addresses of Derry folk living in Ireland, and headed south. Gerald, O'hEara, and Eddie showed up on doorsteps and were taken in as family. They earned a few pounds washing windows, as bar backs at pubs, working as day-labour, and as plaster men. The three slept in the same bed, wore the same clothes, earned their few pounds, and missed their families, but mostly it was like being on holiday, not like being on the run from the law. After all, nobody was scouring the countryside for them.

They bummed about from town to town seeing the sites, meeting girls, and leaving broken hearts, not crime, in their wake. The boy's southern adventure took them through Ennistymon, Shannon, Limerick City, Tipperary, Clonmel, Cashel, Kerry, Killorglin, Clinnon, Cork, and Dublin. Living, working, and playing, they saw more of the south in those six months than most Derry folks saw in a lifetime. They frequented pubs like Dirty Nellie's and Gerald entertained the others with his silly off-key homemade songs but it was really no life for a teenager. The boys eventually tired of it and started thinking of returning home.

Taken to court and sentenced in their absence, O'hEara's solicitor got his charge reduced from riotous behaviour to disorderly behaviour and his result was a three month suspended sentence and a fine. Gerry and Eddie got six months. This news kept them in the South until they heard that internment had been reintroduced. While in Dublin, which they didn't care for anyway, the lads heard the no-go areas had been re-established and again considered returning home. They thought they could go home and live safely within the no-go area.

The lads returned to Limerick and while staying with a woman named Bridgett, a Derry man, Paddy Brown turned up for a visit and the desperadoes asked him for a lift back to Derry. He told them to meet him at Joe Quinn's pub; he was going to have a pint and they'd be off. He sat and drank from early afternoon until half eleven and then they all got in the car and drove six hours home.

The lads arrived to find a dramatically different Derry. Cars were smouldering; CS gas hung in the air; barricades cordoned off the neighbourhood; stones and broken bottles littered the streets. Armed soldiers and armed civilians patrolled their respective sides of the conflict. Arriving home, their families were more worried about them than when they were gone. The lads thought their families would be really pleased to see them as they'd left without so much as a nod. But they were not, because Derry was on fire.

Gerald, O'hEara, and Eddie got back into the swing of life and started sneaking out. Technically they shouldn't have left the no-go area, but they started sneaking out on a Friday or Saturday night to a pub on Foyle Street. Not that the RUC was scouring the streets for them. The arrival of the British Army, internment, and the no-go area kept the RUC busy enough. The three lads enjoyed their outlaw status nonetheless. There was notoriety in being home from a run from the law in the Free State.

The Metropolitan Bar hung between the Loyalist and Nationalist communities and was home to all of Derry, Protestant and Catholic. It was here that Gerald met Hester, a Protestant girl from the Waterside. Hester lived in a very strong Loyalist area and the two Gerrys would walk over to her house together because her neighbourhood was a dangerous place for Catholics. But they were quite daring, being desperadoes and all.

Gerald got really serious about Hester, decided he was in love with her, and that they were going to get married. But Gerald was an outlaw and that didn't square with Hester's Protestant upbringing. Her pro-establishment view of the world was that you served your time and then got on with your life. So he did. He decided that he would hand himself in and he got his brother Patrick to walk down with him. His friends and family said their farewells, he walked down to the barricade, and went off to serve his prison term. It was October, 1971.

Gerald arrived in prison and immediately settled in. Having already experienced trauma in his life, he took this temporary lifestyle adjustment in stride. A teen with a preference for blue jeans and long hair, Mary didn't recognise him on her first visit. 'Here I am Mary!' The familiar voice came from a man sporting a dirty pink waistcoat, a wide-collared blue and white striped shirt, and short-cropped hair.

Mary received three letters from Gerald during his imprisonment. His words, through his letters, reveal his personality and his plans:

Dear Mary,
I am doing great. I have got my hair cut as you might have guessed. The food is very good and the prisoners are mostly from Belfast. The prison officers treat us very well. I was wondering if you could send someone up to meet me when I get released. Could you send me up a pen, some soap, toothbrush and toothpaste, that is all.

Dear Mary,
Just a few lines to let you know that I am keeping well. Thank you very much for the visit. Aunt Annie was up to visit me on the first of this month and left me some cigarette papers and books. I wonder could you send me up a lighter and petrol also some flints. Also could you send me up a few magazines like Weekend or Reville and only send up journals not daily papers.

Well this is all for now. P.S. Don't forget the lighter and tell everybody I was asking for them. Love, Gerry

Dear Mary,
Just a few lines in reply to your letter. I'm sorry I didn't write sooner but you know how it is you kind of forget things. I'll bet

you think that I've forgotten about something but I haven't. I wish you a happy anniversary, it's only the first but it won't be the last. No news yet of a bundle of joy some company for Denis or are you thinking about it.

Well how's young Denis keeping does he still keep you awake at night or is he quieter now? I'm sorry I can't be there for the anniversary. I was wondering could you get me a pair of Wranglers and a Wrangler jacket which is a jean coat with the money in the credit union and get yourself a present and a few drinks on me. What's this about Hester saying I wasn't writing, she mustn't be receiving them. I'll write my last letter to Hester and address it to the factory so that she will get it.

P.S. Don't forget about the jeans coat size 34, trousers 29 make sure that you get the Wranglers. All for now. Best of Luck, Gerry Donaghey

Dear Hester,
Well, I arrived on Wednesday night at about nine o'clock and the time has flown by very quickly. It is Saturday night already. I miss you very much Hester love and the first month I get back we will get engaged. I will have my hair cropped when I am released. Please write as soon as you can but only one letter a month. This is all for now Hester love so goodbye till next time. All my love goes with this letter, Gerry

Gerald was to be in Crumlin Road Prison for six months. If he served his time he'd have been far from harm's way on 30 January 1972. As luck would have it, Ian Paisley was arrested and jailed at Crumlin Road. Paisley's supporters caused such a ruckus outside the prison that the powers that be decided to grant amnesty to everyone serving less than three years thus unburdening themselves and the neighbouring public of the riotous beast and giving a whole host of minor offenders, just-plain-innocents, and their families a happy Christmas gift.

Just before his release date, Mary wrote to Carlin's asking if Gerald could return to work when he got home. The letter she received from the Brewery was not as cheerful as Gerald's correspondence from prison. She was curtly told there was no longer a place for Gerald.

Gerald's letters reveal he was still very much a boy at heart. They certainly don't sound like the letters of a dangerous felon. His big concern is new jeans, 'coat size 34 trousers 29.' But he was finding his way. He had struggled a bit in the prior few years; struggled to find himself, to figure out who he was and what he wanted. He'd started college and dropped out to get a job. He worked diligently for Carlin's brewery and attended the training centre. At some point, unbeknownst to Mary, he joined Fianna Eireann but never got the chance to meaningfully participate. His arrest for riotous behaviour was just unlucky and the decision to run off to the South the rash decision of a typical teenager.

Even so, Gerald was coming around. His experiences in the south helped him understand a world existed beyond the Derry walls. His time in Crumlin Road gave him time to think and evaluate his future. His love for Hester made him want to settle down. Gerald was growing up, becoming a man. When he was released from prison he was ready to step into adulthood and start a new life for himself.

On 29 January 1972, four weeks after Gerald returned home from Crumlin Road, a bullet came through a window and lodged in the wall by the upstairs landing. The occasion was blamed on sporadic violence related to the barracks at Bligh's Lane. Nobody thought it was an ominous sign.

The next day Mary and Gerald would attend a peace march against internment. It was Mary's first march. The people of Derry had made great strides in their quest for civil rights, marching for equal access to housing, jobs, and voting. Marches were designed to be peaceful demonstrations, and although several incidents of violence had been perpetrated upon march participants over the years, the marches typically went off peacefully, as intended.

Mary put her son Denis in his pram and went out to the march. Halfway through the march Mary decided to take Denis home, get him out of the cold, and prepare tea and sandwiches. Gerald said he would be home for his tea at seven o'clock as he was going to meet his girlfriend at six. It was now just half three, but Mary had some tidying up to do to prepare for the coming week.

At home, Mary cared for her Denis, straightened up around the house, and waited. A wee while passed and then a friend, Kathleen Flood, called at the door. She asked was there anyone home with Mary? She then told Mary that she heard Gerald had been shot in the leg. To her relief, Mary soon learned that it wasn't Gerald that had been shot.

Unfortunately, Mary's cousin Damian was the victim. He and an older man had been shot as they crossed the waste ground at xxx Seven o'clock came and went and Mary began to worry. She felt guilty about feeling relief that it was Damien shot and not her Gerald. But where was Gerald?

More rumours of Gerald being shot prompted Mary's husband to go over to Altnagelvin Hospital to find Gerald. Jackie made several trips between home and hospital that night only to be told Gerald was not there. The waiting was terrible. Mary hoped there was a mistake, that he was with his girl and lost track of time.

She prayed. It just wasn't possible that another member of her family would be so tragically taken away. He must be alive. Her emotions moved from hope to despair. She tried to remain positive, but the hours ticked by and fear of the worst crept in. Gerald's friends came to the house and reported that Gerald had been shot. But it wasn't until Father Rooney arrived that Mary knew with certainty that Gerald was dead.

Gerald's body was not delivered to hospital until ten o'clock that evening. John's final journey to hospital was to identify Gerald. He returned home heavy-hearted, bound with the terrible task of telling Mary that another member of her close-knit family was dead.

Gerald and Mary had grown-up and grown stronger after the sudden and tragic loss of their parents. They had survived and built a lovely life together. It was good. And then, it was over. A quiet pall came over the house. For the third time in her twenty-four years, Mary contacted Patrick to report a death in their family.

Gerald's body came home Monday night. In the twenty-four hours home, the house never emptied. It seemed as if all of Derry stepped out to wake its dead. Thousands of people moved from house to house offering solace to as many families as they could reach.

On Tuesday, the caskets containing the bodies of the men and boys murdered by the British Paratroopers were delivered to St Mary's chapel. The caskets, carried by friends and family, streamed down from Creggan and up from the Bogside all through the evening. Gerald's body, tucked quietly in the shining wooden casket, was carried to the chapel by his closest friends and family. And then, Mary was alone.

It was months before Mary learned the whole story of her brother's death: Gerald had been shot running for home. He was cut down while seeking safety from the recklessness of soldiers who had been ordered to stop firing. Gerald was wounded, but the injury was not imminently fatal. He was alive and likely to survive with prompt and proper medical attention.

Two men, Leo Young and Raymond Rogan, lifted Gerald into a car and raced toward Altnagelvin Hospital, determined to save his life. In spite of his desperation in not being able to find his own brother, Leo cradled Gerald in the back seat, talking to him, comforting him, urging him to hold on.

British soldiers stopped the car and Leo and Mr Rogan were dragged out, their lives were threatened, and then, they were arrested. They watched helplessly as the car, with Gerald still in it, was driven away. Gerald lay alone in the backseat of the Cortina, his life slowly seeping away. When Leo Young was released two days later, he would learn his brother John had also been murdered.

Mary left the maisonette at Meehan Square at Easter of 1972. Unable to continue living in the house so close to where Gerald was shot, she took a house in Carnhill. One night shortly after moving, Mary saw Gerald. Sleeping in the front room she woke up with the feeling someone was there. Gerald stood dressed in his Wranglers and his shirt with the orange and fine green stripes going down it. He stood there, just as he always had, hands shoved in his pockets, relaxed, smiling. He looked at Mary for a moment and then, he was gone.

Patrick is now a priest in America and Mary lives in her home in Carnhill. Mary and Jackie's lovely children would have adored their uncle Gerald, just as he adored his first nephew, Denis. Mary survives her father Charles, her mother Rebecca, and her dear brother Gerald.

Each died too young, lost to tragic circumstance. But it is Gerald's death that tears at her soul. Shot and left to die alone in the backseat of a car hijacked by British Soldiers, what was Gerald thinking in his last hours of life? How long did he lie in that car before he took his last breath? Did he wonder why his sister didn't come to him? Why his family wasn't there to help him? Why he'd been left alone?

Mary prays that his death was peaceful; that the pain from his wounds was masked; that he was gone when they handled his body and planted the nail-bombs so he didn't suffer that further deprivation and pain. Gerald's visit to Mary's room offered her comfort in the knowledge that Gerald has been granted peace in the arms of his creator. Mary's peace will come when her brother's name is cleared.

Michael Kelly

'Saw poor Mrs Kelly down the town today, she's suffering so, yer heart just breaks for her.' - Bridget Nash

The seventh child of thirteen, Michael Kelly was seventeen when he was shot and killed while standing near the Rossville Street barricade. William Nash, John Young, and Michael McDaid fell moments after Michael went down. All well-dressed young men, headed for the safety of the barricade. That was their refuge. The Army never went past the barricade. Michael was wearing a blue suit and yellow jumper. He had a half-eaten chocolate bar in his pocket. Sunday wasn't the day for rioting. The boys were out for the craic.

Mrs Kelly knew her son and it is she who I hoped would tell his story. As the interview process commenced, Mrs Kelly suffered a stroke. Her family gathered to help and support her. Their busy lives of work and family, the stressful days of the Inquiry, and their mother's illness all occupying their thoughts and hours, they found time to talk with me about their mother and her Michael. Here is her story, as told by her son John.

We were just like everyone else. We had very little. My father was unemployed. There were twelve [23] children around the house, so there was a lot of to-ing and fro-ing.

My mother was the mainstay. She reared the children. She didn't drink. She didn't smoke. She was very religious. My father was the opposite. Like every Derry man he had his pint and did his wee bit of smoking. So it was down to my mother to ensure that the wains were looked after and brought up right.

What my mother did was a miracle. Bringing up that many children was a lot of heavy work. She was a normal

---

[23] One child died in infancy.

Derry woman. She looked after her children, brought us up correctly, taught us to respect our elders, and to do what we were told. As a result, there were very few occasions that we had to be chastised because we showed respect to everyone.

It was a struggle on a daily basis to feed all of us. For example, today people take chicken for granted. In those days we had chicken only at Christmas. I remember going to school and traveling home at lunchtime. It was two miles round trip for just a slice of bread, but it was adequate, because we knew we'd be getting dinner when we got home. And my mother always had the dinner on the table.

In those days, you knew what kind of dinner you were going to get. It never changed. You got your soup and spuds on the Sunday. Reheated soup, which I hated, with spuds on the Monday. Stew on Tuesday. I hate stews now. She always put turnips into it and I hate turnips. Wednesday and Thursday were typically centred on spuds and Friday we had fish. In the morning it was porridge. There was no such thing as cornflakes, cornflakes didn't exist in those days, or maybe they were too expensive, I don't know but they never came into our house. That was more or less how we lived at the time.

My mother ran clubs to earn money. This meant she collected payment from people who bought things on tick from the shops. She earned a small commission and that was what she had to feed and clothe twelve children as well as keep up the house.

My father was one of these guys who didn't have steady work. Then at one time he did get a steady job and things were grand! He cycled from Creggan to the Waterside, but he worked at night so he had time for a few pints during the day. So, when I say cycle, it's a relative term. He leaned on the bike to get into work and back again – like Lee Marvin and his white horse. He was a man, a typical Derry man with the drink, that's all I'm saying.

For my mother it was all about her wains, all about the house, all about rearing them and bringing them up right, and that's exactly what she achieved. No matter what the problems were or what was thrown in front of her, she'd look after her children first. It was always a massive undertaking for her and she achieved it. She created a good family.

At that time we all left school at fifteen and went to work.

Every Friday we handed our unopened wage packets to our mother. But we only worked for four or five years and then got married, so my mother had only four or five years of each of us handing in a wage packet. The boys worked at what ever we could find and the girls, every one of them, worked in a shirt factory, which was the only work for the majority of the people in the city at the time.

It was important that you went straight home on the Friday and handed in your wage packet. You didn't give it to your da. You gave it to your mother. She looked after the money. She looked after the main running of the house. Everyone was the same. Every child was expected to turn over their pay.

It certainly was a struggle in those days. We had nothing. It was a massive undertaking for my mother to buy a TV but she saved and she did it. In fact, we were the first on our street to get a TV and all the wains came up to the window to see it. The sum of our amenities was a TV, a record player, and a radio. But we were happy. Maybe even happier in those days then people are today because we were such a close family.

My mother worried about her boys. Work was hard to come by in Derry and as we reached our teenage years, the Troubles were starting. She didn't want us involved in anything. She wanted us to learn a trade and get jobs. She knew her boys would have to be responsible for a family and she wanted her boys to be good providers.

At that time girls got married, had children, and depended on their husbands to be the breadwinners. Our mother was happy with that as long as the girls got jobs to help cover their expenses until they were married and out of the house. In fact, my mother would have worried more about her boys than the girls because at the end of the day she knew where her girls were and what they were doing. She knew the girls would get married and start a family. But the boys had a multitude of distractions, and she worried, 'Would they end up on the dole? Get mixed up in the Troubles? Become drinkers? Struggle all through their lives?'

That was the way she was, but in saying that everyone in our house was treated completely and utterly fairly. If she came into the house with a packet of sweets, everybody got one. If you got two, I got two. Everything was shared equally. She never made a difference in anyone at all. If she spent money on a pair of shoes, the next person coming along would have the same amount of money spent on them. If a dress was bought, the same amount of money was spent on the next dress, and so on.

My mother always put her family first. She protected her family. She looked after the family very, very well. I look upon my mother as a Derry woman, which to me is a woman who takes joy in bringing up a family. My mother took joy in bringing up our family, and I think she took even more joy at the fact that we all turned out well.

Saying everything was equal, there is one exception that is Derry mothers in relation to their sons: I think I can say Derry mothers think the sun shines out of everyone of their arses, to put it crudely! I think they see their sons as doing no wrong at all, unless, of course it is something extreme. That's the way my mother was. As far as she was concerned she brought us up right. She expected us to behave ourselves and to give respect to everyone.

She was my hero, if you want to call it that. She was a wee woman who took it upon her shoulders to rear a family and she achieved a good family. Just look at her now, she's still there and still fighting even after a major stroke, she is still with us – her family. As far as I'm concerned, that's a Derry woman, and a good woman. Your family comes first.

Michael was a quiet soul. When he was three years of age he went into a coma. The morning he became ill my mother came in and had us all kneel round his bed and say the Rosary before he was taken away in the ambulance.

My mother was a very religious person. She went to Mass every morning until she lost the use of her legs. But I remember the morning Michael went to hospital. We were told to pray for him, that he'd come round. I think he was in the hospital for about three weeks, and we weren't even allowed to go in and see him. He was in a ward of his own, and he went into a deep sleep. I think it was a virus of some sort he'd picked up that affected the brain. My mother was told to offer him up to God, but she refused to do it. She said, 'No! I'm going to pray for him.' She prayed steadfastly until he was well. My mother has a great belief in the power of prayer. She prayed and Michael came back to us.

My memories of Michael are few between that time and when he went to work. I was seven years older than he and so to me he was just a brother. I know my mother helped him build a large pigeon loft out in the back yard. She helped to get him the wood and all the pigeons, too.

When he was working in Derry, he would take a couple of pigeons down to his work and release them, and she would wait for them to fly back. Then, when he was in Belfast my ma cared for the pigeons while he was away during the week, feeding them, exercising them, and making sure they stayed well. It was almost as if by looking after those pigeons she was watching after Michael.

My mother looked after Michael so closely she actually followed him on the march. She saw him a few times and was more or less trying to keep an eye on him. I think when the march got to William Street, she lost track of him so she went to her sisters flat in Kells Walk. She maintains that she looked out the door into Colmcille Court, and saw Michael running along as the Paras moved in. She called to him but he didn't hear her, and that was the last time she saw him alive.

Much later she learned that she was directly above the wall where Soldier F fired, so Michael's murderer was directly below her and that fact was devastating to her. Here she was taking shelter oblivious to what was happening to her son just below.

We held a wake in the house. Thousands of people came to the house to give condolences. Even an ex-RUC man came in, devastated, and admitted that the men and boys were murdered.

My mother was heavily sedated but on the Tuesday in the early hours of the morning she lifted Michael from his coffin and hugged him. She was crying and saying, 'Michael son, Michael son.' We had to restrain her and put Michael back into the coffin.

Michael's death affected my mother very badly. We were a very close family. My mother could not find a way of coping with his death and we were very worried about her for many years. She regularly went to the RUC Station on the Strand Road to remonstrate and had to be calmed down by Superintendent Lagan.

One winter we found my mother in the cemetery with a blanket trying to keep Michael warm at his grave. My mother had a nervous breakdown after Michael's death. She has no memory of the five years after Michael's death. She just existed.

We all saw our mother suffering, but we never knew the pain our da felt until he died, when we found a wallpaper sample book filled with twenty-one years of Bloody Sunday newspaper clippings and photos of Michael. He was a typical Derry man to the end – he suffered in silence.

Our ma kept Michael's clothes, the Mars bar she gave him every week before he returned to Belfast, and a half eaten whole-nut chocolate bar he had in his pocket the day of the march. She's up the stairs now, a year after her stroke, having good days and bad. When she goes, she'll take the last of Michael's physical remains with her. She will be buried with his clothes. She would have done it if it was anyone of us killed. In our house everything is shared equally, especially the love.[24]

---

[24] Mrs Kelly died 21 June 2004

Barney McGuigan

54 people witnessed Barney McGuigan's murder.
All 54 people saw the same thing:
Barney McGuigan stepped out with his hands raised over his head,
waving a white handkerchief.

Barney McGuigan was a husband. Barney and his wife had six children and were very happy together. They were an extremely good team, dividing the running of the household between them. Bernie took care of the day to day running of the household cooking, cleaning, baking, knitting, and making dresses for their daughters. Barney earned a living at the Ben Sherman shirt factory and Birmingham Sound Reproducers. They were a couple totally in love, whose children never witnessed an argument between them. Over thirty years after Barney's death, his wife is still in his corner. She kept their family together after his death and remembers him fondly to their children.

Barney McGuigan was a family man. He placed a lot of importance on family and family relationships. Family was something he valued tremendously. He was home in the evenings and regularly took his eldest son to Derry City football matches. He planned for his children to be well educated and attend university. The McGuigan home had an open door. Barney and Bernie encouraged their children to bring their friends home. Barney had an exceptional singing voice. His children heard him singing in the house regularly. The McGuigan children lived in a happy house with happy parents who made them feel very safe and secure.

Barney McGuigan was a dedicated employee. During his tenure at BSR, he was promoted to charge-hand. As charge-hand Barney was responsible for twelve men; a very dedicated worker, his section was very efficient and required little oversight. There were never any complaints from Barney's section nor word of any problems. Barney was a very quiet and mild-spoken man. Because of this he was well-liked and respected by the men who worked for him. When Ben Sherman's shirts revolutionised the shirt-making industry in Derry Barney was involved in constructing the expansion of their Abercorn Road factory. He was very affable and got along well with the other employees, most of whom were women.

Barney McGuigan was an important member of the community. Barney represented young people in housing. He was involved in the Tenants' Association. He interacted with the housing executive to ensure the neighbourhood was maintained and there were lights on in the area. Barney called on the fathers in the district to stop stone-throwing near the primary school and to try to restore some semblance of discipline to the local teenagers and to improve their behaviour. Forty fathers attended a meeting set up by Barney and organised themselves to take care of the school to prevent any further damage to it. They did their very best to bring the stone throwing to an end and eventually did so.

Barney McGuigan didn't look for glory or recognition. All the things he did to help people he did very quietly. Only a week or two before he was killed he went out to take up a collection for a family who were getting their electricity cut off. He found shoes for shoeless children, took collections for families in need, worked as a community liaison between families and the government housing association, and advocated for children to have safe passage to and from school. Barney told his children, 'If you do something to help someone you don't need to publicise it and you don't need a pat on the back for doing it.'

Barney McGuigan was trusted. If someone confided in Barney, they knew it would remain confidential. People who were having a problem such as their electricity getting turned off were quite happy to talk to him about it knowing he would keep their private business private.

Barney was outgoing. He had a good personality and enjoyed a bit of fun. Barney could tell a joke and enjoyed the craic with his friends. He was always concerned for people in difficulties and if he was in a position to help them he did. Barney's friends, Protestant and Catholic, visited the house where they enjoyed time together. They speak of Barney fondly to this day.

Barney McGuigan was a good neighbour. The summer before he died a friend of his asked him could he make a headstone for this fella's mother who had died? This particular family couldn't afford a headstone at the time and so Barney made the headstone in his back yard. As the McGuigan's lived overlooking the cemetery, Barney and his sons took it down and placed it at the woman's grave. As a result, Barney was inundated with people who wanted a stone. Before he died, Barney made nine in all. The nine headstones stand in the City Cemetery today. Made in the McGuigan backyard; free of charge. Barney McGuigan was compassionate. If Barney had stayed by the phone box he likely would have survived Bloody Sunday. But he heard Paddy Doherty crying for help so he took a handkerchief, and waved it over is head saying, 'They won't shoot me. I've got to go help this man,' then he stepped out to go to Paddy's side. Barney's compassion led him on Bloody Sunday to go to the aid of a dying man. For his compassion he was shot through the back of the head. With his compassion he laid down his life for another.

William McKinney

'He seems to have been roughly the most boring man on the march. His temperament was mild in the extreme. He didn't go drinking or stoning the army, didn't even do any dancing.'
           - Notes from RUC investigation into Bloody Sunday.

The kitchen is where many of us find our fondest childhood memories. It was the place we rushed through and slammed the back door 100 times a day. Where warm biscuits emerged and love was doled out. In the McKinney house, like many others in Derry, it was the centre of life, where the meals were prepared, the washing done, the shirts ironed, and for the better part of her life, the kitchen was the only place you would find Mrs McKinney.

Ten children, a husband, the Granda, sisters, and assorted friends and neighbours dropping by kept her kitchen open from sunrise to sunset. The McKinney kitchen opened to the alley, where Granda got hit by the car and where Willie locked Peter in the shed.

Mrs McKinney's sharp mind and activity belie her eighty-four years. She's always out and about, 'George comes on a Wednesday night and he comes on a Sunday night; Ann comes on a Wednesday night; Patrick comes on a Friday night; and Peter comes on a Thursday night. They all run me to Bingo, and they all come back for me, I take another woman that lives up the street, and we go to bingo. Peter runs me down to the Marian Hall and George collects me. Patrick runs me to the Stardust on a Tuesday night, Peter runs me on a Thursday night, and Kathleen runs me on a Monday night and Joe collects me. They all take turn about. Oh they're wile good. Kathleen says, "She's a better life than I have at night! We have to book now when we're coming in. She's always out at bingo!"'

Daily Mrs McKinney sits in her chair by the front window of 62 Westway where she has lived for forty-six years. The window overlooks the green where her children played. It overlooks the footpath to the front door where thousands of mourners queued to pay their respects when Willie was murdered. Mrs McKinney's chair faces the fireplace – the same wall where Willie hung a sheet and entertained the family with Mickey Mouse cartoons on his first film projector – and, of course, there's a view of the kitchen.

From her chair she tells stories of her children. Stories of Willie and George: brothers, eleven months apart but different as night and day; the Granda, whose antics cause Mrs McKinney to roll her eyes and chuckle; Willie's loves: his first teacher, his work, his fiancée, music, and photography. She told me about those who loved Willie most: Joanna who fell for the first born baby as she walked the floors, cradling him in her arms; Elizabeth, who loved Willie for six years, patiently waiting for the day they would be married; the grandchildren who never got to meet their uncle, but who no doubt would have loved him just as he adored his first darling niece.

A patient, kind, and generous family, they shared Willie's life. A life filled with passion and dedication. At twenty-seven, a life just beginning to blossom: a good job, lovely wife-to-be, search for his first house underway, and growing talent in photography. Come into the house. Sit. Have a cup of tea and listen. Mrs McKinney will tell you about her son.

Willie was born on 27 February 1944. Each and every one of them was born at home. But Willie, George, and Kathleen were born in my sister's house at 36 Saint Columb's Wells. Willie, George, and Kathleen used to say, 'I was born in the Wells you know.' St Columba is the patron saint of Derry and the Wells were the heart of the Bogside (even before it was the Bogside) so being born there is an honour.

As a baby, Willie never slept. We walked the floor with him at night. During the day Joanna wrapped him in her shawl and walked him around town. At the weekend, Granda tucked him in his pram and walked him down the quay. He wasn't fussy. He just always wanted up out of the cot. When George was born, their father was raging, he thought we had Willie spoiled, because George slept away.

But Willie never slept his whole life. If he wasn't up late working at the Journal Office he was developing pictures or lying awake listening to his wireless. Many a night I went into his room and he'd have it to his ear hearing everything that was going on down the town. Thinking he was sleeping, I would go to pull it out, and he'd say, 'Let that alone.'

After Kathleen was born we moved to 6 Orchard Lane. Orchard Lane was where Willie started school. Miss Johnston was Willie's first teacher. Willie's primary school was one street over from our house on Orchard Lane and Willie would come home and say things like, 'Miss Johnston sent me, could you lend her an egg?' No matter what Miss Johnston wanted, she sent Willie round for it. And I would say, 'have they nothing in that school at all?'

There was a place at the bottom of the street where the rough crowd ran about and a place at the top of the street where the reserved crowd hung out. George's pals came from the bottom of the street and Willie's from the top. This woman, they called her Mrs Rabbit, used to come into the lane and shout, 'Mrs McKinney take this George! He's keeping all these ones going down here!'

One day George went with Willie's friends over to a car park to learn how to ride a bike. There was a crowd that came from the far end of town to pick fights with Willie's choir crowd. So they asked George, would he come learn to ride the bike with them? He didn't know they invited him along knowing the crowd was going to come and fight with them and that George would take care of them. The crowd turned up, George turned on the crowd, and Willie and his friends had no bother after. So even if they didn't run around together, Willie and George were brothers.

Willie and George took turns working in a fish shop. The proprietors couldn't wait for George to finish school and find another job, but they loved Willie. They near enough wanted to adopt him. They had a room ready and all. When we moved from town up to Creggan, the wife sent up word to see would we let Willie stay the weekend? She said it was very late for him to go home, and they had a spare room. So I said to him, 'Are you going to stay?' He says, 'I don't want to stay, I want to come home at night.' So he came up at night.

At the bottom of the street where all the roughs were, there woulda been footballin' or stealin' or down the quay makin trouble. Four priests come out of the top of the street crowd. When we left Orchard Lane the lads that Willie was pals with lit a bonfire cause George was leaving. Mrs Rabbit said, 'Oh I am glad to see the back of that young fella. All he did was fight down here. He'da fought with his shadow.' Willie and George only fought once. Caught fighting in the street by their da – it didn't take much for him to convince them that wouldn't be tolerated. So George went on to fight another lad, another day and Willie went back to his group of quiet friends.

Willie took an early interest in music and took piano accordion lessons. He practiced up the stairs here. You can see from the window here that there are three buildings around the grassy square. Well, in those buildings someone played a trumpet and another played the drums so between

Willie and what was going on across the green, all of Westway could hear the music. Willie used to take his accordion along to play on bus runs – which were outings with the Hibernians or the men from work. One night I saw him coming up the back alley with the accordion. He said to me, 'You think I am coming up here drunk.' And I said no, but course I did.

But Willie didn't turn out that way. If it was George and somebody said to me, 'Where's George?' It woulda been George is down at the club or George is pegging stones or he's away playing football or table tennis. You'd always known what George was about but Willie was a quiet fella. He minded his own business. He was private about his own life for the most part. Willie would have been interested if something happened or somebody wanted to tell him something. If something went on, he'd enquire about it, but ordinarily he went his own quiet way and bothered about nobody.

Their Granda lived with us from Orchard Lane until he died and he contributed his own chaos to the mix. The wains would go up the stairs to their beds and Granda would call down, 'I can't get to sleeping with all these wains! They're wild!' Well that was some going! Sometimes it was wild, the carry on, it was desperate! Whoever lay on the bottom bunk pulled down the bottom sheet through the spring, and then the pillows were getting flung. The Granda would shout, 'They're going to kill me up here! I can't get sleeping with these ones carrying on!' But it was him winding them up!

Granda was a fowl-plucker. The boys visited him at work and knew about the big fridge that kept the chickens cold. They called the shop owner Wiggy on account of his baldness! The wains would be washing and warming themselves by the oil fire at night and Granda, lying in the back room you see, would shout out again, 'They're going to kill me up here.' And they would say, 'Aye this is like Wiggy's fridge!' Granda would say, 'They're killing me. They brought me out of Wiggy's fridge! This is like Wiggy's fridge!' And then they all laughed and carried on, and then they all got a hiding, and it was Granda keeping them going! Sometimes it was wild you know – they were all at one another.

There were only two places Granda could work and that was either the shop on Carlisle Road or the one on Ferryquay Street. So if he wasn't in the one he was in the other. George and Willie used to get money off the Granda for the matinee. So they would go to the shop and ask the man who owned the shop, 'Is our Granda in?' and he would say, 'Aye, he's in the back.'

The Granda would be in a little room at the back with 100, maybe 200 chickens. He'd see the lads and say, 'How youse know I was here?' Willie and George said, 'Well, we just knew' and hold their hands out for money. They went to the Rialto and soon enough we would all be looking for them. We were worried sick and they'd be lying sleeping in the Rialto.

Granda loved the wains in his own way. He walked Willie and George in their prams down the quay. He handed out money to the boys. When Kathleen was small he took her shopping down the town. At home he let her powder his face. I would come in from the shopping and she'd have him all made up.

He was a character but we missed him sorely when he died. He was coming home one night and a car knocked him down. Apparently the driver was speeding, and he knocked him some thirty or forty yards when he hit him. The damage was mostly on his legs. One of the feet had to come off, and he would say to Mickey, 'How am I going to walk home from Altnagelvin? How am I going to get home with only one leg?' The nurses were wild about him. They brought him beer and took good care of him. But the day came when they rang and when Mickey went over Granda was dead.

My sister Joanna was wild about Willie, too. She walked him when he was a baby and later took him, George, and Kathleen on summer holiday. Joanna and her friend Lily took Willie all over the island. George and Kathleen would have gone along at the summer but it was Willie they were attached to and they took him everywhere. Joanna and Lily took the three to Buncrana, Malin Head, and Bundoran from the time they were seven or eight until they left school and went to work. That was a gift to me. With those three gone I only had seven left to deal with and that was a holiday for me too. When they went to the Free State, they could get things cheaper so when George got home-sick they wrapped fabric around him under his clothes, put a label on him, and put him on the bus for home.

We moved to Creggan when Willie was fourteen. At that time he worked at a chemist shop in William Street. He didn't like that job at all. Every time he came into this kitchen after his work he cried about it, and I would say, What's wrong?

'I don't like it.'

'And why do you not like it?'

'Because it's all women work in it, and I would rather work with men.'

Joanna pleaded his case to his father. She came up on the Sunday night and Willie would be sitting here and Joanna would say, 'How are you getting on in the chemist Willie?'

'I don't like it.'

'You don't like it?'

'No.'

'Why Willie?'

'I don't like working with women.'

'You don't like working with women?'

Joanna would turn to his father, 'See here Mickey. You gonna do something about this young fella? Get him outta that chemist.'

Luckily, a friend of mine met me at Joanna's one Sunday and says, 'How's the family doing?' I says alright, but I got a young fella breaking his heart down at that Chemist. So my friend says, 'Wait till I tell you this – I have a grandson leaving the *Derry Journal* office. Tell your son to go down in the morning and see if he can get into it.' So Willie and his father went down in the morning and the *Journal* said the job is only running messages. Willie says, 'I don't care. I'll run the messages as long as I get in with men.'

So he got the job and they liked him and he liked the job and soon he was bringing home a big typewriter to practice as they were training him to become a compositor. He brought a big keyboard home to practice and it wasn't long before he was off the messages and typesetting the paper. He worked steady. Monday and Tuesday nights until four or five in the morning setting the paper for the Tuesday and Friday. When he came in from work on the Monday and Friday he brought five or six Journals for relatives, which his brother Mickey delivered: one next door, one to the Wells, one to the fountain, one up the street, one to Joanna, and one to Lilly.

One night the father got on to Kathleen about coming in late. The father was very strict about the time, and then he was terrified because Kathleen was going with a Yank. He was afraid the Yank would just take Kathleen away and that's all woulda been about her. So she was late one night and she came in and he checked her about coming in so many minutes late. Willie came in behind her and the father says, 'And that goes for you too.

Willie said, 'No way. No way am I coming in early. I work at the *Journal* office until two or three in the morning. I go with a girl who lives on the Waterside and I have to leave her off. I don't know what time I'm gonna get in. I'll go and get a flat.' That was awful for me. I said now Willie you don't need to go get a flat. You stay here. And that was that. It got Kathleen off the hook too. The father had plenty to be worried about with the Troubles and all, but these wains were twenty-three and twenty-five then. But their father was right about one thing, Kathleen married the Yank. When they left Derry, Willie posted the *Journal* to her every few weeks.

Willie's late-night walk home from the Waterside meant he saw all that was going on down the town. He would have walked up Great James Street and cut through the park to come home. One night as he crossed Waterloo Street, he found himself between a group of kids running up and the Army coming down the street. He was scooped along with the rest of them but when he and his father went to court, they explained Willie's hands were black from his work as a typesetter at the Journal office, not from pegging stones, and they let him go.

My husband was Michael McKinney, but all he got was Mickey. I met him at a dance in 1939. We were married in the Long Tower Chapel in 1943. I was twenty-four and he was twenty-one, and he played on that. He says to Mary one night, 'Mary when your mother dies I'm going to get a big blonde in here, and you call her mummy!' He went in front of me anyway. He was sixty-three when he died.

Life was hard at first. Mickey worked steady but one income with all these children was hard. We had seven when we moved to Creggan. I thought I was finished – but then there was Patrick and Peter and then John. It was wild at times up here with all the children in the house.

I once went to Lourdes with some friends and they were all sitting waiting on me when I came in. Mickey was left with the wains and when we came back he says, 'I never was as glad to see anybody coming back in my life.' My daughter Ann said 'He came over to me and said, 'I wish to God I could see your mother back, my brain's turning with them crowd.' Not only was he glad to see me, the wains were glad to see me. They had eaten all their meals from the chip shop while I was gone. I left the meat and spuds out for him but when I came back it was still sitting. I said, Mickey, you didn't cook for them? He says, 'They didn't want it. They all went out and bought outside.'

I was in this kitchen morning, noon, night. Cooking, feeding, and washing dishes while Peter kept the whole lot going. When the television was on he wouldn't let the rest of them listen to it, all I could hear was, 'Ma come on in to Peter!' It was just wild. I never got out again.

That Peter fella called Willie, 'Specky.' When Willie went out the back door, to leave for work at the *Journal* office, his bike was left out the back you see, Peter would call, 'Bye Specky,' and I would say to Willie, Go on and give him a skite! Don't let him call you that. But sooner than give Peter a skite, he'd lift him and carry him out and put him in the shed. There was a bolt on the door, so he bolted him in and said to me, 'As soon as I'm away, let him out.'

It wasn't long till Peter needed glasses too. One day I was here and the nurse comes up and says, 'Peter just got glasses and he can't see the board.' So I took him to the doctor and the doctor says, 'Let me see your glasses.' He took out a cloth and cleaned them off. Peter had been sticking them in his pocket as soon as he left the house, and they were so dirty he couldn't see the board. But he wasn't the only one to take his glasses off. I once found a photo of Willie at a dance. There he was dancing without his glasses. I don't know how he ever danced without glasses. He couldn't see a thing.

Willie had a country and western record collection, and he bought a big music centre to listen to the records. It had two big speakers and took up the corner of the living room beneath the stairs. One night George broke the centre – we don't know what he did but it wouldn't play and I said, Oh, George they'll be murder when Willie gets home! Well, we sat up shakin,' waiting for him to come home. He came in and said, 'Look at youse. What's wrong? There's something wrong.' I said, George broke the record centre. Willie said, 'It'll be alright' and he turned and went up to bed.

Willie was sensitive to other people's feelings. He didn't approve of gossip. If the young-uns were talking about someone, he would say, 'Where did you hear that? You don't know if that's true.' He made sure his younger brothers and sisters finished their homework. He told them to get home if they were out. He was quiet but he was principled, and if you were wrong – he would tell you.

One night when Willie and I were chatting in the kitchen, he told me he remembered how much I baked when we lived down the lane. We had a range there and it was wile handy to bake in. When we moved to Creggan, I didn't bake anymore. With so many wains, I just didn't have time. So one Sunday night he's sitting here talking to me and says, 'Go on try a scone.' I said, Willie, it's that long since I done one, I couldn't. He says, 'Go on try it. I'll watch the timing so it doesn't get too hot.' We tried it. It was like a pancake! We had to throw it out!

Willie talked to me in this kitchen, but he was quiet about his personal life. My sister came into me one Sunday evening and said, 'You'll never believe who I saw today going up Shipquay Street with a girl.'

Who?

'Willie.'

My God, I can't believe that.

'Aye, I saw him. He even looked over at me.'

That was Elizabeth. She lived on the Waterside. He was wild about that girl. She was all he'd have talked about then. One morning I came down the stairs, as usual I was up early, and when I came into the house, what was going round the house but a rabbit! Oh my God! And I went up the stairs and said Willie, you were the last in, did you let in a rabbit? And the mess with it! He says 'No. I bought that for Elizabeth.' Well, I said, get on now and go take it to Elizabeth! He bought her a rabbit! She loved rabbits and he bought her one.

Elizabeth was the last girl Willie went with. They were together for six years. They were supposed to get married but they never did. George even put off his wedding waiting for them to get married. But then George got tired of waiting so he went ahead.

Willie was camera-mad. His first camera was a small projector. He hung a sheet in the living room and we all sat on the floor watching black and white Mickey Mouse cartoons. His next camera was a small Pentax 35mm. He was always after me with that camera. He took pictures of me washing socks, cooking dinner, watching television, and many with my hand covering my face. Everywhere I went there was Willie with that camera. I used to try to chase him away. After the camera, seems like all he done was take my photo. He developed his film here at night. When we were all in bed and the house was dark, he stayed up developing all those photos.

He also loved taking pictures of Kathleen's daughter, Elaine. He snapped her photo when she was a baby bouncing in her chair and as she toddled up the footpath and through the gate. Every time he took her picture, he said 'She's powerful!'

His first film was of Elaine. We were all sitting here on a Sunday night and here comes Willie with a light and his movie camera. We were all sitting around Elaine as she played in her wee bouncer and he filmed us playing with her. While the rest of the family sometimes grew weary of his cameras, the wee-one never tired of her uncle Willie taking pictures.

When he got his first movie camera, he began filming all the civil rights marches. He would get in as close as he could to take in whatever was going on. He filmed the funerals, including the funeral of Sammy Devenney who was beaten to death by the RUC. He filmed the baton charges of the RUC. When they came at him, he didn't move. He stayed on filming. His brothers had to pull him out of the way. He wanted to stay to the last second. He'd be getting a battering to get all the action.

When Willie left for the march, he had his movie camera over his shoulder. I said to Mary, They'll think our Willie's a reporter today, nothing will happen to him. It was only a march, you know, for Civil Rights. But that was the next of it then, you know.

Willie saw two of his sisters on the way to the march. He pretended to film them as they mugged for the camera and then he sent them home. He tucked his camera under his coat to protect it when the army opened fire. But it was him who needed protecting. The army murdered him as he took cover, crawling by a low wall, crouching in the grass. A woman who saw him just before he was shot said he looked absolutely terrified.

There was a Dr McClean that was with Willie for the last. He went over to him and Willie said, 'Doctor am I going to get better?' Dr McClean says, 'I told that fella a wee white lie, I said, "The ambulance is coming now and they'll take you to Altnagelvin and you'll be all right." It's wile lonely when you're dying, so I held his hand until he died.'

Willie suffered two gunshot wounds. Well, the experts say it is unknown whether the wounds came from one bullet or two, but it doesn't really matter, the army shot him in the back and killed him. He was just there to film the march and they shot him.

Willie used to meet Elizabeth at the Guildhall, and the day that it happened she was standing waiting on him. We had to go down and tell her. She waited six years for him to be ready to marry. But they didn't get there. There's honour in being a widow. It must be hard to be the girlfriend of a murder victim. It's easy for people to disregard the depth of the relationship when you are just 'the girlfriend.' But to us she was his fiancé and so, part of our family. He loved her so much. We were so happy for her when she found love again, married, and had a family.

Miss Johnston came to the house for the wake. She was so sad. She must be nearly ninety now, but she still waves over to me at the Long Tower Chapel every Sunday at eleven o'clock Mass.

Kathleen was in Puerto Rico when Willie died. She arrived in Derry the day after the funeral. They held Willie's body back at the chapel and buried him the next day. I thought I was going to go to the cemetery the day Willie was buried. But that big car pulled up out there for me and I said, I think I am going to his wedding with the like of this car. I couldn't go. I used to go up on cemetery Sunday, but it's a long time since I've been up there. I won't go near it.

We never talked about Willie after he was shot. There were six sons left, and we were afraid they would have got into bother with a soldier or something you know, so we never talked about Willie. But one night they were all sitting, you see, after Willie died, and the father says to them, 'Are any of you in anything?' He meant IRA. And they said no. He said, 'Well keep it like that. One sore heart's enough. We don't want any more.'

The story ends. Mrs McKinney sobs. The shrieking piercing wounded cry of a mother grieving for her son. It makes your blood run cold and heart break. What healing can there be for the mother of a murdered son? This lovely, kind, generous woman left this world on 16 July 2005. In Mrs. McKinney's death I hope her grief has healed and she has found peace.

William Nash

Alex Nash and Bridget Doohey, the Boss and the Duchess, were married at 6:00 p.m. on New Year's Eve, 1942.

Wille, Alex and Bridget's sixth son, was murdered by British Soldiers on 30 January, 1972. He was nineteen.

Alex and Bridget Nash were in love. No huggin'. No peckin'. For Bridget and Alex, a whack at the end of a night's drinking was love. Their children never heard them utter the words, never saw it expressed, but they knew. They felt it. In the absence of pats, hugs, kisses, or words, it was there. A presence in the house no one could deny. Can you imagine feeling something so strong you never need to hear it? Knowing something so deep in your soul it never need be expressed externally? Could you spend the rest of your days secure in the love of your partner if he or she never again uttered the words? Alex and Bridget Nash, the Boss and the Duchess, they knew.

Alex and Bridget's son Willie never got the opportunity. No lucky girl ever got to be wrapped in his strong arms, run her fingers through his brown locks, lie next to him, her head on his chest on the cold Derry nights, watch him lift his children in the air and spin them around, tease him about his hair turning grey, bother him about the bills needing paid or the car needing repaired.

Photos of Willie don't reveal what an enormous presence he was, even at nineteen. His height hardly matched his long strong arms capped with the large rough hands of a man with docking in his blood. When he mounted the last stretch of road up to 38 Dunree Gardens at the end of a day's work, the children on the street ran up to him calling, 'Swing me around Tarzan!' And he did. The children squealed in delight as he scooped them up and spun them around.

The giggly one with the lopsided grin, Willie could melt your heart. But he was also a shit he played so many pranks and practical jokes. At first it was a boot or a shoe on top of the door. Willie left the door slightly ajar and the minute you walked in the door, bang! Down came the boot and smacked you on the head. If you were clever enough to steal a kiss in the back garden, you could count on passions being cooled with a pan of water, compliments of Willie.

As he grew so did the complexity of his pranks. For one of his favourites he removed the light bulb, filled a pair of trousers with clothes, and waited. The unsuspecting victim mounted the stairs up to the second floor and the screams that followed were undeniable. Willie had struck again. No matter how many times he did it you never got used to the figure dropping down from the loft.

His genius was in his patience. The other children would help collect the bottles and tie them together with the long, clear string but they soon became bored lying in wait. Willie got the joy of pulling the bottles behind the unsuspecting passer-by. When the victim walked, the bottles followed along. Every time the walker stopped and looked, the bottles rested until, with one big tug, the bottles smashed and sent the victim darting into the night.

Willie's boldness earned him the pleasure of knick-knock, because before you got to watch the neighbours open the door to an empty porch, getting more upset each time, someone had to sneak up and tie the thread to the knocker. Willie's project management skills allowed him to enjoy the consternation caused when he executed the Mini-cooper relocation plan, moving the car from the street down the way into the garden in front of a neighbour's house.

Though he's been gone a long time, you still half-expect him to reach out and grab your leg as you pass by that shrub in the front of the house or to feel his long arm reach in the window and whack you with a stick as you watch TV.

In the spirit of, if you can't beat him, join him, the whole Nash family played jokes on each other and it continues to this day. Was the donkey in the bedroom a pint-sized attempt at a prank? Banty will have you believe it was just plain earnestness. That donkey's owner was really mean to the donkey. He loaded it down, drove it too hard, and was just a mean spirited old coot who clearly did not have the donkey's best interests at heart. Six-year old Banty led the rescue. Once the donkey was in the house, he managed to get it into his bedroom. But it just wouldn't hide under the bed when Banty heard his parents coming.

The prize for the most elaborate prank pulled, however, goes to Bridget. When Alex turned sixty-five and applied for his pension, the office requested a birth certificate. In the days when Alex was born, recording births was not a high priority. A child was born at home and when someone got around to it, they went down to the office and recorded the birth. Family bibles and baptismal certificates were a family's record of a birth, not a government-issued certificate.

To apply for the pension, Linda sent off for her father's birth certificate and received a stern letter asking if she were aware that giving false information to the registrar was a serious offence. Linda knew exactly what her father knew – he was born 27 December 1919 on Blucher Street. She learned he was actually born on 28 June 1920 at 3 Howard Street. Alex, like the Queen of England, now had two birthdays- a real one and a celebratory one. When Alex learned the news, he thought it was a good thing because at Christmas he felt he was always done out cause his birthday presents and Christmas presents came together. Now he had 28 June. However, when he realised Father's Day was around this time, he needed to move his birthday again to different date.

The family speculated about the possible explanations for the misplaced birthday, but when Alex realised that his 28 June birthday made him a few months younger than Bridget, he realised he'd been had.

Back then, you couldn't fall asleep because if you did, they'd pour water in your ears or paint you with soot from the fire. Nobody took naps during the day. Everyone tried to be the last one asleep at night.

Today, you can't walk down the hall of a hotel with one of them. They will knock on all the doors and dash off leaving you standing there as the rooms' occupants answer.

Like his friends and siblings, Willie left school at fifteen. Few Irish went on for higher education in Willie's generation. Unless you were going to be a priest, what was the point? Families needed to be housed, clothed, and fed. Work was work. You were lucky if you could get it, with or without a university degree.

As children, they were trucked to the Waterside farms for work. Later they looked for anything that helped them contribute to the household. Girls went to work in the shirt factories, boys to whatever they could find, work in shops and pubs, the brewery, the quay. Some found their way to the training centre to learn a trade, such as painting, plumbing, or electric.

Willie went to work for Jackie Doherty's grocery on Central Drive. For two years he made deliveries on a bicycle with a basket on the front, his sister Maggie trailing after him. At seventeen, Willie joined his brothers, da, and granda down the quay.

The Nash men: Stiff, Tombstone, Banty, Allen, and Willie, three generations of dockers, dressed in layers – shirt, jumper, jacket, and cap. It was their movement, more than anything, protecting them against the raw wind each day at sunrise. The morning walk to the quay was two miles straight down. From Dunree Gardens, left onto Broadway, down the New Road, down Eastway by Essex Army Base, down Westland St., across Rossville St., up William St., through Waterloo Place, to Customs House Street. Head down; collar up. .

The Nashes worked for McKenzie's import/export business, which meant when the boats were waiting and the spuds delivered, they were guaranteed work. Twelve hours a day of eight stone bags from the lorry to the shed explains the massive upper-bodies the Nash-men still possess, even though the quay closed years ago.

The quay and the men who worked there are an essential part of Derry history, and the Nash family is part of the fabric of Irish families who made the Derry quay the most efficient docking system in Europe for generations. The quay was the only place where for years Irish men could find work and be rewarded for dedication and a job well-done as recognised by the button system. Here, they ran the show. The tradition of Derry dockers is of men so strong, it is hallowed in the lore of dockers. The world the Derry dockers made was steeped in a pride of steadfast dedication to the job, strength, and efficiency that far outpaced even their fiercest competition in Belfast.

Half-seven the men gathered for an 08:00 start. The Nashes reported to the Liverpool shed at the back of the Guildhall. Smoking cigarettes, doled out by the Duchess, they stamped their feet and chatted to ward off the damp cold wind. Dock work was a winter activity, but no matter the season, it's always cold down the quay. Granda Paddy (Stiff) worked the coal boats where a gang consisted of fourteen men and the gaffer who was employed to hire the men and collect dockets from the lorry drivers. These men were proud of their long-standing tradition of efficiency and endurance, and it is recorded that twelve men could discharge 120-150 tons of coal between the start of a boat at 8 a.m. and the 10 a.m. 'smokoe' or tea break. To put this into perspective, that is the equivalent of the twelve hold-men shovelling one ton of coal out of the hold every minute.[25]

For Alex (Tombstone), Willie, Banty, and Allen, work was on McKenzie's spud boats. The most labour intensive cargo of the lot, the potatoes arrived at the quay by lorry. Two planks were laid from the wharf to the boat. Two long ropes or slings were positioned at the bottom and two dockers would lift and place an 8-stone bag onto the shoulders of one of four men who carried ten such bags from the lorry to each sling. The sling was then tightened over the bags and secured onto the hook of the ship's winch which in turn deposited the sling load into the hold. Another four dockers then stowed the bags. These men were also proud of their reputation: Derry dockers took two and a half days to Belfast dockers' six to load the same tonnage.[26]

When they came of age, Willie and his friends were often found at the pubs. The Rushes lived two doors down, Pat Ward and Tommy Hazelet rounded out the group that went out for the country music at the pubs down the town. Banty made friends with the Americans who learned soccer and in turn introduced basketball. Basketball never really caught on in Derry, but Americans and Irish have a common love of

---

[25] John P. Coyle, *Down the Quay*, 18 (1990).
[26] John P. Coyle, *Down the Quay*, 20 (1990).

drinking and, God Bless America, the soldiers had a line on a steady supply.

Alex took full advantage of his sons' early forays into Friday night drinking. Saturday mornings, the Nash sons slept soundly through measured commotion rising up from the kitchen, each movement carefully timed and taken so as not to rouse the Duchess. Alex knew where his sons had been each Friday and the condition of each on Saturday morning. Patrick and Edward had moved out. Joe and Michael were still school boys. But Alex was a lucky man, there were still the four in the one room, ripe for the picking.

First he shook Willie's shoulder, 'Wake up, son I've got a breakfast here – made it just for you.' Willie turned over, his long, lean frame stretched under the blanket, mop of brown hair showing signs of a deep sleep.

'It's early, go on da'.

'Now look here son, the eggs are fresh, there's bacon and sausages, just the way you like 'em.'

Willie reached for his trousers, 'Here da', if I give you a cupla bob will ya leave me be?'

'Aye Willie, that'll do.'

Next came Banty, 'Wake up, son I've got a breakfast here – made it just for you. Here let me get it down where you can smell it. Have a good sniff. Isn't that grand?'

'Aw, da' not again, hand me my trousers, there's a few bob in me front pocket.'

Alex shook Allen's shoulder. He kept his head under the army blanket. But a quid came out from under the covers, 'Here ya are, go on now.' By his pre-emptive strike, Allen avoided the nausea that washed over the others at the sight and smell of the full fry swimming in steaming lard.

Alex approached a waiting Charlie, upright in bed. As a non-drinker and boxer he was always the last to get the offer. On his way to becoming a seven time all-Ireland national champion, he passed on the shakedown, relishing the grease laden plate of eggs, sausage, black and white pudding, toast, and beans, preparing him for the training-day ahead. Willie missed his brother's success. Willie's grave was still fresh as his family sent Charlie off to compete in the 1972 Olympic Games. He wasn't there when Charlie turned professional winning the Irish Title, the British and Commonwealth Title, and the European Title, which he retired to fight for the World Title. Keeping his collection complete, he came back to re-claim the European Title.

After Alex's breakfast scam, Bridget took the rest of the boys' money on the Saturday night. The wage packets came on the Friday and just like her mother and mother-in-law before her, Bridie collected the money from her children and husband. Of the £4-5 the kids each earned, £3-4 went to the household and £1 to the worker. Bridie was the ruler of the roost and this included the distribution of cigarettes for the week: three fags in the morning, three for after lunch, one for the evening. The weekly dole of forty-nine cigarettes had to be paid for on the Friday. After the household contribution and the cigarette fee, the kids had about enough for a dance on the Saturday night.

But what Bridie didn't get from them for expenses and fags, they lost to her at cards. To say Bridie was a crack poker player is an understatement. You'd have a better chance playing against the devil, in which case you might have stood a chance to win a hand or two. Bridie held court at the kitchen table, presiding over games that lasted through the wee hours of the morning. You have to admire a woman who can raise thirteen children, manage a husband, and beat the pants off you in poker.

When Willie was eighteen, he experienced the right of passage that took many Derry lads from boyhood to manhood. He spent six months at Crumlin Road Jail.

The Select Bar stood facing Foyle Street, across from the present day bus station. The three-story building held a shop on the ground floor and to the side a door that opened to stairs leading to the bar on floor two and the toilets on floor three. The space provided just enough room for a small bar, a few tables of four or five, and a three-piece band.

Eight friends out at the pub. There is probably not a single more ordinary happening in Derry. Banty, Allen, and Willie Nash, Paddy, Joe, and Noel Rush, Tommy Hazlet, and Pat Ward sat at a table on the second floor smoking and talking over a quiet pint. Danny Doran, alias George Washington, local country and western singer, was playing that night.

As the lads left the bar, they alighted down the one-body wide staircase and encountered a police contingent. As the friends attempted to exit, an RUC arm came across and blocked the way out, 'Where the fuck you think youse are goin'?'

'We're leavin',' was Willie's reply. Banty didn't hear the details of the conversation, but he deduced that words were exchanged. No big deal, they were accustomed to verbal jibes from the RUC, but when the baton was raised above his head, Willie didn't flinch. He floored the cop. He wasn't out that day to be harassed and abused. One RUC man down, the friends scattered.

Unfortunately, Allen and Willie were lifted. Banty and Paddy watched helpless from the Derry walls as his brothers were loaded up and driven to Strand Barracks; Willie taking a baton beating in the back as they passed by. On 10 May 1971, Willie was sentenced to six months. He went to jail, served his time, and earned his 50% remission.

Due to be out in August, as Willie's release date drew near the RUC decided he'd been in an earlier brawl that deserved another six month sentence. Without the benefit of trial, Willie was sentenced and served that six month term as well, once again earning his remission. He was out of jail just two months before he was murdered.

On 26 January 1972 Bridget had a heart attack. She was in hospital when Willie was murdered, waked, and buried. She never got to stroke her dead son's hair, gaze on his face in his casket, kiss him goodbye. Bridget didn't get to escort her murdered son to his grave. Instead, Bridget was locked away in a hospital room helpless, unable to take his last steps with him just as she had been present when he took his first.

Was her heart weak from the physical strain of an attack, or was her heart broken grieving for her murdered son that took Bridie just seven years later? Her family knew a woman who never recovered from the news her son was murdered, waked, and buried while she lay in hospital helpless to care for him, to be with him, to say goodbye as he left the world.

The bullet that ripped through Willie's heart seemed to tear her heart as well, but Bridget never spoke of her own grief. 'Saw poor Mrs Kelly down the town today, she's suffering so, yer heart just breaks for her.' Bridget wasn't the same woman after Willie's death. She stopped visiting her children. She was completely shattered. Her family watched helplessly as she struggled to mend her wounded heart, as she was diagnosed with diabetes, as she ached for the other mothers of dead sons. She was buried with her Willie on 19 May 1979.

Bridget suffered the fate of other Derry mothers of murdered sons. Alex was afforded an opportunity denied the other Derry men whose sons were murdered on Bloody Sunday. Alex was there. He was close enough to shout out, to race to Willie's side. But before Alex could call his name, a bullet entered Willie's chest and exited through his back. Before the sound of his father's voice reached him, Willie lay dying on the Rossville Street rubble barricade.

Alex raced to his son's side. He raised his hands over his head in an attempt to stop the shooting. For his heroism, for the love of his son, Alex was rewarded with two gunshot wounds. He was rewarded with the sight of his son being tossed like an animal into the back of a Saracen. Lifted by the hands and feet, Willie was tossed in with the bodies of Michael McDaid and John Young, who were also taken from the rubble barricade and contaminated by the poisonous hands of British Soldiers, filthy with gunshot residue.

Alex Nash changed after Bloody Sunday. He blamed himself for Willie's death. A father is supposed to protect his sons. A father is supposed to die before his sons. Alex stepped into to a hail of bullets but he couldn't turn back time. The bullet that ripped though Willie's heart, through Bridget's heart, tore open Alex's as well. He often said, 'You should never bury a son or a daughter, they should bury you. It's not the natural way of things.'

Alex suffered. For years he had travelled to England to paint in the summers, earning essential cash. Money that fed and clothed his family. After Willie was murdered, Alex never returned to England. Alex seemed desperately to want to die. He taunted the soldiers and the RUC so relentlessly they crossed the street to avoid him. The British Army raided the Nash home just as relentlessly, gathering the family into the small sitting room at the front, and then ransacking the house. But they never entered the room where Alex slept.

Did he believe he should have died too? Was he haunted by the sight of his son's murder? Was he tortured that he could not stop it? Was Alex further destroyed because he couldn't protect his family from the hate mail, telling them their son deserved to die; the British press that excoriated the men and boys killed, calling them terrorists; and the constant pursuit by the British Army that terrorised his children and particularly his daughters?

Years after the Duchess was buried, Alex was still talking about her as if she were just out in the kitchen. She was always there with him. The night Alex died, the night he was finally granted the gift to be with his wife and son, he was peaceful and serene. At that moment, Banty learned that the best measure of a life is the love you leave when you're gone; that what counts is how you care for and look after your family.

When we come to understand the tragedy of Willie's death, the injustice of it, and the pain it caused, we release the truth hidden in the moral rubble of Bloody Sunday. And the truth, eventually, will set the Nash family—and countless others—free.

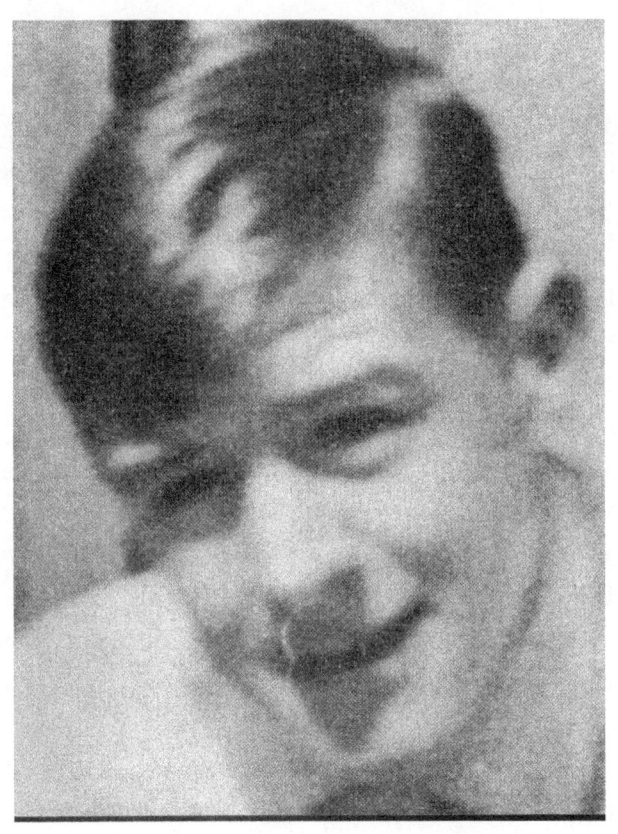

Michael McDaid

Michael was the second youngest of our family of twelve.
At the time of his death he had seven brothers and four sisters.
Michael was twenty years and four months old when a
British Soldier ended his beautiful life, and put a bright light out
in my family. - Bridie Gallagher

An old machine washed two bottles at a time but Michael preferred to do it by hand. The whole operation was set up in the wrong direction. The optic measure attached from right to left. The brass rod threaded through the siphons from right to left. Michael was left handed. He adapted. He bottled three barrels of Guinness a week. At fifty dozen bottles a barrel, Michael washed, dried, filled, and tended 1800 bottles every week.

Monday he washed the bottles. Tuesday they dried. Wednesday morning the delivery arrived. The three barrels of Guinness in place, corked and waiting, Michael set up the bottling machine. Bend over; lift four bottles; dispense beer; cork bottles using foot pump; place bottles in crate to brew for two weeks. Repeat 450 times. Monotonous, hard work, dedicated attention to detail, customers to tend to in the bar, week-in, week-out. Michael loved it.

The day-patrons: retired teachers, milkmen, postmen, accountants, factory workers, coalmen, dockers, and the unemployed supervised operations while perched on crates set in a half-circle around the bottling line. Lengthy discussions on international politics to the rhythm of the process were the order of the weekdays.

Thursday and Friday the bottles rested. The crowd picked up. Danny Doherty used a crutch and always sat at the table to the left of the bottling process. Jim McBride, 'Hambone,' who worked with horses and was big strong man with a great toothy smile, joked with all the customers. The sheepskin curer turned out some fine skins but look at him crossways and he mighta said – 'What are you looking at?' The two men engaged in conversation between the glass divides were oblivious to the others.

Bang! Michael slammed the bottle of stout on the bar, There ya go, Leo, drink up! Leo Carlin lived behind the Brandywell, the football pitch just across from Bradley's. Displaced from his local through redevelopment, Leo started drinking in Bradley's just before Michael came over from the shop. They became fast friends. 'Michael worked every Friday night. He served forty or fifty patrons and knew them all by name. He knew their personalities and how to wind them up, but they all loved him. Michael was a great man for pranks, especially on the older men. He liked to keep them laughing. Mickey would get Danny talking to somebody and then lift the crutch and hide it.'[27]

The bar was 'The Celtic' but everybody called it Bradley's. The family owned it and the attached grocery for three generations. Tall and gray, Bradley's stood at the corner of Elmwood Road and Stanley's Walk. If you entered the corner door for the grocery, you found four hundred square feet of spuds, turnips, beetroot, bread, sugar, flour, tea, everything required for the family larder. Order at the front of the shop, and it was sent out by delivery.

Upon exiting the grocery, a left turn onto Elmwood Road took you to the bar. The first door was the snug. A wee place where maybe a man and his wife would have a bottle or wee drink on the quiet. The snug kept secrets. Like men who enjoyed the company of their wives and sons who didn't want their fathers to know they drank.

The second door opened into the bar. A man's bar. Guinness bottling to the right, bar to the left. A few tables seating three or four each dotted the back wall. The bar was divided by panes of glass, four or five at two-foot intervals

---

[27] Interview with Leo Carlin.

which allowed the patrons to enjoy a quiet drink and conversation.

Bradley's was a quiet bar during the week but come Friday and Saturday, Mickey's forty or fifty drank and sang. According to John Bradley, 'some of them had been professional singers so they sang songs and had a tremendous time. At that time money was not plentiful, so they drank a little and sang a lot. The craic was good. It was a friendly place and very much because Michael was part of the whole. The Celtic was a place where everybody had a very enjoyable time and he took part in the fun.'

The Bradley family had operated the grocery and bar for three generations when Michael joined the staff. In the two and a half years he stocked and delivered, he became part of the family. When Mickey started at Bradley's, he worked as a messenger boy for the shop. Delivering the spuds, turnips, beetroot, bread, sugar, flour, and tea, Mickey got on very well with all the customers, especially the older ones. He always made sure they had everything they required. Nothing was too much to ask of him.

John Bradley recalls:

Michael worked very hard. He was a unique young man in the sense of his age group. I was a contemporary of his. I lived and was reared only 200 yards away so I'd known him since his childhood, and he had a very respectable family. The reason I say he was unique is because he dressed in a manner uncharacteristic of young people in the sense that he wore a collar, tie, and a sports coat. His trousers were immaculately ironed. Never was a crease in them. His shoes were always shined. He was this way when first he came to work for us at sixteen. He was very different from the other young men running around at that time. He was respectable, quiet spoken, and a hard working industrious young man as well.

In the autumn of 1968, the Bradleys' long-time barman got an offer to join DuPont, a good job with great pay and benefits. For Derry men such jobs were a long time coming, so when offers from DuPont finally came, they took them. It was a hard blow to the Bradley family who had depended on him for a decade. Mr Bradley, getting past the age of long hours and bottling Guinness, had looked to his manager to take over. The family was devastated.

John Bradley, just off to university, decided to abandon his plans to become an accountant and return home to take over the bar when his father had a brilliant idea. Why not Mickey? He'd been at the shop for two years. In that time he had worked hard and been an asset to the business. Lately he'd been helping out more frequently at the bar. He didn't smoke or drink. He was always well dressed and polite. Everyone liked him. He loved his work. Why not let Mickey have a run at managing the bar?

It wasn't long before the Bradley's realised they had struck gold. They'd had the perfect match with them for the last two years and Mickey found the perfect job – this was what he was supposed to do. Bradley's bar and the Bradley family soon became Mickey's second home and family. Before long, the elder John Bradley was grooming Mickey as he planned to groom his own son to run the bar. No doubt Bradley's Bar would be Michael's some day.

According to Leo, 'Mr Bradley put a lot of trust and faith in Michael and Michael was loyal to Mr Bradley. He never let him be interrupted. Michael handled the daily business of the bar and took over the bottling process as well. In fact, Mickey would've been one of the last of the young people to bottle Guinness'.

Michael's work ethic and enthusiasm for the bar and patrons was very important to John, who went on to become a successful accountant. 'I remember very well my father writing to me and saying Michael McDaid had been doing a very good job in the grocery shop and had graduated essentially into the bar and was doing a few evenings work in the bar. He had proven to be a fantastic worker, very popular with the customers. There needed to be no question of my giving up a university career. That was very significant to me. I was always grateful to Michael for that.'

At the close of business Saturday, Michael closed out the tabs, bid goodnight to the few still lingering, washed the glasses, wiped the bar's mahogany finish to a deep glow, shined it's glass divides, stood at the door, and surveyed his work. Someday he would be the proprietor.

Michael turned off the lights, locked the door and left. He walked 100 yards along Elmwood, then left for number 22. Click. Click. Click. The sound reassured his mother. Her Mickey was coming up the street, his iron tipped heel ticking on the concrete footpath. Now she could sleep.

If the staccato of the bottling process, the repetitive nature of the bar business was the rhythm of Mickey's life, his mother, Cathleen, supplied the melody. Michael's mother infused joy into her family. Every morning, 4.30 a.m. saw Mickey's mother in the kitchen making dough. As it rose, so did her children. Twelve, all told, up for school or work, washed, dressed, fed, and out. By 7.00 a.m. she was cutting the gravy rings and doughnuts. Sent with one of the boys to the shops in town on the weekdays; lined in boxes for the morning queue outside her door on the Sunday. Scones, apple cakes, gravy rings, wedding cakes, Cathleen's kitchen and front room supported a cottage industry.

Pre-dawn to dark of night she worked. She hummed. She sang. She never complained. She lived a Derry mother's life: she loved her children, was dignified, strong, and happy. She created a place to which her children always returned. When the McDaid children left home, they didn't scatter to the wind. Beechwood Street, Stanley's Walk, and Marlborough Road are all a stone's throw from the family home in Tyrconnell Street. Some went to England for work, but the McDaid family was always in touch, and Cathleen's children landed home regularly.

In 1970 Michael and Cathleen bought a dark green Ford Cortina. The 1600cc, four-door with radio was Michael's pride and joy. He kept it immaculate and it changed his family's life. Before the car, a day-trip to the beach was a huge production. It meant planning, packing, and riding the bus forty-five minutes each way.   After the car, it was just a matter of jumping into the car and away they went. Before the car, a day-trip to Buncrana was the extent of the family holiday, a trip to Galway or a night's stay was out of the question. This suited Michael's father, John, he preferred to sleep at home, in his own bed. But that fact didn't necessarily stop the rest of the family. The car meant Mickey and his mother could scheme a weekend holiday. As Michael's younger brother Kevin remembers it:

Mickey and our mother must have cooked up the plan, because when we loaded into the car that morning my father and I didn't know the boot was packed. We headed toward Bundoran, about an hour and a half down the road. We stopped for tea and sandwiches and it was still early so Mickey says, 'Why don't we just go on a bit further?'

Well, it ended up we arrived in Galway about eight thirty or nine that night. My father ranted and raved – 'you planned this!' Ordinarily we could ply him with a stout or a whiskey, but not this night. We really did ourselves in. We booked into a caravan park for the night and were going to go into town to hear some music but if dad wasn't having any fun – nobody was having fun so we were sent for take-away and ate chicken, fish, and chips in the park.

Galway is the gateway to Connemara National Park, Corrib County, and the rugged, beautiful Aran Islands. The city is filled with shops, pubs, restaurants, museums, and galleries. The Salthill suburb of Galway boasts fairground attractions and sandy beaches for swimming, sunning, and fishing. At the time of their trip, the weather was brilliant, sunny and warm, perfect for a few days' sightseeing but the McDaids saw none of it. They set out for home as soon as the sun rose the next morning. Kevin recalls:

It was an adventure for me. I was only sixteen then and it was great to get in the car like we never had a worry. Galway was over the border, just 175 miles, but it was really the other side of the world for us. It might look like it turned out to be just a drive but it was an amazing trip. We had a lot of laughs. I enjoyed it from the minute we left till we got back. Me and Mickey had a great laugh that night. Our father was a good character and we enjoyed the craic.

Before the car, most Sundays passed uneventfully. After the car, most Sundays Michael took his mother, sister Bridie and her boys, Seamus, Hugo, and Damian to the beach. Bridie's house sits on Beechwood Street, smack between Bradley's and the family home. From Bradley's, Mickey watched for his nephew Seamus walking to and from the Long Tower School. He thoroughly enjoyed the boys and called in daily to play with his nephews. He got Seamus to take his first steps and say his first words. 'See you later,' Michael called. 'See you later!' Young Seamus called back.

In the summer of 1971 Cathleen rented a Buncrana beach house for the month of June. Bridie and her sisters took their youngsters out of school and went off to the beach. Mickey landed down on his nights off; husbands and brothers at the weekends. It was a brilliant month. The weather was great. Just a half-hour walk to the beach, the three-bedroom concrete bungalow had an old range – in the mornings, the women prepared the dinner and left it in the stove. The stew or steak, gravy, and spuds were ready when they returned in the afternoon. Then, back to the beach in the evening.

Bridie's boys had just received their first boxing gloves and part of the craic at night was their first attempt at Derry's most popular sport. The house was near Buncrana next to a farm and the children had hours of fun chasing chickens and 'tending' the other animals. Filled with a lot of play, some drinking, a whole raft of singing, laughter, and much joy, it was the last summer holiday they would share with Michael.

No one knew that beginning at 20:16 on 30 January 1971, the year preceding Michael's murder, every day with him, every memory of him, would be the last.

Memories like the tape recorder. Bridie recalls when Michael won it at a rickety wheel a few weeks before Christmas 1971. He brought it to her house, sneaked up the stairs and taped the boys chattering before they went to sleep. The tape recorder went back and forth between Bridie and her mother's house with messages for a bit of craic. The McDaid family song – a well-kept secret - is stored on one remaining tape, one with Mickey's precious voice and laughter.

Memories like Christmas, 1971. As always, after midnight Mass, the family landed at Cathleen's for a fry and time together – women in the kitchen, men in the living room – they chatted and joked until half-two or so in the morning and then carried tired children home to bed and parents' final preparations for Christmas morning.

That Christmas morning Michael and his parents arrived early at Bridie's. Bridie and her husband Hugo gave their boys a large Lego set, and over the next few weeks Michael spent hours building cars and castles with the boys.

The next Wednesday Mickey collected his mother, Bridie, and his nephews Hugo, Damian, and Seamus. The merry band drove off to Strabane, Cathleen's birth place. They visited her family home, school, and parent's family homes. Cathleen told lovely stories of her school days, and of old friends. It was a wonderful afternoon.

The morning of 30 January 1972, Bridie and Hugo met Michael at Tyrconnell Lane. He was on his way to Creggan, where he was meeting Leo Carlin, Paddy Doherty, and Eamonn McLaughlin for the start of the march. They were jubilant. They were going to see the biggest crowd that had attended a march. They spent a few minutes talking, said good-bye, and parted ways. It was the last time Bridie saw her brother alive.

The day, and life as they knew it, ended for the McDaid family about half-eight. It was natural for the family to gather at their home on Tyrconnell, and they did. They gathered and waited. Rumours spread that Mickey had been arrested. His family was not officially informed that he was dead until the evening. A pall set upon the house. The click of Mickey's heel on street letting Cathleen know her son was home safely was silenced.

Michael's family was devastated. His mother was never the same. No one in the family ever heard her hum or sing a tune again. His sister remembers him as *'a fine, decent, honest, hard working, loving human being. He had so much to offer, yet he was gunned down. My family was not the only one robbed by his death. The people of Derry were robbed also. They were robbed of a special person, someone who cared for others more than himself, someone who could have made a difference.'*

Her sentiments are echoed in the words of Michael's friends. Leo Carlin was traumatised by the events of Bloody Sunday, he was shot at, marched with a rifle to his face and arrested. He lost two close friends, Mickey and Paddy Doherty. He still grieves deeply for the McDaid and Doherty families' loss, and reflects:

He was only twenty. Michael was only twenty when he was killed. Michael was a great lad. His whole family, his mother and father were brilliant people. When I gave my statement to the Inquiry it was terrible hard to do because I never spoke to anybody about Bloody Sunday. In fact you're the first stranger I've ever talked to about Bloody Sunday. I never spoke to my wife about it. Michael was along with me that day he was shot. We were together he, and I, and Paddy Doherty. They were both killed.

John Bradley says:

Michael was very popular with the customers and his death was a terrible loss to everybody. Michael left his mark on all the various people that came into the bar and his death left a terrible void. My father, who died in 1973, was a father figure in totality. When anyone was in crisis, he was the man to come to. He was very respectable and would have been regarded as a pillar of society. He regarded Michael as one of the family; as a very important member of our family and so we all got very close to him. His death at such a young age was such a terrible loss. As a family we take Michael's murder very much to heart and it still affects us.

Michael's brutal murder by callous, indifferent soldiers stands in stark contrast to his warm and kind humanity. By any criteria Michael McDaid was the opposite of a Derry Young Hooligan. Like thousands of others he joined the march as a witness to the injustices heaped upon Catholics in Derry. He was no different than the countless Americans who marched in civil rights demonstrations. He was no different than his neighbours who were clean of the IRA but clear in their intent to send a message: 'Internment is wrong.'

Michael's intent was to attend the march, meet his girlfriend, go home, have his dinner, and go to bed. The next day he would return to Bradley's to do his work and pick up conversations with his friends and customers. Michael died as an innocent and his death touched the hearts of family and loved ones in a profound way.

Thinking about Mickey one afternoon, Bridie sat down and wrote about her brother. Her words conclude:

The last time I saw Michael alive was shortly before the march on Bloody Sunday. My husband and I were taking our sons to my mother's house, she was minding them, as Hugo and I were going to the march. It would be my first ever march. We met Michael at Tyrconnell Lane. He was on his way to Creggan for the start of the march. He was like myself and everyone else in Derry that day – jubilant, we were going to see the biggest crowd that had ever been at a march before. We spent a few minutes talking, then we said good-bye. Little did I know that the next time I would see Michael, he would be in a coffin!

Twenty-six years on, my brother Michael is still held in high regard, and spoken of frequently by those who knew him. This speaks volumes for the type of person he was, and encapsulates fully the essence of why his death was so very wrong.

The trigger-pullers glee was short, shallow, and hollow. Michael's memory shines bright, vibrant and everlasting. It will be passed from generation to generation with love.

Paddy Doherty

*Paddy just loved his children. He was a very simple man.
He never wanted anything. He lived for us, that was it.*
- Eileen Doherty

Three months after her 11th birthday, Karen Doherty became a fatherless daughter. Karen's dad died when he went off to walk in a civil rights march one day. She loved her father wildly.

After her father's death, Karen became largely responsible for her five younger siblings. Karen was her father's daughter – resolute, proud, passionate. But she didn't know how to be a fatherless daughter. Paddy taught his daughter to tie her shoes, cook the meals, and mind her brothers and sisters. He never taught her how to live without him.

Paddy Doherty was thirty-one years old when he was killed. He had been a husband and father for eleven years his wife, Eileen, giving birth to six children. They had the first four in four years, a five year break, and then two more. They were all born at the start and the finish of the month: Karen on the 31 October; Patrick 27 November; Tony 1 January; Paul 1 February; Colleen 28 February; and Gleann 2 June, so it might be said that the happiest days for Paddy Doherty were at the start and the end of the month!

Eileen's mother proposed. She called Paddy in and said, 'It's done. You'll be getting married now.' The dress was pink satin with three-quarter length sleeves and a full skirt. Pink veil, white gloves, and white shoes completed the ensemble. Paddy, the handsomest man in Derry, was dashing in his navy single breasted suit. She had to kneel outside the altar but she was marrying the man she'd loved for two and a half years. He smiled, held her hands in his, made his vows, and kissed her. Everything was perfect.

The Easter Tuesday 8 a.m. wedding Mass was followed by a fry for a hundred guests at the house at the top of Central Drive. While the guests stayed on to toast the couple, Paddy and Eileen departed for their honeymoon. Eighteen years of age. The eldest of thirteen. Her first time away from home. Tears fell as Eileen waved goodbye to her father on the platform. She and Paddy were too young to be getting married. Too young to be parents. But it was done.

They were in love. They would do the best they could. Six months later, Karen arrived and Paddy found great joy in being a father. He loved his daughter wildly.

Karen only knew her father for eleven years. She had all of those wonderful 'being in awe of your dad' years. The time in life when your father can do no wrong. The time when his punishments are justified, his expectations reachable, and his praise lavish. A time when a girl's desire to please her father is rewarded.

Karen was first born. A place of privilege in her father's eyes. Long walks by the River Foyle after her siblings were put to bed was a special treat. Working by her father's side in the kitchen while he prepared the Sunday dinner made her feel grown-up. Placing her small hand in his large one when they walked to Mass and then standing at the back of the chapel with her father and the other men solidified for her – she was Paddy Doherty's daughter. Paddy Doherty – strong, hard working, respected in the community, liked by his peers, and loved by his family – she was his daughter.

Paddy wasn't just Karen's best friend, confidant, and role-model, he was her protector. He punished her brothers when they wronged her. When she returned from school one day to find her prized possession, an Elvis poster the size of her bedroom wall, suffering an injury of graffiti at the hand of a brother, Paddy lined up the three potential suspects, Tony, Paul, and Patrick and interrogated them like a Chicago cop on a bad day. The fact that the poster was a gift from Paddy to Karen didn't help the boys' case.

When a drunk neighbour stumbled into Karen's room one night, Paddy went to the man's house, knocked on the door, said, 'Excuse me Madame, I'm real sorry to have to do this,' took the man outside, and taught him some manners, Karen knew he would always defend her honour.

Paddy was a renaissance man. The father of a new generation. His house was one of equality. He and Eileen both worked and everyone in the house was expected to contribute a fair share. For the children this meant everyone had chores – boys and girls alike hoovered, scrubbed, and cooked.

This was a dramatic departure from the way Paddy and Eileen's generation was raised. They were treading unchartered child-rearing waters, but their children didn't know that. The boys knew they were hoovering, cooking, washing dishes, and cleaning the yard while their friends were playing football. They knew that other girls were kept in while Karen went out for late-night walks with her dad. In the Doherty house it was age and family-contribution, not gender that earned you perks.

In retrospect, the Doherty siblings think Paddy was concerned about making sure that his family was brought up as properly and decently as possible. He wanted his children to be productive members of their community.

Paddy was aware of social justice. He wanted his children to have the same rights and privileges as their Protestant peers. It certainly wasn't going to be anything they did that brought on governmental mistreatment. Paddy was raising his children to be equal members of what he hoped would become a just society.

To this end the children got paid sixpence every Friday night. They all contributed and they all got. They also attended Mass every morning. Every week-day morning they rose at six, dressed, and were sent up the hill to Long Tower Chapel. They went to Mass, trudged back home for breakfast, then back over the same route to school. Paddy worked to ensure there would be no spoiled children in the Doherty household.

Even so, Paddy seemed to know each of his children's special desires and he particularly indulged their wishes on their birthday: a big red bus for a very small Paul; a secret camera for Patrick for whom Paddy lined up all the other children in the back yard for a photo that turned out to be a hosing of water and a host of laughter from Paddy and Patrick; a bike for Tony.

Paddy made them each feel as if he knew them. He made a connection with his children as individuals. Colleen can't remember it but it was she that spent the most time snuggled in her father's arms and sitting in his lap. It was she that brought him home from the pub so Paddy spent more evenings helping with homework, wrestling, and laughing with his children than he did drinking with his friends.

Paddy was a family man. But he didn't just spend time with his wife and children. He got on great with Eileen's parents, too. Mrs Quigley set high expectations, telling Paddy in very specific terms how she expected him to treat her daughter and grandchildren, but she doted on him as well. Eileen's father was a traditional Derry man. He worked. He drank. He gambled. As different as Paddy was in that respect, Eileen's father had a great affinity with Paddy as a man's man.

Eileen's parents and her twelve siblings lived on Central Drive. A favourite destination of the Doherty children, they had no idea how intimately acquainted they were fated to become with the household. In contrast to the Doherty's, a white-glove house of order, the Quigley house was a whirlwind of activity. Packed full of teenagers, the house reverberated with The Beatles, Rolling Stones, and The Kinks. Mrs Quigley was a prolific baker and the house always smelled of breads and buns.

The Quigley's was also the place for parties. Christmas especially, when the lorry pulled up to deliver beer and lemonade; Sinatra crooned from the record player; stories were exchanged; and toward the end of the evening, men sang to their wives. Except in Paddy's case, his wife sang to him. Eileen was a great singer and was always prompted by her father to sing for the crowd. After all, Eileen was her father's daughter.

Paddy's desire to raise his children right: to be productive members of society, respect their neighbours, and participate meaningfully in their religion was reflected in his civil rights activities. Not only did he want his children to be good people, he wanted them to live in an egalitarian society. Just like fathers of black children in the southern United States, Paddy took to the streets to make his desires known.

His children were only vaguely aware of Paddy's participation in civil rights marches and contributing his strength and determination in the Battle of the Bogside, when Eileen and the children evacuated to Central Drive for protection and waited anxiously for Paddy's return. After three solid days of defending the Bogside, Paddy was safely home. His hands and face pure black, he emerged from the Bogside walking up Westway to Creggan. Exhausted, he went inside, ate, went straight to bed, and didn't get up until the next morning.

On 30 January 1972, Paddy joined Leo Carlin, Michael McDaid, and Eamonn McLaughlin on the Civil Rights March against internment. They were a good way back in the crowd and reached Barrier 14 as the crowd began dispersing. They didn't know why the crowd was running away from the barrier but they joined them and took off down Chamberlain Street. Here Leo split off from his friends.[28]

When Soldier F gunned down Paddy he didn't know Paddy was a family man. He didn't know that six young children would be fatherless. Soldier F was a paratrooper; a soldier trained to do a job. He was given orders, which he executed. After all, if he violated orders by killing Paddy, his commander certainly wouldn't have been decorated by the Queen for their actions that day.

The Army thought Soldier F was a good soldier. They say the paratroopers are the best of the best in the British Military. What kind of soldier shoots an unarmed civilian in the back?

Doherty had been shot between the rear of Block 2 of Rossville Flats and Joseph Place while crawling along the ground holding a handkerchief over his face. He had been hit from behind by a bullet which passed through his body almost parallel to his spine. Lord Widgery found that he had not been carrying a weapon when he was shot.[29]

It wasn't Soldier F's job to know Paddy was a family man or to know he had six small children at home. It was Soldier

---

[28] Statement of Leo Carlin to Bloody Sunday Inquiry, 6 October 1998.
[29] Walsh, Dermot. *Bloody Sunday and the Rule of Law in Northern Ireland*, 210, (2000).

F's job to execute an operation according to orders, not to concern himself that his actions would lead to the devastation of a family.

This soldier's actions left Karen Doherty a fatherless daughter. He left a young girl with no strong arms to protect her. No shoulder to cry upon. No man to confide in. No more Sunday dinners to prepare. No walks by the Foyle. No father to walk her down the aisle. No grandfather to greet her newborn children.

Though Soldier F took Karen's first love on a clear day in January, he did not darken the light within her, because Karen is Paddy Doherty's daughter.

Jackie Duddy

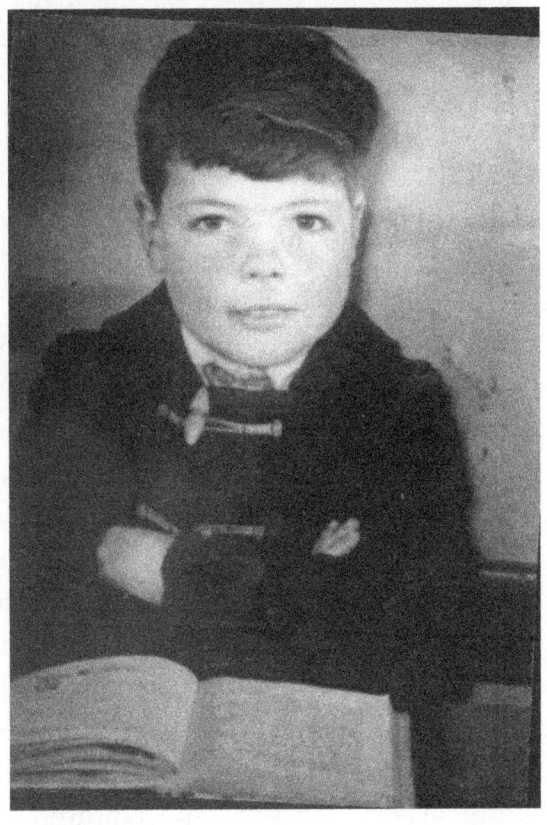

    My sisters Maureen, Bernie, and Kay loved Jackie. They'd say, 'He was so sweet and placid. He was always smiling. You could never rile him. He was so good to the young ones. He had a lovely nature.' Well, he punched me up in the front hall and made me carry his boxing gear to the gym and back every night and that was one hell of a walk!

    He was nothing special, just my older brother.

- Gerry Duddy

My name is Michael Duddy. I was born on 21 October 1960. My dad wrote a note to get Kay out of school to watch the little ones, 'Please excuse Kay from school as we have been blessed with another gift from God.' I was the fourteenth. Kay's school teachers were amazed at how the letter was worded – that it was still considered a gift from god even though it was the fourteenth. Pauline arrived three years and ten days after me, and she's the baby, so there's just the fifteen of us. Well, fourteen now, since Jackie's dead.

My brother Jackie was born on 7 July 1954. That was when they still lived in Springtown Camp. My mother loved Springtown. There are stories of water running down the walls and disease and children dying, but my parents were one of the first to move their family into the huts so at that time they were still in good condition. They were damp and there was no central heating or bathroom. Maureen and Bernie and Kay remember the tin bucket where they bathed in front of the fire. Considering the condition of the houses in town at that time, this was definitely an upgrade.

Ma used to say she wished they had knocked her hut down and built a house there 'cause there was big rooms and lots of land around. But for the children, moving to Creggan Heights was like moving into a three bedroom mansion because it was a brand new house with a bathroom, hot and cold running water, a fire, and a big back garden.

Everyone called Gerry, Patrick, and Jackie the three musketeers. Jackie and Patrick were a year and twenty days apart. Gerry came along another eighteen months later but he was the biggest of the three so a lot of people referred to Gerry, Patrick, and Jackie when it was actually Jackie,

Patrick, and Gerry. Nonetheless, they looked near enough alike to be triplets.

When Gerry was born we outgrew the kitchen and started eating in shifts. At Christmas we set up a table in the sitting room so we could all eat while the food was hot, otherwise the wains were fed first, then the school age group, and the ones out working would eat their dinner when they got in after work.

The bread man delivered maybe eight or ten loaves a day. On the bank holiday, when the bread man couldn't come for two or three days, there was something like twenty-four or thirty-six loaves delivered to our house, because no matter what you ate you had bread along with it to try and fill you. At least two loaves of bread always sat on the table at any dinner regardless of what the dinner happened to be. The bread was the filling bit. There might not have been much meat or spuds in the stew but there was gravy and you dipped your bread into it and got your fill. We always had friends in, especially the boys, and there was always enough so they got their share as well.

Each week the girls were given this wee note and they went down to the shop and left it off for the delivery man. The note would have listed maybe six pounds of butter, six pounds of jam, and twenty pounds of spuds, peas, fish, roast, chicken, and cabbage. The dinners were set for each week and there wasn't any such thing as two or three dinners being made to satisfy the fussy ones. You ate it or left it and if you didn't eat it you would have plenty of bread and jam to fill you in. Funny enough, Gerry was the fittest and he was the one who lived mostly on the bread and jam.

Saturday's Jackie and his pals went to the pictures. Jackie liked the westerns. There was a time that all these European film production companies made westerns. They made something like 600 of them between 1960 and 1975. The critics hated the films and because most of them were financed by Italian companies, they called them Spaghetti Westerns. Jackie not only liked the films but he bought the records and listened to the scores over and over again! His favourites were all Clint Eastwood films: *A Fistful of Dollars*, *A Few Dollars More*, and *The Good the Bad and the Ugly*. He loved how Clint always 'rode into town.'

When Jackie was twelve he started boxing at the Long Tower Boxing club. There was a boxing bill every week, Creggan one week, then Long Tower, St Mary's, St Eugene's, Strabane, etc.

In only four years he'd won hundreds of trophies. There were two sports in Derry at the time, boxing and football. Our family did more boxing. Gerry started after Jackie but trained at St Mary's and as soon I came up, I joined the club as well.

Long Tower Club was a converted terrace house on Alexander Place just off Foyle Road. After dinner we left the house and walked down Bligh's Lane, down Stanley's Walk, up over the fly-over, down Bishop Street, and turn left into Alexander Place. We lived at the top of Derry and the Long Tower Club was at the bottom just before the river.

In between the workout of walking to the club and back home, we got warmed up with jacks, sit-ups, lunges, and skipping. Then we broke up into speed bag, heavy bag, and sparring. You did so many exercises and then the groups switched around. Depending on the night, you could get some rest waiting your turn.

The only heating was this old fire and that was only when the club was open. Nights when Jackie had a fight coming up, the club wasn't open, and he wanted to do extra training, he needed a sparing partner so Muggings (Gerry) had to go down with him and then get the head punched off him in the cold just so Jackie would be prepared for the fight. Jackie dragged us down to that club in all types of weather – from the top Creggan down to Alexander place and then back up again.

I got my first boxing lessons in the hallway in Central Drive. In the short narrow hallway Jackie could get us up against the front door or against the stairs and use us as his punching bag. There were six boys and it seems like he practiced on all of us. Jackie was our first sparing partner and eventually we all took a turn at boxing, but Jackie was the only one who went anywhere with it.

Jackie trained to win. He boxed to win. Winning is what kept him going. At the time, to work so hard that your body is exhausted, your arms hang at your sides, until you are battered and weak, all for the possibility of winning one match seemed a little over the top to me. But to be the best was Jackie's driving force. Winning was the thing that motivated him to keep on. He became obsessed. It was his first and only love in life. For a while, everything took a backseat to boxing. But by being obsessed he was successful. If you are obsessed about other things – a girl, the drink, a job – they might lock you up. If you are obsessed about a sport, you are a hero.

At only fifteen years of age he went down to Dublin to compete in the All-Ireland Championship. He got beat in the finals. The people he boxed with all went on to become champions so he was in a good class of fighters. Dad loved it —him bringing in his trophies. He was so proud of Jackie's boxing.

Me da always said he was an ambassador for Ireland. He was in the Merchant Navy for a time and he said this was his role in life – to be in the Merchant Navy, travel the world, and be an ambassador for Ireland. He told us it was very important no matter what we done or where we went to always uphold this ideal that we were ambassadors. He always said he was a cosmopolitan. Later, when the Army came in, he was like, 'Why are youse raiding us?' and be looking for his medals. We never knew what the medals were for. He had these medals – but we never knew what they were for or even if they were his or his fathers!

Me Da was a very private person and tried to bring us up that your business was your business. The world and his brother didn't have to know. If we were fighting in the street he was always, 'Get them in here! Sort it out in the house! The world doesn't have to know!' We were brought up keeping everything within the confines of the house. It was, 'Nobody needs to know your business but you.'

Da was in the town one day and, I don't know how many youngsters he had with him, but he met this man and he hadn't seen him in a long time and the man said, 'God Willie haven't seen you in a long time. How many wains have you?' Me Da told him the count was thirteen then. The man replied, 'God! Look at the grand way they've turned out!' Me Da turned and he said, 'What did you expect, them to be in their bare arse because we have a whole lot of wains? We do look after them you know!'

My dad was a merchant seaman, and his father before him. He wasn't a sailor per se, he was a boiler man. It didn't matter to him though, he sailed the world and loved it. He even lied about his age to get in. When he was 14 he was sent out to deliver some linen and never went home. He went to the docks and the sailors made him a special shovel so he could manage the coal along with the rest of them. Our Eddie joined the Navy too for awhile but he was only in six months till home sickness brought him back. Then Jackie tried to sign up but he was just over the age limit. It was kind of a tradition in our family, but I always thought Jackie wanted to join to get away from the hassle from the Army.

Jackie quit boxing about six months before Bloody Sunday. Gerry says he was tired of all the hassle he got walking down to the club and back. He had to pass through the barricades and it seems like he got a lot of grief from the soldiers. I don't know if he'd have gone back to it if he hadn't been killed. But even though he wanted to join the Merchant Navy, I think he would have returned to boxing because he had a great love for it.

Jackie used to go out in the morning and run around the wall round Westway and Glenowen. It was one hell of a run. I mind Jackie getting up in the morning, when he just started work. He was working for Thompson McGlinchey's. I used to walk down Westway with him, I would have headed on down to Rosemount Boys School and he went on down Park Avenue. But he'd have already run twenty-five minutes around the park before he left for work.

Seems like he was always running and I'd be running after him whenever I could. Jackie delivered the papers from McCool's Shop. I went with him and my payment at the weekend was an outing to the swimming baths or to the city picture house. He liked Spaghetti Westerns but he took me to see Batman and Robin. It wasn't like what you see now but it was a treat for me.

Treats were few and far between but we got one trip every year. We went even if it was rain, hail, or snow. My mother with her lot and my Aunt Dolly who had nine or ten of a family. They planned the day to coincide it with the 12 of July because it was always said the sun always shone on the 12 July. So the way it went was, 'Go down and ask your aunt Dolly would tomorrow be OK?' Right.

So I would run down to the next street where Dolly lived and Dolly would say, 'We will try it tomorrow, OK.' I would go back up and we started making sandwiches, packing buckets and spades, and extra coats in case it rained. The packing that went on for this day was enormous. Then all this stuff had to be carted on a bus to get this one day trip out. The bus to Buncrana was a double-decker and our two families managed to fill the top and no one else was allowed up.

That's the way it was. Sometimes it happened that we woke on the day and it was pissing rain so I was sent back down to Dolly's to ask, 'What will we do?' The answer was always, 'Ah bugger it, the weather could pick up.' So the trip went on anyway, you know regardless of what the weather was like. That was our big thing. That was our summer holiday. The rest of the time the boys went out to the fields and played football and the girls made rag dolls and played at skipping and hopscotch.

All the boys in the neighbourhood shared the one ball and one summer day me, Gerry, Liam, Jackie, and Andy were playing football. Patrick was in the house and our ball went over the wall and into the Doherty's garden. As usual, I got cheesed up to go and get the ball. I went up and was told, 'F-off! Ye're getting no ball!' I went back to the lads and reported, 'We aren't getting no ball.' Jackie said to me, 'Go over to the house and get Patrick.' The next thing I know he's over the fence and Gerry, Patrick, and Jackie are in the back garden fisticuffing over this ball. Jackie wasn't ever one to start a fight but he'd surely finish one. He soon got our ball back.

Another time we were standing over at Coyle's shop and two guys from a very tough family walked up. I mean, you just wouldn't mess with them. Jackie said to one of them, 'Were you shouting at us down the town?' The way he asked it seemed friendly enough to me, but they musn't have taken it that way because the next thing I know is Jackie tellin' them to buzz off.

The three of them squared off and Jackie put the both of them down. Big Coyle came out and said, 'What's going on here? Get away!' When Jackie came home he said, 'Thank God Johnny Coyle came out. Them boys would have kilt me!' Later Johnny Coyle drove up to the house and said, 'God young Duddy, them was two great punches!'

Kay was assigned the Christmas shopping for the wains. She always went for six pairs of trousers, six underpants, six pairs of socks, six shirts, and six jumpers at a time. The shop was on the Waterside so six sets were all she could carry at once. Then they were all tried on and this matched and that matched, and this fitted her and that fitted him, and so on. Whatever didn't fit had to be taken back to the shop and Kay started the whole process over again until everyone had one new outfit from head to toe.

Shoes were another process. My parents kept a list and you got new shoes when your name came up. There was no such thing as outgrowing them before your turn came around. We cut holes for our toes and cut out cardboard to cover our toes – you slid in the cardboard then put your foot inside. We used bits of carpet and lino sewed into them – anything to keep them together. You had to wear them until they literally fell off your feet. Then we had a go at mending the shoes ourselves. Somebody got some scrap leather and nails and you hammered it in. At one point my dad found an old shoemakers stand and then we really got into sophisticated repairs.

Maureen was the first to get married. Seventeen people in the house (ten of them female), one bathroom, and the wedding Mass at 8.10 a.m. Kay and Bernie scrubbed all the wains the night before, and washed, ironed, and laid out their clothes. In the morning the curlers were flying and the wains getting stuck into their clothes and the rush out the door was madness.

The night before Maureen's wedding Eileen took ill. She was so sick, in the morning Kay wanted to send for doctor, but Eileen wouldn't hear of it. This was her first wedding and she was not going to miss it. When we got back to the house after the wedding, we sent for the doctor and Eileen was rushed to hospital and had to have her appendix out. We could have killed her taking her to the wedding!

Two years later 'the big woman always in the kitchen' died. We missed her sorely but we had to get on with things too. That October Pauline would just turn four and Da needed someone to look after the household. After retiring from the Merchant Navy, Da was unemployed for a long time but at the start of that summer he'd gotten a job as a boiler man in St Columb's Hospital in the Waterside. Maureen, Kay, and Bernie were married, which left Ann as the oldest in the house. She gave up her work and took over running the house. When Ann met and married the love of her life, as luck would have it Kay's marriage broke up so she took over running the house and it just sort of moved down the line that way, whenever one moved on, another picked up the reins and ran the house till we were all raised.

Kay and Bernie always had us organised from the night before. We were scrubbed, our clothes laid out, and shoes lined up. Breakfast was tea and toast and a run out the door. The older ones took bread and jam to school and the younger ones were home for their lunch.

The boys would have you believe that it was the girls that always got into spats but if Gerry wore Jackie's shirt or

Patrick's jumper there would have been a whole barney about it. There were nine girls and six boys, so in a way, we had it easy. The boys were only three to a bed but the girls were four and a half – Pauline was the half – she was so small she just jumped from bed to bed.

We fought about everything under the sun. He got more dinner than I did; I took a lend of his shoes or dirtied his jumper; she wore her knickers; he was watching something on the TV and I turned it over; I sat in his favourite chair. There were about a million things that could have started an argument. Gerry was the instigator of a lot of it. He still pushes our buttons today. Back then all you'd hear was our Da shouting, 'There's not a family in this town that fights the way you crowd do! I'm sending for the priest for you!'

Our father told us to stay away from the march. Jackie went anyway. He said he was going to see his girl Bernie. Bernadette Devlin was speaking at the march and Jackie said you could always count on good craic from Bernie. I went to play cards at Johnny Coyle's. From down in the shop I heard people yelling, 'They're murdering people down the town!' I came running up the stairs then and I seen all these boys jumping into a car and roaring off.

I went home and said, I heard our Jackie was killed down the town. My sisters gave me a hard time saying that of all my five brothers, Jackie was the least likely to get shot. Kay gave me a skite and got it out of me that I was just mouthing off. I was only carrying on, you know. An hour later the knock came at the door that Jackie was killed.

Me mammy was eighteen when she married. She died at forty-four and had fifteen children in between. Our Da said he couldn't begrudge my mother one of us. That's how he came to terms with me mammy and Jackie's deaths. He said he knew why the Scared Heart took her. She wasn't meant to be here to go through this. She wasn't meant to be alive to see one of her sons die.

Before he died, Jackie left a note for Patrick, 'Dear Patrick, I have borrowed 4 bob from your trouser pocket and I will give it back to you when I get paid. – Jackie'.

Since Bloody Sunday, the privacy our Da treasured has been taken away. We are no longer Maureen, Bernie, Kathleen, Anne, Willie, Eddie, Susan, Eileen, Patrick, Gerry, Margaret, Theresa, Michael, and Pauline, but 'Michael, brother of Jackie Duddy killed on Bloody Sunday.' The photo of Father Daly escorting my dying brother as he was carried is something we learned to live with.

Jackie was the first to be killed on Bloody Sunday, but his is the last life-story recounted in this book. That is because Jackie's story isn't finished. It will never be finished until his name is cleared and all of the Bloody Sunday victims are vindicated. At this moment, Justice Saville is deliberating. Will he clear the names of the brothers, fathers, and husbands wounded and murdered on Bloody Sunday? Soon we will know. But no matter how the Inquiry is resolved we will never stop telling Jackie's story. I hope that Jackie will never be forgotten not because he was a Derry mother's son but because he could have been any mother's son.

The following people spent many hours with Jennifer Faus sharing their memories of family and friends lost on Bloody Sunday.

John Nash	John Bradley
Linda Roddy	Eileen Doherty
Patrick Nash	Paul Doherty
Tommy Hazelet	Karen Carlin
Bridget Nash	Kay Duddy
Bernard Gilmour	Bernie Duddy
Gerry Doherty	Gerry Duddy
Maura Young	Michael Duddy
Leo Young	Charlie McGuigan
Helen Young	Annie McKinney
Joe McKinney	Mickey McKinney
Brian Rainey	George McKinney
Mary Doherty	Ann McKinney
Gerry O'hEara	Kathleen McKinney
Fr Patrick Donaghey	John Kelly
Liam Wray	Ita McKinney
Margaret Wray	Kevin McKinney
John Duddy	Regina McKinney
Bridie McDaid	Louis McKinney
Kevin McDaid	Mickey Bradley
Leo Carlin	Ivan Cooper

Excerpt from Jennifer's forthcoming novel: *Rathlin*

JOHN

The note read:
rare roast beef sliced thin, corned beef, one meaty slice of real turkey breast, creamy coleslaw, the crisp end of a romaine lettuce leaf, two hearty slices of heirloom tomato, a bit of shaved white onion, swiss cheese, russian dressing, and dijon mustard on lightly toasted rye.

It was John's first communication to Emma, this note, this recipe, written on a white paper lunch sack and handed over the deli counter.

On the night he met Emma Barlow, John Thacker was thirty-five years old, educated, well-employed, and still lived at home. The phrase "lived at home" was really an inaccurate description as he rarely crossed the threshold of 12 E. 79th. It wasn't mommy-issues or a particular desire to continue living in the palatial 16,000 sq. ft. home of his childhood; he was simply too busy.

It seemed as if the past seventeen years were simultaneously a grind and whoosh of time moving from high school to college, Yale, like his father, then a Wharton MBA to please his mother, and a job sufficiently demanding as to render him lifeless where social responsibilities were concerned. If not on the road, he simply lived at work shuttling between the gym and his office.

John's life was either delivered to him or collected and returned: meals, laundry, shined shoes, tailored suits, all within the confines of the Manhattan building that housed his office. In an emergency, Brooks Brothers was directly across perched at the transit entrance. John thought Brooks Brothers had chosen an ideal location, for the many shirts and ties purchased as the result of a cup of coffee combined with a jostling in a crowded subway car.

He now realized why a large well-appointed office was one of the features often highlighted, discussed, and debated when he and his MBA cohort took to the streets in search of employment. If your building did not provide showering facilities and your office lacked a couch that was long enough to sleep on comfortably, you became one of those poor sacks living in a hole within walking distance to work or you were constantly shuttling between office and gym. You could always tell the ones with the bad offices: the guys carrying duffle bags on the subway. The ones with just a newspaper in hand; the ones not sweating from carrying their lives on their backs; they were the ones who had showers and couches and closets.

John often thought the only fresh air he breathed was between the doors of his office building and LaGuardia when he rolled down the window of the cab, inhaled deeply, and let the wind blow though his hair. He laughed at this, thinking that what his Ivy League education and fancy job had ultimately bestowed upon him was a deeper understanding of his father's Bloodhound who insisted that no matter the weather, when riding in the car, his window must be lowered and his nose out—just enough—to enjoy the air.

It was no way to live. This was, his mother reasoned, why men had wives. To this John invariably rolled his eyes. His mother and grandmother were graduates of Penn's medical school. How could the women who influenced him, these Renaissance women, advise him so absurdly. "I'm just being practical. John," his mother brushed him away with the tips of her fingers the way she always swept away dissent or unpleasantness whether real or imagined.

Without considering the emotional aspects or any other benefits that might come with marriage, as John edged away from 30 and considered the inevitable: 40 years of age!; he reasoned he would either have to get married or formally move out of 79th Street.

The subject of a wife (or lack thereof) and grandchildren (or lack thereof) was bound to come up with increasing frequency and this was a lecture he wanted to limit to Sunday dinners. Which, unless one was further than a five-hour flight from JFK, one was required to attend. And so, John absconded from work at noon one Friday determined to find a place of his own.

"Look, it gives you a place to crash. Buy it for the investment. At the very least it gets you out of that basement," George told John for the 100th time, when their paths briefly crossed at a function. "That basement" was the offhand way George had always described John's room at 79th. When his mother allowed him (her baby) to move out of the nursery, John chose a room in the basement for two reasons. First, it was the room furtherest from his parents and second, unlike every one of his cohort, the Thacker family didn't escape to the Hamptons during the oppressive summer heat and the basement was the coolest place in the house.

Much to John's disappointment George had escaped the Upper East Side by enrolling at Stanford, ostensibly to study math, when he was just 16. Not satisfied with breaking family tradition and his mother's heart (her words) after graduating Stanford with a fine arts degree George went on to live like a gypsy (again, his mother's words) at Taliesin where he studied architecture at The Frank Lloyd Wright School.

True to their blood-brother pact at six years of age, George and John never lost touch and always remained the best friend to the other. Both men stood at 6'3" and at 35 were as fit as they were at 20 years of age. George's looks and personality were dark and intense to John's fair and pleasing. A dog lover, John's father once suggested George was a Rottweiler to John's Golden Retriever. The boys had to admit the analogy suited them.

Safely returned to New York, George dedicated the next ten years to designing and developing high-end residential buildings but today dusted off his broker's license to show John every pied-à-terre in Tribeca priced under $2 million. When John protested, he did not wish to steal time from his busy friend's schedule to shuttle him around looking at potential homes, George waved him off saying, "The last thing you need my friend, is my mother and her cronies showing you apartments."

As the sun set and the masked Manhattan stars began to twinkle, John and George had traversed every listing from Vesey to Canal. Twelve hours into what George was now referring to as their epic journey and John hadn't found a single apartment he liked, so George thought he'd get to the heart of the matter; the rationale all their friends used when when giving each other the get your own place speech: "Aren't you tired of sneaking women into your parent's place?"

"I only have sex when I'm on the road." It was a relief to John that he could speak plainly to George. In the entirely of his space, real and theoretical, it was only that space between he and George in which John felt comfortable being utterly candid.

"Is that why you are always on the road?"

"It avoids entanglements for which I have neither the time nor interest."

"You are a wise man. I seem to be constantly entangled. From one to the next."

"Your mother would tell you to get married."

"That is a whole lot of entangled I intend to avoid for as long as possible."

"We seem to be the last two hold-outs. They say if you wait too long women go from seeing you as that desirable unattainable guy to seeing you as just a weird guy."

"We've got another twenty years before we transition from desirable to weird and I plan to enjoy every minute." As the two men said goodbye, George implored John to keep looking at apartments; they would find the right place and if not the right place, at least "a place to crash that is a good investment." In their parting, they were true to themselves and their lives: George in a cab uptown to meet a woman and John on the subway back to the office.

He'd wasted a day tromping around Tribeca. He'd enjoyed getting out of the office and reconnecting with George. But, John thought, wouldn't time off work for both of them have been better spent relaxing? What if they had gone sailing on a Friday or flown to Vail and skied for the weekend? John was annoyed with himself. He abhorred wasting time. But on a larger scale, what was he really accomplishing working all the time? Wasn't that too, in a sense, wasting time? What was he working for? George built something. When George finished a project you could see it, touch it; it would shelter you. When John finished a project there was just another project. Money in the bank, paperwork filed. Nothing tangible.

John spent his whole life preparing for the next thing. Throughout his grade school years he'd worked to get into the right high school. Then high school was preparation for the right college.

Yale prepped him for Wharton which prepared him for this. This demanding job. He made money. A lot of money. But for what?

Was this demanding job simply preparing him for retirement? His parents worked. They had real jobs. Demanding jobs. The Thacker family had always had money. They were monied as far back as England so his parents had never needed to work (if having enough money was the gage for who needed to work). But in addition to earning a living, the work they did was meaningful. His mother, a pediatric neurologist, his father a judge, both not only worked hard but volunteered tirelessly. Their lives had meaning. Their work had meaning.

John's life had been dedicated to fulfilling the expectations of his parents. With the exception of getting married at the right time to the right woman, he'd done so admirably. John drew the line at marriage. He was not going to attach his life to another person simply to please his parents. Putting that aside, John's conundrum still existed. The question remained: what now?

Was this it? All those years of preparation earned him 80 hour work weeks, which were simply to earn money, to save, to prepare for retirement? No wonder so many people dropped dead when they retired. With this approach, retirement was simply in preparation for death. At that point, why wait? John tried to dismiss his thoughts. The wasted day was simply unsettling because it was wasted. Neither he nor George would get those hours back.

John never considered that he might be on the wrong path. Not once in his life had he doubted his journey; his goals. Everything had gone according to plan. Everything in his life had worked out. How many people could say that? So why was he so disquieted by one fruitless day of apartment-hunting?

In all aspects of his life John knew exactly what he wanted: midway back in first class on the captain's side by the window; an old-oak Barbera with pasta, Cabernet with steak; his suits were Italian; his women foreign-born models with short attention spans; he eschewed polo and rugby and (God-forbid) rowing; he preferred South Beach to Nantucket; but he had no idea what he wanted in a home.

Safely returned to his office John made up the wasted day. He decided to simply tuck it into the "goofing off" category of his life and went back to working until his eyes glazed. He would make it up to George with a good, no, a great bottle of scotch. And the next time they goofed off, John would see to it they did it over Delmonico steaks followed by cigars at the Grand Havana. If one was going to do it; that was the way to waste time. Sufficiently satisfied that the day was behind him, the time restored, John decided to run the five and a half miles home. 79th Street always centered and grounded him. Wealth hadn't spoiled the Thacker family; they never let any one in their enclave feel uppity or behave like an entitled brat and John felt that a return to 79th Street would set him to rights.

One stand-out feature of the Thacker household was that the staff was dismissed at noon on Friday and did not return until late-morning Monday. His young friends were at first horrified that Friday-night sleepovers were sans-nannies and cooks. His friends soon came to covet the casual family-centered weekends at 79th Street. Thanks to Thacker family weekends a generation of Upper East Side boys knew how to cook, do laundry, and scrub floors before they left for college.

Getting dirty was encouraged so long as the boys cleaned up after themselves. Eating the Thackers out of house and home was fine so long as the boys prepared their own meals and there was never anything in the Thacker's larder that came from a box or could be microwaved. Though John's mother would never admit it; it could be convincingly argued that George's talent for painting was fostered during weekends at 79th.

If they weren't so wealthy, well-connected, and powerful, people in certain circles would have called the Thacker family "mid-western" (folksy, down-to-earth, these were derogatory labels affixed by Upper East Siders to those they deemed beneath them). Knowing this, John was surprised and delighted when long-absent friends, now adults, turned up at Sunday dinner.

They showed up because of course, everyone knew there would be Sunday dinner at the Thacker's. Everyone knew that one could simply show up, roll up sleeves, pitch in, and enjoy a splendid meal among good company. This tradition was a source of pride for John and he decided he would go home and spend the weekend in the mid-western environment that reminded him not to behave like a wretch.

Running helped him think and the late hour meant he could run up 5th Avenue, a straight shot to 79th where a bath, a fire, a scotch, and a conversation with his parents would correct his bearing. It was decided. He just needed a weekend at home. So, into his running attire, down the elevator, out the doors of his office building, and John was off.

But he didn't go straight up 5th Avenue. He zigged. He zagged. He meandered. Up West Broadway, over on Chambers, along Lafayette, across the park to Center street then north again to Canal...his mind buzzing, his thoughts a jumble. He was unsettled. John always thought himself as the perfect combination of focused and spontaneous.

He was always focused on work that is certain. But he would often ring a friend and say, "Grab your passport and meet me at JFK." There they would choose a destination from the departures board. The game was, it had to be leaving within the hour. The friends would purchase their tickets, race for the gate, and fly off for the weekend. This was his spontaneous side and the part of him that enjoyed his hard earned money. This was how he showed the world: I am a successful businessman. But I'm fun too. This is who I am. Serious and fun. Seriously fun. My brand: John Thacker, seriously fun.

His feet pounded the pavement harder as he repeated his raison d'être to himself. Business and fun. Tall, handsome, fit, free. That's me. Serious and fun. Serious and fun. Serious and fun. Serious and— his toe caught a crack and John went down hard. Hands scraped, knee bloodied he sat on the curb catching his breath.

"No," he thought, "I am a fraud. I live a manufactured life. I have a practiced and polished personality. The surface looks flawless but there is nothing beneath the veneer. My life lacks substance."

Why should looking for an apartment, a normal thing for any grown man to do, throw him for such a loop? "Because fundamentally—I don't really know who I am or what I want from life." This he said aloud and the sound of his voice shocked him back to reality. He looked around. He had no idea where he was. Nothing looked familiar. The streets seemed dark for New York.

Looking up, John thought he saw a star. Up through the branches of the tree hovering over him, past the leaves, hanging in a cloudless sky twinkled a star. Shaking his head at his absurdity John took a breath trying to get his bearing. Behind him the sign for Zelda's shown brightly. He turned, thinking, "Well, you can't miss that."

John picked himself up and limped to the door, the bell jingling as he entered. He plucked a bottle of water from the case and a package of wet wipes off a shelf.
"You alright there?"
"This street's not lit so well. Missed the curb."
"It's residential. A neighborhood. Bright lights keep people awake at night."
"Don't you worry about crime? Muggings?"
"The muggers live here. Come home here to their beds. When they are out for muggings they go downtown where the money is. You know, tourists, businessmen. Easy pickings."
John pulls a wadded-up ten from the tiny pocket of his running shorts, pays for his items and tears open a wet wipe.
"I'm Wally," offering John his hand, "and I'm teasing you. About the muggers. You know that, right?"
"He knows. He knows!" came a woman's voice from behind the deli case.
"Now really. Are you alright? Looks like you took a terrible spill. Truth is the streetlights are so old they won't take those new bright bulbs. Sodium bulbs? Seems like they just recently switched them over from gas. Someday the city will get around to changing them out. In the meantime, we just do our best, you know, looking out for the cracks in the sidewalks. Mae? Will you unlock the toilet for this man?"
"I'm OK. I don't want to put you out."
"No trouble. Go on clean yourself up."
"Thanks. I appreciate it."

John followed the short lithe old woman to the back of the store. He noticed she wore a cotton dress patterned with tiny yellow flowers and a white butcher's apron. She was so thin the strings were wrapped around her waist twice. She unlocked and removed a padlock then pushed open the door revealing a pristine white-tiled restroom. His bathroom at 79th wasn't as clean as the sparkling room opened to him. This corner store toilet was well-lit, polished, and smelled fresh. It was so far removed from what he was expecting, he exclaimed, "Wow. This is beautiful. So clean!"

"I work here seven days a week. Why would I pee in a dirty washroom?" She shook her head matter-of-factly, did an about face and returned to her post. John smiled at the frankness of the old woman.

John emerged looking fresh and fit. His composure restored. As he walked back toward the register he noticed the old woman was not alone. A young woman stood next to her behind the deli counter surrounded by piles of meats, cheeses, and condiments. They were deep in conversation. The old woman was insisting: "It's got to have pastrami!"

"But everyone has pastrami on rye."

"That is because everyone eats pastrami."

"I thought it was going to be unique. I think we have to go with three meats. Ham, turkey, and roast beef."

"Not enough flavor. Corned beef, turkey, and roast beef."

"That will up the price."

"It's going to be special, they will pay."

Reaching the register John smiled and thanked Wally then said, "I'm a little embarrassed to tell you—I'm lost. I was running along, I guess you'd say I was lost in my thoughts, and I just got turned around."

"You are at the corner of Mulberry and Spring Streets."

John's blank stare prompted Wally to say, "Let's get out the map. Where are you visiting from?"

"Well sir, I live here."

"Little Italy?"

"In New York, yes, Manhattan. I work downtown and live North of here. Not far."

"How long have you lived in New York?"
"Most of my life."
"Don't get out much?"
"I guess I've just never been on this particular street. You know, everything looks different at night."
"I'm just giving you a hard time. Mae says I tease too much. Don't know when to stop, she says. I've lived in this neighborhood my whole life. Can't say I'd know every borough. Let's get you sorted out."

John felt shamed. He was just reveling in his jet-set life, thinking about how worldly he was and yet how grounded and for the second time in a day, the city of his birth had turned him on his ear. How could he not know where Spring and Mulberry were?! He hadn't run that far off track. He was just thinking what a genuine guy he was.

He was just moments ago convincing himself that though he may be privileged; he certainly wasn't pretentious. Now he wondered, was he just a spoiled rich-kid who had no real experience of the world? Why was he so mixed up? John's head began spinning again. He turned and looked over to Mae but it was the young woman who looked up at him and smiled.

She was tall and fit and beautiful. She could have been a model but she didn't look like the models John dated: pale, blank, starving. This woman was golden, natural, wholesome. Her blond hair was pulled back in a loose pony tail and her eyes smiled at him. John thought she should be standing in a wheat field under a blue sky with the summer sun behind her, not standing behind the deli counter of a corner store. She looked at John for a long moment and then returned to her discussion with Mae who was lamenting, "It's got to be Russian dressing, Jews don't eat mayonnaise with meat."
"But Mae, it has cheese, you can't have meat and cheese together and keep kosher."
"They can order it without the cheese."
"They can order it without the mayo."
John felt warmed by her quiet smile. The girl's deep blue eyes disarmed him. He felt exposed and yet he had a sensation of Sunday dinners and soft rainy mornings and Christmas.

"Here you are. Have a look at this map. This is where you are, see Spring and Mulberry. Now, where are you going?" But the fact was, at this point, John didn't know.

That such a simple question was suddenly turning him inside out: Where was he going? 12 E. 79th? One World Trade Center? How could it be these were the only two places John could think of? When had his life become so provincial?

Wally waited patiently, smiling at John, but after a few moments Wally covered John's hand with his. "If you can think of the address, we can hail you a taxi. It will be alright. You'll get where you're going." John looked at Wally's hand, rough with work, and felt comforted; he felt his senses returning. He looked at his kind face and wondered if Wally had a son, then, fully regaining his composure and his sense, John spoke with conviction, "If you'll direct me to the nearest subway station. I can find my way from there. So sorry to have bothered you."

"No bother, you can see it from the doorway. Just turn to the right and walk one block."

John turned to go, then stopped. "Could I trouble you for just one more thing?"

"Absolutely. What can I get you?"

"A pen? and a piece of paper?"

Wally produced a pencil from his shirt pocket and a white paper sandwich sack from under the counter and John set to writing. It took several minutes to compose and Wally smiled as he peeked at the missive John penned. After a period of focused attention and careful penmanship John folded the sack. He returned the pencil to Wally then, before he departed, he walked to the deli counter and handed the deli-sack over to Emma and Mae. As the bell jangled announcing John's departure, the women unfolded the note, which read:

rare roast beef sliced thin, corned beef, one meaty slice of real turkey breast, creamy coleslaw, the crisp end of a romaine lettuce leaf, two hearty slices of heirloom tomato, a bit of shaved white onion, swiss cheese, russian dressing, and dijon mustard on lightly toasted rye.

Mae whistled, "Well I'll be."

"Very specific. I like that." Emma said as she studied the note; the precise penmanship of it's author.

"He was cute too." Mae elbowed Emma and, no longer arguing, they set to constructing the sandwich they would soon christen The Triple Threat.

When they introduced the sandwich, the note had been framed and hung at Zelda's. After they were married, John and Emma placed the treasured note on the bookshelf that flanked their fireplace. In the five years that had passed since their meeting, this place of honor had become a jumble of memories and experiences shared by John and Emma; once two, now one.

John knew it the minute he saw her. Emma was his home. Home wasn't a two-bedroom in a Tribeca co-op. It was a blond haired woman standing behind a deli counter. Taking a liking to the young man, Wally and Mae quickly became his allies when John faced resistance from the shy, reserved young woman. It was Mae who suggested John help Emma home with a box of books Mae had "collected" for Emma. Wally chastised Mae for her scheme but truth be told, he thought it kind of brilliant. Books were the one thing Emma couldn't resist and Mae had managed to put together a plum of a collection so really, in the end, Wally admired his wife's contribution to bringing two fine people together.

Setting the box of books down, John surveyed her apartment, "I didn't know you were Amish. It's so sparse I can hear my echo." Frugality was Emma's way. It never occurred to her to buy more than what was needed. "You sit in the chair. Why would it need a decorative pillow? A cashmere throw on the sofa? I just drag the blanket from my room if I'm cold. If the purpose is to shut out the light isn't the blind achieving that? Well, yes, now that you mention it, I can see how someone might conclude those blinds are ugly."

Painted white, walls were devoid of adornment. There was not a knick-knack in sight. Books, Emma's one weakness, her love, lined the shelves flanking the fireplace and the singular silver framed photo was of Emma and her parents. Her fifth birthday, June 21, 1971.

Every year Emma's mother told her she was glad Emma was born on the longest day of the year because she wanted as many hours as possible to celebrate the best day of her life.

John opened Emma's eyes to her apartment's shortcomings and its possibilities and by sitting with her and meticulously going over her finances he convinced her she could pry her pocketbook open a little. After a few mis-steps in the world of decorating, plaid didn't play nice with polka dots and guests slid down the modern plexiglass chairs, Emma delighted in transforming her functional apartment into a luxurious and comfortable home.

Once spartan, the apartment became warm and inviting. It surprised Emma finding this talent in herself. Emma felt the only frame of reference to build from was her distant memories. The memories of a five year old. Encouraged by John to follow her heart and draw from these earliest memories of feeling warm, safe, and loved, Emma let go of what she thought she was supposed to do. She dumped the design magazines in the bin and created a home.

More important than the artwork that covered the walls, the muted colors, the deep luxurious chairs, the large dining table that invited guests, the heavy silk moire curtains at the windows keeping the winter winds at bay was John's reaction, "I cross this threshold and peace sets in," he said. Emma had fought for independence and control in her life for so long she did not acknowledge or recognize the lonely space inside her. John exposed the emptiness while simultaneously filling it so completely and satisfactorily that Emma didn't mind it's discovery.

Encouraging Emma to decorate her apartment was another sort of a ruse. Emma Barlow didn't let people in easily. After her parent's death, Emma didn't get close to people. Shuffled from one foster home to the next didn't make for lasting attachments. Mae had helped John to get past the gate and inside the castle. It was up to John to figure a way to stay. Encouraging Emma to decorate her apartment gave John myriad excuses to stop by, to go shopping with Emma, to suggest they stop for a meal together, to drop by his parent's house ("I just have to let the dog out"). As John learned to know her, he realized this ordinary activity of decorating one's home, gave Emma Barlow her first opportunity to dream. It was a wonder and a delight to watch and to be included in this awakening in another.

Like John's life, Emma's life was a series of benchmarks, of goals to be achieved. Emma never allowed herself to dream of possibilities. She worked toward certainties. The A's in school were certain because she worked tremendously hard to earn them. Finishing college in three years was a certainty; she'd laid it all out with her advisor; it was just a matter of ticking off the boxes. The next item was to find work, then start a business, buy a house, check, check, check, each box ticked as she trundled through life. Everything according to plan.

She hadn't planned for John. Yet here he was and Emma felt as if every pore on her body was open. Like lying in the warm sun and just when you're feeling hot, a cool breeze passes over—this is how she felt when she thought about John. In John she found her harbor and with him Emma knew her stormy life was finally calm. John changed Emma. John was certainty. She felt safe with him. With John there was permanence and with this she was able to open her mind to possibilities. John gave Emma the confidence to dream, to fly, and with his encouragement Emma replaced her fortress with a nest.

In spite of her feelings, Emma was surprised when she spontaneously asked asked John to stay and she was delighted that he said yes. George teased Emma that she'd cost him a commission. Wally and Mae brought over a bottle of scotch. John's mother did not ask when they were to be married, though secretly prayed they would. Two people who had been lost were now found and without a thought in their heads, without a plan or a goal, they simply embarked on a life together.

On her 30th birthday Emma and John stayed in. His parents had sent lobsters down from Maine. John cringed when after he killed and cleaned them, Emma hacked them into pieces, wrapped the pieces in lettuce leaves and carried them up to the roof where she unceremoniously tossed them on the grill.

Adding to this insult Emma opened a bottle of wine and filled two tumblers with a cabernet so rich it was almost purple. Though

John could feel the collective eye-roll of his blue blood relatives, he reasoned that with Emma out of the kitchen he could lay out the most important pieces of his plan, which he did when Emma sent him down from the roof to clarify butter. She laughed when he returned with a stick of butter in a sauce pan and placed it on the grill. "Well, we are grilling," he said.

"Why not!" Emma placed the lid on the kettle and ten minutes later they were ripping into hot bright-red shells and pulling out the luscious white meat. Emma loved hers smothered in melted butter and her hands and face were smeared with the stuff. Even the red-checked napkins brought out for the occasion were gloppy with butter. Thankfully the pesky yellow-jackets held off until Emma and John finished both the lobster and the bottle of wine. Which, he had to admit, complimented the meat very nicely, but as the fire died, the bees moved in and Emma and John took the celebration indoors.

John opened another bottle of wine and built a fire while Emma degreased her hands and face. "You know one day they are going to find us here, dead." Emma said as she settled on the floor next to John.
"And why would they find us dead?"
"We are always eating too much rich food and drinking wine and then lolling around in front of the fire. It's shameful. We are the only people to have a fire in June. It's so decadent."
"Would you like another glass of wine?"
"Of course. It's a beautiful cab. So deep. I don't like a red I can see through."
"Is that why you don't like white wine? It's transparent?"
"You my dear are transparent. Plying me with wine, lobster, a fire."
"Lobster? I think you ate an entire stick of butter for dinner! As my father would say, 'would you like a little lobster with your butter?!' You are right though, they are going to find us dead here one day,"

John cupped Emma's face in his hand, "We really are gluttonous sloths. We've got to join a softball team or a running club." He looked into Emma's eyes, studied her face for a moment then kissed her deeply to which she replied, "OK. If this is how I must die, so be it," and kissed him back.

That was the thing about John, Emma could kiss him intensely for long stretches and never feel self-conscious. She could look in his eyes and not feel as if she needed to look away. Whenever she was vulnerable with him he made her feel protected, stronger, more confident. Emma knew John would never judge her. He would never use her fears or insecurities against her. She trusted him utterly.

"I was thinking October."

"Hum?" Emma refilled their wine glasses and while she was sitting up tossed another log on the fire. Not-gracefully she reached for the poker and encouraged the flames. She settled back again next to John and tried to snuggle in closer but he was far away, thinking, mumbling to himself and then suddenly he sat straight up, looked at her, and said, "I was thinking City Hall. What do you think of City Hall? My parents will host a big reception, there will be no getting out of that, but then we can go to Maine and do anything we want. Just the two of us. No work, no phones, just us."

"John, what are you talking about?"

"Our wedding."

"City Hall?"

"Or a church? The yacht club? A hotel? What would you like?"

"City Hall. That's good. I like that."

"Do you think Wally and Mae would close the store and come and stand up with us?"

"Maybe we could get the first appointment in the morning. Then they could just open late."

"Very practical, yes, but my father is a judge, we don't need an appointment."

"Oh yeah, that's handy. What about your parents? Your siblings? Their spouses and children?"

"When I suggested City Hall I was thinking small. If you start adding my family the numbers will very quickly get out of hand."

"Yes but don't you think if Wally and Mae come your parents ought to be there?"

"OK. Wally and Mae and my folks."

"And us."

"Yes. The bride and groom. To City Hall."

"October?"
"Yes."
"Will it be too cold in Maine?"
"Not for what I have planned."
"You are very naughty when you've had too much wine."
"Just enough. There's just one more detail."
"What's that?"
"You have to get up for this part."
"Oh but I'm so comfortable."
"Come on, it'll be worth it."

John and Emma struggle to their feet, their legs heavy from lounging by the fire and John leads Emma to the kitchen.
"I've chilled Champagne. Will you get it? I'll get the glasses."

Emma opens the fridge and next to the expected bottle of Dom Pérignon is an unexpected small velvet box. Shocked, Emma quickly closes the fridge. She is even more surprised to find John in the kitchen on one knee to which Emma says, "Now this is just getting weird."

"Shhhh. I played to your practical side, now play to my romantic side. Emma Barlow, you've given me a lifetime of happiness. Will you let me spend the rest of my life trying to give you the same? Will you marry me?"

"Yes John Thacker, I will marry you."

John leapt up and opened the fridge, excited as a small child getting a cookie, "This is the best part! I've been waiting all night for this!"

The chilled velvet box in hand, he opened it with some ceremony and the brilliant single round diamond set in platinum stunned Emma. Tears poured down her cheeks. It wasn't the size, though it was enormous in her eyes, it was the significance of John placing the ring on her finger. The outward sign telling the world she was not alone. There was someone soundly beside her. The tears please John. The sure sign he got it right.

An awkward proposal some may think, they might have to come up with a different story for the purpose of telling friends and family, but perfectly fitting for Emma. Getting her to casually agree to the wedding before the proposal, John saved his future bride too much surprise. She dreaded surprises, refused to acknowledge the unknown, and he didn't blame her. Few men would have grasped and understood Emma's complexities born of witnessing her parent's deaths. John understood Emma and accepted her and now he would be by her side forever. He felt satisfied, filled, complete.

"This necessitates a Sunday dinner at my parents."

"I love your mother's pot roast but I may never get accustomed to your Upper East Side side. Will that be OK?"

Opening the champagne John pours them each a glass. "Everyone there loves you. Just the way you are."

"Except Charlie."

"Charlie is a snob."

"I never thought of Bloodhounds as snobbish. A Great Dane, a Doberman, I can see. "

"You never met his father. You think Charlie, excuse me, Charles is snobbish? His father was Best in Show at Westminster."

"Oh my. Who had time for all that? Your parents are superhuman."

"Now my dear, we have news to share. Shall we take our bottle and go to Zelda's?" Emma wrapped a shawl around her shoulders, slipped on the flats she always left by the door, and carried the bottle out, skipping down the stairs.

John retrieved another bottle of champagne and two extra glasses and followed Emma. They made their way into the night walking arm and arm down Mulberry Street. They caught Wally and Mae just as they were switching off the lights and the four friends stood on the corner of Mulberry and Spring drinking Dom Pérignon and talking late into the night. As the summer solstice ended, John and Emma's new life dawned.

As planned, Emma and John married at City Hall, attended a boisterous and extravagant reception in their honor at his parents Carnegie Hill home, and then scampered off to Maine where they spent two weeks on the Thacker Family Island. When the two weren't wrapped around each other they donned jeans and sweaters and hiked along the water, drank wine, and indulged from a hamper of decadent treats packed as a wedding gift from Wally and Mae. "If your honeymoon is anything like ours was, you're going to need sustenance."

"Oh stop telling tales Mae," Wally interjected, "they can spend their honeymoon however they like." Then handed John a bottle of whisky with a wink and an elbow. "It's restorative," he whispered and the two men giggled as their wives rolled their eyes.

A young couple in love, alone on a Island, John and Emma did require sustenance and were grateful for the dates, figs, nuts, caviar, crackers, pates, artisan breads, and—direct from Europe brought over in Granny's purse—rich cheeses and cured meats. It was a glorious two weeks and it was what a honeymoon was meant to be: celebrating the two of them bonded together, believing it would last forever.

By their 5th anniversary, John and Emma had made good on their promise to spend more time being fit. The two were serious competitors in cycling, running, and swimming. They were presently training for the IronMan triathlon. Hawaii would be the longest trip of Emma's life and her first time on a plane but John felt certain once she went, a whole new world would open up for them.

The international markets were beckoning and John longed to work outside the US. He thought his wife, if she were willing to take the plunge, would thrive in Paris or London. John had decided long ago his wife had an adventurer inside her. Emma filled their precious free hours exploring New York City. There wasn't a borough, a park, a museum, library, or coffee shop his wife hadn't visited. She took him to star-gaze in Brooklyn and on a "cruise" to Staten Island. Emma's joy in sharing her city with John was enchanting. If his wife could make John's home-town come alive for him, imagine what she could do with a brand new city.

The only thing John would change about his marriage was his wife's commitment to his longevity, in other words, his health. Every year there were fewer steaks and more salads. Champagne? Chocolate? These were for celebrations. And his beloved Triple Threat? Emma called it the Heart Attack on Rye and reserved it for a very rare treat usually only gotten after a long training run.

OK, so, yes, he was actually in better shape than he was at 35 and he hadn't thought that possible. Emma was a goal-achiever. He knew that going in, but he hadn't counted on his health being one of her goals!

John decided if Emma could be so diligent in pursuing goals on her husband's behalf, he was going to use this to his advantage. If he could get his wife to decide he should have an international position he felt certain they would be moving within a year. Hawaii was the first step in his plan. But first he had to get them to Hawaii and it was exhausting. They had been doing training rides in the middle of the night to avoid the heat and be free of traffic but this meant they were on this crazy 24 hour schedule of sleeping and training. Needless to say, John looked forward to completing the race, just to be done with it!

They had exactly one month to go and tonight was their final "cheat meal" there would be nothing off-plan for the next 30 days so John made it worth it. Emma's idea of a cheat meal was a small piece of chocolate for dessert or one glass of wine. Tonight John had other ideas: there was cake with buttercream frosting, the Triple Threat, a bottle of wine, and a small serving of a really fine whisky just to top things off, "A bit of a digestive" he reasoned to his wife.

The next morning, on little sleep, feeling the slight pangs of a hangover, and wanting to stay in bed with Emma working off the calories and the hangover, John nonetheless left for work early. He needed to prepare for a meeting.

Emma, desirous of her husband and wanting to stay in bed with him had long ago accepted his work demands. Besides, if they waited until after work to make love, they might just skip the night's workout and as much as she wanted to do well at the competition she was so tired of training! With John off to work at this ungodly early hour Emma decided to get herself out of bed and work on a novel at which she'd been plucking away for the last six months or so.

Though she reveled in this new hobby of fiction writing, found it enchanting, freeing, a diversion from her sometimes dreary client work; at the moment she was stuck. She had it in her head that the supporting character had to die. It actually wasn't just in her head, it was crucial to the story. This death was essential to the eventual rebirth and renewed joy her character would find on the other side of his grief. That was what she wrote in her outline, anyway. Right now, all she could think was, "blah, blah, blah."

But Emma felt that maybe there wasn't re-birth and renewed joy after unexpected death. The loss of her parents was still with her. Her parent's death left a wound that still ached. She had not yet been able to "leave it by the side of the road" as she once read, and walk on.

She could point to Wally and Mae and John as joys in her life that came after that tragic night. Her world had expanded when she met John. It now included dear George, an assortment of friends made in the racing world, a large extended family, and a stubborn but lovable Bloodhound.

She could say she was a happy person. Even so, she couldn't bring herself to kill off the character and with the glorious time to devote to her novel ticking away she sat and stared. No matter how much she crinkled her nose, cocked her head, and scrunched her mouth from side to side the words did not materialize.

So with a pad of post-its and a pen in her pocket she walked out into the brilliant September day. The back-to-school blue sky stretched out above and her beloved city beckoned. In two miles she could be at Battery Park. In the opposite direction Washington Square was less than a mile.

In addition to the shortness of the walk, she knew she could depend on there being a friendly dog or two in need of a belly rub or an ear scratch at Washington Square. She also knew she could depend on the men playing chess to give her plenty of material on ways to kill her character. They never tired of telling their greatest generation war stories and so long as a game wasn't too intense, they delighted in Emma's presence.

She walked north enjoying the beautiful day, composing in her mind a picnic for John. If she could get him away from the office before sunset they could meet. She would bring a basket with cold roasted chicken, vegetables, and red-beet eggs. Emma couldn't stomach the eggs but John loved them and he needed the extra protein. She knew he a was taking a beating with their crazy training schedule and she knew he was doing it for her. She also knew he wanted to take a position overseas and she wanted to be able to support him, go with him.

If she survived their trip to Hawaii and didn't expire doing the triathlon, she would figure out a way. Maybe. It was too much to think about. How could she leave New York? Her parents were buried here, Wally and Mae were her safe haven, her home....She reverted to her short term goal planning so her heartbeat and respiratory rate could return to normal.

Before she reached the apex of Mulberry at Bleecker Street, Emma had planned her visits to two parks today, Washington in the morning for inspiration, and Battery tonight where she would meet John for a picnic. She thought perhaps she would even tell him she wanted him to pursue his dream of working overseas. She would see, she didn't want to promise something she couldn't deliver.

After their picnic, they would walk home where Emma planned to close the deal on the romance they'd missed last night after over-training and over-eating. Her over-worked husband was not going to fall sleep tonight without first engaging in some serious lovemaking. The deep intimacy and passion she shared with John was one of the great and enduring joys in Emma's life.

Emma's life before John was bereft of physical closeness and she was surprised and delighted to learn it was her circumstances and not her personality that gave other's the impression that she was cold; had walls up around her. With John, Emma learned that she thrived in a relationship with no boundaries, no walls, nothing unspoken.

Emma thrilled at John's touch. Whenever Emma felt alone John always took her hand. He knew. She didn't need to ask. He was simply there. John's presence was so strong that when he was away on business all Emma had to do was close her eyes, breathe deeply, and John would take her hand. This comfort, the stillness she felt in these moments soothed Emma's soul.

Walking along Emma contemplated the death of her character. Death was a subject she avoided. So why was she writing a novel in which one of the primary characters dies? It was more than that. As she worked on the story she was coming to realize that death wasn't just the death of a character, it was the central theme of the novel and she wondered if subconsciously her novel was a way for her to think abstractly, tangentially about death, perhaps even her parents' deaths.

Emma didn't kill anything. Spiders, ants, even the mouse family lived happily and in some degree of comfort in her apartment. Occasionally these beings were re-located to a more appropriate home but none were ever killed. Emma avoided the subject of death entirely and now she had made herself responsible for killing a person. It was up to her to kill the character, she had to do it, she could not bring herself to do it, and there stood before her the question: why?

Emma was certain that entering Washington Square Park was neither the time nor place to delve deeply into her parents deaths and what emotions she might ought to recognize and rectify around that night. Instead, Emma did what made her comfortable. She set goals that could be checked off as she moved through her day:

1. get ideas on how to kill her character from men playing chess
2. give a snuggle to a needy canine
3. complete a client project
4. meet her husband at sunset.

If she completed each item on the list, she could count it a perfect day and indeed it looked promising because Emma's timing was spot-on. As she approached the dog-run a dog walker entered accompanied by an impressive variety of dogs.

Emma thought what a well-rounded bunch they were and wondered how ever had this dog-walker acquired such a mishmash of clients. At her feet waited one that looked like a scraggly stray, another fresh from the groomer, mutts and AKC's, those sitting patiently and one or two behaving most atrociously.

In spite of the chaos the young dog-walker appeared unruffled and Emma felt comfortable enquiring, "Would you mind if I played with your dogs?" The girl replied, "Your landlord doesn't allow them?"

"Nope!" It was easier than saying she didn't own a dog because she knew some day it would die and she just didn't think she could deal with that.

"I understand. Mine doesn't either. That's how I got into this tricky business! Here," she said, scooping up the smallest of her charges and, struggling into her backpack for a tennis ball said, "this little guy likes to play ball and the bigger ones crowd him out. You could take him to the small-dogs run if you want."

"A dachshund that plays fetch?! Adorable. I would love to play with him! Thank you!"

"Bring him back when you are finished, not when he is. He'll play all day if you let him! His name is Fredrick."

Emma and her stubby-legged, long-bodied companion made their way to the small-dogs run and played together, each delighting in the other's participation. Fred-the-dachshund was thrilled with Emma's adherence to the singular rule of the game: throw the ball punctually each time he drops it. Emma laughed as Fred's enthusiasm built each time she threw the ball. They played happily, enjoying the beautiful day until Fred suddenly stopped in his tracks, dropped his ball, and cowered at the monstrous boom echoing across Manhattan.

Emma scooped up the terrified dog and rocked him holding him close to her. Each and every one of them in Washington Square Park turned and gazed silently south-west as smoke billowed from the tower. The City fell silent as the collective breath of Manhattan was held.

Emma's trembling friend licked her face for comfort and she whispered, "It's just an accident. It's going to be OK." As minutes passed and breathing sporadically resumed, mobile phones began to ring. Hellos could be heard from all over the park.

The minutes ticked by. Emma tried to remember where John was. Was the meeting at the office? What time was the meeting? Do he go to the office early and then leave for the meeting? Maybe he wasn't at the office at all. Maybe he forgot something and was at home, wondering where she was. Well, maybe she should call, so he wouldn't worry. Then it hit her and just as Emma thought, "Oh God.

I forgot my phone," she felt the vibration in her pocket. Holding Fred with one arm, she fumbled for her phone. "Hello?"

"Emma?"

"John! John. Are you OK?"

"I'm at work. There's been an explosion. There's a lot of smoke. I can't breathe. We're trying to find our way out."

"I can see it. I'm at Washington Square. I can see the smoke from here."

"Emma it's hot. It's so hot!"

"It's OK. You're going to be OK."

"I have to get down on the floor I can't breathe."

"Don't hang up."

"There's water all over the floor Emma. It's black. I can't see anything. There's no air. I can't breathe. It's hot. It's so hot. It's really bad Emma."

In the moments of hellish helplessness Emma searched for words that would convince her husband to get up. To get up off the floor. To get up and get out out of that building and come home to her. Emma wanted to speak words that would blow away the smoke, lead him toward light, guide him down out of the Tower. Once on the street, if he walked north up Broadway and she walked south, they would be together in only fifteen minutes. But she needed the words.

John always wanted her to be more spontaneous. He'd say, "Let's go away somewhere together," and she would put him off. There was always some excuse for Emma to stay in the city. With the exception of their honeymoon she'd never been further a far than Rhode Island. New York was her home. John, Wally, and Mae, were her family.

New York was the place she felt safe and she feared she'd loose her footing were she to leave. Faced with the prospect of losing her husband, she realized it wasn't the city; it was John. He was her home. He kept her safe. With John everything was OK. Why was she coming to this realization now? She needed John to leave his office and come to her now.

With rising panic she says, "You're going to be OK. You're going to get out of there and come home and we are going to go away somewhere together. You won't even have to ask. We'll just go. Just like you've always wanted."

John's breathing is labored and in the background on John's end Emma hears voices, people are calling to John, "There's light! This way!" and Emma urges her husband forward, "John. Go! Get out! I need you to come home. I want you..." John interrupts her saying quite forcefully, "Emma." It was a tone she'd never heard from her husband. It stopped Emma in her tracks. He blood ran cold. Her heart stopped beating. Her world went silent.
"Yes John?"
"I love you."
"I love you," she replied
and with a deep sharp inward breath he was gone.

Fred wiggles. He wants down. She is holding him too tight. Unconsciously, Emma pulls the crown of her father's watch, stopping time. She adjusts Fred, he licks her face, she carries him back to his walker, sets him down among his canine companions. Then calmly, in a matter-of-fact manner Emma hands the ball over saying, "Thank you for letting me play with Fredrick. You are very kind," and walks away.

John told Emma he loved her, took a deep breath, and closed his phone. He thought it would be better for Emma if she didn't know. Crawling across the wet floor through the choking black smoke, the group already knew that all escape routes had been destroyed. The exits were blocked, the stairways collapsed, the smoke impassible, the heat was rising. The floor was becoming so hot it was burning their hands as they crawled. Death, they knew, was coming for them. The discovery of the light streaming through the broken window gave them an option.

Moments before the smoke cleared revealing the opening, the group had come to the terrible realization that there was no way out. Lives that were full of promise, opportunity, choices were over. It wasn't going to be cancer or old age that claimed them. They were going to die in a fire. They could only hope the smoke rendered them unconscious before the fire reached them.

And then, there was light. The glass had been completely blown away and what remained was a perfect rectangular opening. It reminded John of the front door of his parents home, standing open in the summertime, the household taking advantage of a rare cool breeze gifted to Manhattan on a July afternoon. Before him stretched an immense blue sky; behind him a raging fire. To his left and to his right black smoke battered the still-in-tact windows, it too, desperate to get out.

John stood in the window. Several of his colleagues had gone already. Their falls were varied: one simply plunged; one paused, turned, and fell backward; some clung to the building as long as they could before falling. Most were crying, distressed that they were forced to choose how they would die: by smoke and fire or by a fall. Death was certain; imminent. The only question remaining was: How are you going to die? John stood to the side as they went out, one after the other.

A woman he didn't recognize sat on the floor across from him. She faced away from the windows her back against the glass, her legs stretched out in front of her, her arms limp at her sides. She was shoeless, sobbing. She looked at John, helpless, and cried, "I forgot my phone. It's in my purse." John stepped toward her, leaned down, handed her his, and returned to the open window.

John knew what he was going to do. To his mind, there was no question that leaving through the window was the better option. But for these last few moments he had been granted, he wanted to admire the blue sky, appreciate the fresh air. John stood looking out at the brilliant day. He breathed deeply in and out letting the oxygen stimulate his senses. Everything felt new. It felt to John like he was at the start of a great adventure. He felt her take his hand in hers. She was there, and with her, he felt safe.

Emma loved to look at the sky, it's ever changing shapes and personality. She never tired of marveling at clouds and stars and sun and so for the last time, John admired the sky, seeing it through his wife's eyes. He felt her squeeze his hand. He knew it was time. He turned his head to look at the woman standing next to him. The stranger was holding his hand. She looked up into his eyes and said,

"I'm afraid. Will you go with me?" John nodded and squeezed her hand. Then he and the woman took a breath, and together, they leapt.

ELLIE

With Paddy's very specific instructions zipped into the front breast pocket of his anorak Jackie readied his boat for the trip to Scotland. He was to select a young Border Collie to replace old Drum who after sixteen years of service lay down for his final rest. Per Paddy's instructions the new dog was to be a female and strictly and most assuredly not a puppy. "She's got to be fully trained but young. No more than eighteen months." Paddy shouted as he tossed the mooring ropes up to Jackie's sure and steady grasp.
""She'll be expensive if she's trained. Why not train her yerself? Ye've got the time."
"I'm too old to be messing around with that."
"Too bad old Ted Hope's gone. He'd give you a run. He trained up til the day he died."
"Just give Brendan the list, Jackie an bring me back my dog."
"Alright da. Don't need to be fussing."

The initial stretch of the trip to Gare Loch could be treacherous. The waters off Rathlin, where the North Atlantic Ocean and the Irish Sea meet are at once passionate, angry, formidable, awe-inspiring, and always dangerous. Sailors operate with reverence for these waters. Jackie sailed these waters daily and this particular route, he took it monthly to Belfast but he never took his experience for granted.

This trip meant turning North into the Firth of Clyde passing Arran on toward Millport from which point the character of the trip changed entirely. From Millport to Garelochhead was 25 miles of wonder. Jackie thought he ought to some day drive up the A78 rather than sail along side it. He could stop to trek through the deep woods, visit the pubs in tiny towns that from the water looked steeped in tradition, and explore castles that dotted the shore. Jackie didn't often wish for company but this particular stretch of earth was one to share.

Mooring at Garelochhead, his boat secured, Jackie's host collected him, "Brendan Kerr. You're Jackie, yes?"
"Yes. Standing in for my father Paddy Doyle of Rathlin."
"I know your father. He is a fine trainer. Drum was a champion."
"He was a loyal dog. Worked until he died. Was he one of yours?"
"Aye. A bit surprised Paddy didn't retire him. Sheep are hard work."
"Me da and Drum just walked around; hung out together you might say. There's not much herding on Rathlin. So long as they don't fall into the sea, find their way to the pub, or board the ferry, there's not much place for them to go. Paddy's been farming so long I recon his sheep could walk themselves."
"Suspect old Drum was good company for your da."
"I'd say that's true."
"Coffee?" the man asked as they pulled up to the barn.
"I don't mind," said Jackie.
"Come in. You can gaze a bit at the wee ones and then we'll go out to the kennels."

The man busied himself heating the kettle and spooning coffee into mugs. "Milk?" Jackie assented. Milk was splashed in on the instant coffee powder and then steaming water poured over. Jackie accepted the proffered pottery mug and tarnished spoon. He walked through the barn gazing at the puppies sheltered there. Each litter was in a different stage of development from one very rowdy bunch nearly ready to go out to the kennels to a pile of wiggling fur nursing at their mother. "What's that black spot there?" Jackie indicated the undulating mass of black and white interrupted by an inky black smudge.

"The neighbor's Newfoundland. Lost her mother in an accident and we hoped she would take. This little mother doesn't seem to mind but the pup's such a wee one, doesn't seem to have the strength."

"Have you a bottle?" Jackie had cut him off, "I mean, if you don't mind." Jackie's sudden interest in the pup took Brendan by surprise but he pulled a wooden box from under the table supporting the coffee supplies. A baby bottle was fished out, and handed over. "Suit yourself. There is some dried milk replacer on the shelf. Best I can do at the minute. Don't have a fresh batch handy." Then, sizing up the volunteer said, "you sure?"

Jackie followed Brendan's gaze to his hands. A person could be forgiven for thinking Jackie's large hands, scared from years of physical labor, were good only for brutish tasks but Jackie's years as a fisherman, tying lures to hooks, made his practiced fingers nimble.

When he cared for his ailing mother, she taught him to knit saying, "If you're just going to sit there you might as well be productive," and he became very proficient over the two years it took Katherine Boyd to die. So proficient was he that ten years on every living soul on the Island possessed and wore a Katherine Boyd jumper. Jackie designed the whimsical pattern in honor of his mother's joy-filled life.

Then too, there were his father's sheep. The lambs that needed nursing were assigned to young Jackie when he lived at home and brought over in a wagon when Jackie had a home of his own. So it wasn't the rough worn paws of this native of the most rugged Island in the Northern Hemisphere that lifted the puppy from her surrogate mother's protection. These were the loving capable hands of a gentle man who'd given his life to caring for others.

Surprised by Jackie's behavior but not one inclined to ask a lot of questions, Brendan returned to his work telling Jackie, "I'll leave you to it then. Come on up to the house when you're finished. My wife, Elise, will look after you."

Brendan departed. Jackie felt for the man who not only bred and trained champion Border Collies but ran a substantial farming operation as well. Jackie imagined he would find a brood of children when he sought Elise at the house later.

As they settled into a corner of the barn, Jackie rested the puppy on his chest. He sensed if the wee girl could hear his quiet breathing and the steady slow rhythm of his heart; if she could feel his warmth and smell the scents of sea air and sheep carried on his sweater that these would comfort her.

In this swaddled place he offered her a few drips of warm milk and she opened her mouth, took in the nipple, clamped, and began sucking. Having been told she wasn't taking, her vigor and enthusiasm surprised Jackie and he relaxed back in the hay enjoying the comforting sounds and smells of the farm.

A few days prior, the wee one had been plucked from the protection and warmth of her family and placed in the midst of a wiggly furry clan. They were puppies, like her, but to the wee girl these animals were big. Their long hair got in her nose and poked at her eyes. There was a lot of pushing and shoving to get to the milk.

She felt so tired. She wanted to curl up with her mother and go to sleep. She wanted her brothers and sisters. She was in a big clump of soft warm fur with breathing and heartbeats but it was unfamiliar breathing, staccato, irregular not the relaxed harmonious rhythm of her family.

These hearts beat quickly; the heartbeats of her brothers and sisters had been slow, measured. This family smelled different, not earthy and nutty but pungent, sweet. She sensed were they similar, that she and they were alike but different too and she felt desperately lonely.

In Jackie's embrace the pup felt protected again. He was large, like her mother. The cadence of his breathing matched hers. Their relaxed heartbeats thumped along together. He moved at languid pace as compared to her surrogate brothers and sisters. In his arms she felt peace. If she was not so hungry she'd have fallen immediately into slumber. Relieved of the burden of fighting for a teat she drank as much as she could and soon, with her belly full and her body warmed and her soul assured, she slept.

Having taken responsibility for this life, Jackie slept in the barn, nursing the pup every few hours, building her strength. Taking pity on him, Brendan offered Jackie a cot and insisted Jackie share meals at the family table. In return Jackie plucked Brendan's to-do list from the cork-board in the kitchen and set to checking off those tasks that seemed to be perpetually moved down in favor of more pressing items:

✓ re-shingle the small shed
✓ white-wash the chicken house
✓ tune-up the kid's bikes
✓ patch the old rowboat

and in the wakeful hours of the night Jackie sat under the stars and knit Elise a sweater with yarn swiped from her "bag of good intentions"—knitting set aside after the birth of her fourth child in as many years.

It was six weeks from the time Jackie motored out of Rathlin Sound until he returned. But for a brief phone call to Cullen's, reporting only that he'd been delayed, the Island would have rung the Coastguard. When the time came that the wee girl was strong enough to make the journey home, Brendan fitted a box together and his children provided a scrap of a blanket for her travels.

Brendan wondered about Jackie. What motivated this man? What did he have or not have at home that he could abandon? What sort of life did he lead that he could just put it on pause to nurse an orphan puppy? A puppy so small, even if she lived would likely never amount to much. Brendan didn't think she would be fit to breed and she certainly would never be a working animal.

Brendan didn't ask. He was familiar enough with the vagrancies and challenges of life to know the answers didn't matter. What motivated a man, any man, was his own private business. Brendan drove the two, man and pup, back to the shore where Jackie's boat was tethered, the men shook hands, Jackie boarded, readied his boat and secured his charge, and headed south for Rathlin oblivious to the storm that await him.

"I couldn't just leave her to die!"

It was the sentence that finally unleashed the flood of unspoken resentment between Jackie and his father. Upon mooring his boat in the harbor that Friday evening Jackie carried the pup in her box to Cullen's to introduce her to the residents, most of whom lifted a jar on the Friday night.

When he placed the box-with-puppy on the bar Paddy launched in asking, "what the hell is that?" following up directly with "where is my dog?" Jackie tried to explain but it wasn't happening. Paddy was not having it. Each attempted sentence was interrupted with another question, an accusation, a slight, an insult, until Jackie exploded shouting, "I couldn't just leave her to die!"

Jackie's feeling that Paddy had left his wife, Jackie's mother, to die alone lay there between them. Paddy's belief that Jackie had overstepped his bounds coming between Paddy and his dying wife bubbled up from under his collar. Dying was their business. A private affair between husband and wife. It was not the place for a child to interfere. After few moments of glaring silence Paddy turned on his heel and walked away.

The residents went back to their pints. They weren't fazed by the exchange. Paddy and Jackie were the only two on the Island who hadn't discussed the bad feelings between them. There was a sense of relief; now maybe the two men could move on from their anger and grieve the death of the woman they loved.

Isabelle was glad when the argument subsided, because now she could turn her attention to the adorable puppy, it's paws at the top of the box, it's head peeking over, it's hind feet searching for something to step on, to push against, to hoist herself over and out of the box. Isabelle helped, taking the little black ball of fur into her arms and nuzzling her face, inhaling the earthy nutty scent of Newfoundland puppy.

Point of fact, if Cullen's stood across the sound in Ballycastle, Isabelle would have had a strict "no dogs" policy. "But I don't live in Ballycastle" she would sigh, explaining to a hapless tourist with a muddy snout resting on his lap, "my pub is here, on Rathlin, where for over 200 years sheep farmers have had working dogs and those dogs have found their way into this pub."

Truth was, never more than a handful of dogs lived on the Island at one time. but one muddy snout, one spray of wet-dog scented sea water onto a newly purchased isle-knit could seem like a dozen, so, part of Isabelle's schtick with the tourists was to fein exasperation with the dogs and shrug her shoulders with an "it's beyond my control" expression.

But this little one. This baby peering up at Isabelle. This little girl kissing Isabelle's nose with her tiny pink tongue. She was a dream. Isabelle's maternal feelings, which she believed had died with her son, roared to life and she promptly and certainly christened the little girl "Ellie."

"Lady Eleanor if she's ever for tea with the Queen, otherwise, Ellie." Isabelle said this with such authority and finality that no one questioned her pronouncement. Ellie she was and Ellie she would be.

A month before her first birthday, Jackie took Ellie to see the Newfoundlands from the Italian School of Canine Lifeguards. Watching the demonstration from Ballycastle Beach Ellie was impressed with their extraordinary skills. Far from shore the giant black dogs jumped off speedboats, leapt off jet-skis, and dropped from helicopters. They pulled people in hauling them by lifejackets or by having the "victim" hold onto their harnesses. They tugged rafts to shore, pulling them by holding a rope in their mouths.

Ellie was astounded when as a finale "Mac" pulled a rubber boat filled with nine of his canine colleagues from far out in the water all the way onto the shore. Math wasn't Ellie's strong suit but she weighed 8 stone at her last check-up so she imagined nine of her would be a lot of stones to pull.

They were admirable animals no doubt and Ellie enjoyed the show enormously but, as impressed as she was with the dogs' abilities she was particularly enamored with their form-fitting rescue harnesses. So captivated was she that Jackie obtained the name of the manufacturer and, armed with Ellie's very carefully and specifically obtained measurements, ordered a custom-made, very expensive life jacket. Ellie waited anxiously for weeks while it was sewn and shipped, visiting Bronagh daily at the post office, to cock her head and perk her ears, which Bronagh interpreted as an enquiry as to the status of Ellie's package.

When Bronagh announced that the anticipated box had been delivered Ellie and Jackie opened it, secured the vest around her midsection, and rejoiced when the sleek jacket fit perfectly. Unlike her previous life vest, adapted from an old human one, this didn't ride up to her chin when she sat down or rub against her legs when she swam. She adored the colors of the jacket: black and blue with strips of silver reflective tape. She thought it made her look like a seal effortlessly slicing through the water.

Sometimes, as they got close to the harbor Jackie would let Ellie leap off the boat and swim to shore. She would swim across the cove, climb out at the beach, and then walk down the road to meet him at their truck. After seeing the Italian Canines, each time she did this she imagined she was rescuing a distressed swimmer.

It was from this practice that Ellie and the seals got to know one another and these friendships were why Ellie often snuck off to go swimming in the cove. She didn't understand Jackie's concern about her habit of cavorting with marine mammals. Certainly, Ellie thought, I am much more like a seal than a Border Collie, sheep, Kittiwake, or cat, which were the other options for animal companionship on the Island. Besides, she had a working relationship with the sheep, the Border Collies were haughty, the kittiwakes were bad-tempered, and the cats were, well, cats.

The last Saturday in September, as Jackie readied his boat for the monthly supply run to Belfast he heard a familiar voice.
"You shouldn't spoil her."
"Oh yeah, hows that?"
"It's not good for her to be at sea all day. Swimming with the seals, hanging out at the pub, waiting at the Post to collect her mail."
"You're a storehouse of information."
"She's too smart to be hanging around on a boat all day with the likes of you."
"I am sure there is a compliment for someone somewhere in that sentence."
"I sent you to get me a dog. Over a year ago. I've been herding them sheep myself."

Jackie couldn't help chuckling to himself. His da walked by Jackie's cottage every morning with his sheep. Those sheep were getting a whole lot of extra exercise to accomplish this but the stubborn old man was hell bent on making sure the sheep bell rang and their hooves echoed on the paved road that passed by Jackie's window at dawn each day.

Jackie didn't let on that he'd changed bedrooms. He'd taken to sleeping in the room on the opposite side of the house and since then wasn't bothered by the sounds of Paddy and his sheep. Still, he couldn't help think what a hassle it was for the sheep.

Paddy didn't let on that for the past year, every Saturday, when Isabelle was supposedly dog-sitting Ellie, he'd been training the giant Newfoundland to herd. Now here he was, fit to be tied. Jackie was taking Ellie with him and Paddy needed her. He wanted to take her to the sheep trials in Ballycastle. Paddy adjusted his cap, shoved his hands in the pockets of his Carhartt work-pants (his only weakness being American goods), and kicked imaginary dirt.
"What is it your wantin' da?"
"That dog of yers."
Jackie silently counted to five before responding.
"What about her?"
"I'm wantin' her. That's what it is I'm wantin'—her to spend the day with me. She's been lookin' forward to it."
"How's that?"
"Could I just keep her while yer away in Belfast? Is that askin' too much?"
"Why would you be wantin' that?"
"You gonna make me work for this Jackie?"
"You gonna keep walkin' past my place at dawn?"
"Is it a trade you're lookin' for?"

The argument might have lasted the day had Isabelle not interrupted, "What are you two going on about?! Jackie, leave the poor girl with Paddy, she's been looking forward to the sheep trials for a month. Paddy, quit waking the earth with your early morning treks around the Island. No reason those sheep need to be traipsing around at sun-up. Now, Jackie, are we ready?"

In her beautiful way of slicing right to the heart of a matter, Isabelle had spoken and it would be done. Ellie trotted down the gangplank toward Paddy passing Isabelle as she trudged up. Jackie helped Isabelle onto his boat, then Paddy helped Jackie unmoor the boat, and each went his way. By sun-down Ellie had her first trophy.

www.ingramcontent.com/pod-product-compliance
Lightning Source LLC
Chambersburg PA
CBHW031419150426
43191CB00006B/324